FEAR OF HAT LOSS IN LAS VEGAS

www.**rbooks**.co.uk

FEAR OF HAT LOSS IN LAS VEGAS

Brendon Burns

BANTAM PRESS

LONDON • TORONTO • SYDNEY • AUCKLAND • JOHANNESBURG

TRANSWORLD PUBLISHERS
61–63 Uxbridge Road, London W5 5SA
A Random House Group Company
www.rbooks.co.uk

First published in Great Britain
in 2010 by Bantam Press
an imprint of Transworld Publishers

This book is a work of non-fiction based on the life, experiences and
recollections of the author. In some cases names of people, places, dates,
sequences or the detail of events have been changed solely to protect the
privacy of others. The author has stated to the publishers that,
except in such minor respects not affecting the substantial
accuracy of the work, the contents of this book are true.

A CIP catalogue record for this book
is available from the British Library.

ISBN 9780593062456

Addresses for Random House Group Ltd companies outside the UK
can be found at: www.randomhouse.co.uk
The Random House Group Ltd Reg. No. 954009

The Random House Group Limited supports the Forest Stewardship
Council (FSC), the leading international forest-certification organization.
All our titles that are printed on Greenpeace-approved
FSC-certified paper carry the FSC logo.
Our paper procurement policy can be found at
www.rbooks.co.uk/environment

Typeset in 10.5/15pt Versailles by
Falcon Oast Graphic Art Ltd.
Printed and bound in Great Britain by
Clays Ltd, Bungay, Suffolk

2 4 6 8 10 9 7 5 3 1

Mixed Sources
Product group from well-managed
forests and other controlled sources
www.fsc.org Cert no. TT-COC-2139
© 1996 Forest Stewardship Council
FSC

For Barry, Provenz and Keith,
because it was the funniest thing I could think of . . .

'A picture is worth a thousand words . . .'
Ad slogan, often mistakenly attributed to Confucius

'Because you don't always have a thousand words'
worth of time to argue your case.'

Brendon Burns

The following is based mostly on bullshit.

1
The Vision

I HAD MY VISION about half an hour before Barry called. Barry's a good guy. Everyone loves Barry. He hates the name Barry which is really so very Barry of him. In stand-up comedy circles you can't say 'Barry Castagnola' without everyone in the room firing back 'fantastic bloke' or 'lovely fella'. If they don't then you know they're a bit of a tosser. Barry's such a good bloke he can be used as an arsehole barometer. If someone doesn't get along with Barry, there's simply something wrong with them.

Barry and I had only hung out a few times before he called but I instantly liked him. Even though he was new to stand-up he was never subservient to anyone nor did he look down on them either. I think that's why everyone likes Barry. He's a rarity in comedy, and in life really, in that he has no sense of hierarchy.

Barry is a blank canvas of a man and possibly the finest character comic actor I've ever known. He's used on hidden camera shows all the time simply because he's so damn convincing and utterly unremarkable-looking. Making him (physically anyway) instantly forgettable and therefore unrecognizable. This sounds like an insult but he's actually just a perfectly proportioned human. If he were to commit a crime he'd get off scot-free, as witnesses would never be able to describe him to a sketch artist.

'What did the man look like, sir?'

'Blond, neat, and everything was in the right place.'

'So, a man?'

'Yes. A man did it.'

By his own admission he is terminally normal. I remember one night at a party I voiced the cliché (in response to what, I can't remember), 'Yeah, but what *is* normal? I mean, who *is* normal?' (We were all extremely high so no one called me a wanker.)

'I am,' remarked Barry flatly as he put up his hand.

'Oh, yeah' – 'Yeah, there is Barry' – 'He's right, you know' – 'Yup, Barry's normal,' came the nodding replies and murmurs.

'Yeah, fair enough,' I conceded, 'that's pretty undeniable – Barry's normal.'

Seriously: picture a blond Londoner with blue eyes. Now make him slightly fat. Bingo! I guarantee you've got him. He once got a plastic model made of himself and the moulder guy couldn't even capture him. He has no distinctive features. One night he took the model onstage with him to show to the crowd. 'Look at it, it's not even fat,' he said as he held it up. 'Ten quid that cost me! Pathetic.' Strangely enough he said the last bit cheerily. He has a love of the pathetic, our Barry. He accentuates the 'th' in the middle perfectly.

Anyway, back in my flat, my lounge in disarray, everything within my grasp turned into a makeshift ashtray, I had a vision of a photo. (I say it was a vision, others might say it was a drunken delusion, but I'm telling the story.) In the vision I was on the back seat of a convertible with the Nevada skyline behind me and I was with two guys. I couldn't tell who they were, but in the photo I was content. I looked handsome and tanned, and I wore a killer smile.

I didn't feel a whole lot like the guy in the photo. I didn't really like who I was back then if I was to be honest. I tried and faked it quite well but I would've liked to be the guy in the photo so much more. I figured if I could get to wherever I needed to be to take the photo, then I'd be that guy. I'd be happy and my problems and pain would be over. I'd have found what they call in recovery circles 'the magic button'. My life was written by me after all. I also figured magic mushrooms would help when we got there.

The phone rang.

'Brendon, it's Barry.'

It was Barry.

'Orright, Barry,' I replied. Attempting my mock English accent. I was short of breath as I'd been working out and drinking. A dangerous combination of self-loathing and self-improvement.

'What's that noise?' asked Barry.

'What noise, Barry?' I continued with the voice.

'That noise you're making.'

'I'm working out.'

'No, the voice you're doing.'

'It's my cockney accent.'

'S'great,' he muttered. (Barry is the only man I've ever met who can actually speak in a smaller font.)

'No it isn't, it's fucken awful,' I replied. (I should point out here that I'm Australian and that's how I say 'fucking'.)

'Well don't do it then,' he said flatly.

'Orright, Barry.'

'S'what'sthescenelikeinAustraliathen?' he went on. (Not only can Barry speak in smaller font, as if to balance out this gift he is also marred with an inability to use the space bar. One can actually hear it being ignored when he talks. I shall limit literal representations of this to a bare minimum. However, rest assured, it happens all the time.)

'Shit. Why do you think I left? Why? You thinking of going out there?'

'Chris left me,' he returned.

Chris was his fiancée. I was totally knocked for six. How could this have happened? The only reason I could think of was that having 'Barry and Chris' on the wedding invitations might have made it sound like two very forward-thinking builders were getting hitched, but she was the girl opting for 'Chris' over 'Chrissie' so if anything she was the weak link here. This was grossly unfair.

'Oh no no no no no no! What? That's ridiculous. You two were getting on so well. That doesn't make any sense.'

It was true. I'd seen them together in Edinburgh during the festival. They were playing with my son as we climbed Arthur's Seat.* She was clucky as hell. This was truly upsetting. They were happily engaged just like me and . . . well. No need to go into that now.

The penny dropped as to why he was really ringing me.

'Yeah, all her friends feel that way too. It's totally out of the blue. I'm in fucking shock.' (Yes, he may have been in shock, but he knew how to say 'fucking' the English way.)

'I imagine none of your friends are any help now either,' I offered.

'Nah, they just think I'm better off and all that. I just saw

---

*A large hill overlooking the city. It is something of an institution for performers to scale it at the beginning of the festival every year in order to delude themselves that they're living healthily during such a month of debauchery.

how you dealt with you and y'know breaking up and all and I . . . I dunno what I want actually.' He was cracking up.

'Well, listen, Barry. Any time of the day or night. I honestly don't care what hour. You call me. I offer no "better offs" nor "more fishes in the sea", none of that shit. You ring me and I will just shut the fuck up and listen.'

'Thanks, mate.' He hung up before I heard him cry.

I openly wept for at least half an hour. It was exactly the same story as me and mine. I took out a framed photo of us in happier times. My tears splashed on the glass, cleaning away the dust. Upon closer inspection I could make out tiny particles sitting afloat in the droplets. I swigged back some more ouzo. It was all I'd had left in the house and as it was sweet it made a makeshift replacement for breakfast. I wished I could do something for Barry. I might have been a lost cause but if I could just cheer him up then that'd at least be something.

Then it hit me: Barry was the other guy in the vision. He had to be.

I rang him straight back.

'Barry! You're coming to Vegas,' I shot down the phone. I was insistent, manic even.

'What?'

'The first thing you have to do right now is something you couldn't do before and that's come to Vegas with me.' I didn't tell him about the vision. It wasn't the time.

'Mate, that sounds brilliant, but I can't.'

'Yes you can.'

'I can't.'

'You can.'

'I don't have the money.'

'I do. I'll lend it to you. You're coming.'

'No.'

'Yes.'

'Can't.'

'Can.'

'Won't.'

'Will.'

'Dude . . .'

'VEGAS! WHOOOOOOOO!' I whooed the full-blown hoarse American 'whooooo', the one that winds up with one's voice in a rasp.

'Brendon . . .'

'VEGAS! WHOOOOOOOO!'

'It's kind of you to offer . . .'

'Gimme a "V"!'

'Mate . . .'

'WHOOOOOOOO!'

'Burnsy . . . I . . . I . . .'

'Gimme an "E"!'

The phone clicked in my ear, and thus began the two-week campaign to get Barry to come to Vegas with me.

I don't know if you've ever tried to get an Englishman who doesn't know you all that well to come away with you on a trip. But it takes work and *both* their mobile and landline numbers.

And let me just say this: I'm annoying. Really annoying.

Take your loudest, most drunken, fucked-up buddy, then make him slightly hard of hearing, with a tenuous grip on reality and common airs and graces in general, and that's me.

I'm loud. Loud for a living, loud at home. Loud, loud, loud, loud, LOUD! Despite being a single dad I am actually incapable of sneaking around at night. My son has learned how to sleep through anything. I realize that sounds a bit paedo, but I just mean I make a lot of noise simply carrying out my business. Twin this with a minimal inner monologue and an even thinner sense of embarrassment (don't get me wrong, this isn't self-loathing, I wouldn't wanna be anyone else today) and fuck me, am I annoying. Being a touring comic, I have to spend a lot of time alone in the car and I can bug the shit out of even me. I've often caught myself literally screaming an argument to a halt and announcing to absolutely no one, 'Whoa whoa whoa. Hang on, hang on. HANG ON! There's no one else here.'

At all hours of the day and night I pestered Barry to come to Vegas. I actually filled his answering machine with garbled messages, all ending with 'VEGAS! WHOOOOOOOO!', like a horny yeti's cry. For me it was a call to arms. None of my other friends were single and here was a new one. A brother in arms. The fellow downtrodden, the broken-hearted. America was the promised land it once promised to be. And Vegas? Well, Vegas was Vegas, baby.

WHOOOOOOOO!

I'd call him on the way to gigs – 'VEGAS! WHOOOOOOOO!'

'Is that Burns?' the other comics in Barry's car would ask. (Comics tend to travel in packs, and even in an industry filled with wee loud mad fuckers I was *still* considered the wee loud mad fucker.)

'Yeah,' would come the flat reply. 'Would it be anybody else?'

'What does he want?' they'd ask sarcastically.

'S'wantsmetogotoVegaswithimdoesnee,' Barry would mumble.

'VEGAS! WHOOOOOOOO!' I'd yell on the other end of the phone, fully audible to the entire car.

Did I mention I'm loud?

In the middle of the night – 'VEGAS! WHOOOOOOOO!'

While he was onstage at his gig in Kingston – 'VEGAS! WHOOOOOOOO!'

I'd get creative. 'Barry, can you tell what type of gas that is?' I'd tease him on his answering machine. '"What gas?" you may ask. And you'd be right to ask. It's hard to tell isn't it? What would be the words one could use to describe a gas of such a nondescript nature? One would almost call it a vague gas. A Vegas even . . .'

Beep! The machine ran out of tape. This happened more times than I cared to count. Naturally I'd always call back to finish the message: 'VEGAS! WHOOOOOOOO!'

There were many of these, designed more to annoy than amuse. My personal favourite came in the form of a three a.m. call.

'Barry, it's Brendon.'

'What . . .'

'Knock knock.'

'Jesus! Who's there?'

'Vegas.'

'Vegas who?'

'That's the spirit! VEGAS! WHOOOOOOOO!'

That one actually made Barry laugh; I'd worn him down. We comics are a funny bunch. By which I mean funny/ peculiar not funny/ha ha. We actually think if something's amusing then it's a logical viable argument.

'Right, lemme look at my diary for November,' he finally conceded.

'Yes, Barry, yes, yes, yes, yesyesyesyesyesyyyesss-eyeyeyeysss . . .' I quickly ran out of ways to say 'yes' so I fell back on the old faithful: 'VEGAS! WHOOOOOOOO!'

(In reality Barry took more convincing than this, but it was

more of the same really and I'm not trying to talk you into anything other than reading on. I'll wager annoying you into it
won't have quite the same effect.)

As luck would have it we both had a week's window in the
second week of November. I saw this as a sign. Comics don't
take weekends off. Ever. We're both irresponsible and
obsessive. Consequently we need the work and we want the
work, particularly during the boom period leading up to
Christmas when most guys are paying off their debts from the
Edinburgh Festival. Clearly my mission was holy. Now I just
needed to gather my disciples.

'I can stay out at my dad's place,' Barry said, 'but it's an
hour outside LA and pretty much a studio flat. Where you
gonna stay?'

And that was it. In that moment I knew who the third man
in my vision was. It was my friend Paul Provenza. It had to be
him. He'd just spent the whole month of the Edinburgh
Festival bugging me to go and stay with him in the US.

Like all American stand-ups, Provenza's a director/
comedian/actor. Unlike most American stand-ups, he's pretty
much the coolest guy everyone who knows him knows. He
can wear leather pants and doesn't look stupid.

'Fuck off!' I hear you cry. 'No one can wear leather pants!'

You're right, and I agree, but Provenza can wear leather
pants . . . and does . . . and can.

Provenza, or 'Provenz', has been around for yonks. You'd
recognize him from something. He was the lead in the final
series of *Northern Exposure* before it got cancelled, the part of
Sam Sebourne in *The West Wing* was originally written for
him (before the network insisted they needed a star like Rob
Lowe), he was down to the wire to host *Late Night* before they
went with Conan O'Brien. That, and countless other shit, got

him the Hollywood nickname 'Mr Almost'. Everyone in Hollywood knows Provenza and Provenza knows everyone.

I found out just how true this is only recently when he finally got his own TV series in the States called *The Green Room with Paul Provenza*. He fought tooth and nail to have me on and I was gobsmacked to see just how many big-name stand-ups knew him and lined up to be on his show to help him get it started. Roseanne Barr, Tommy Smothers, Robert Klein, Jonathon Winters, Sandra Bernhardt, Larry Miller, Bob Saget, Drew Carey – all real heavyweights, some of whom I'd grown up watching and learning from. And here they were raving that he'd finally got his own series. He hadn't told me a lick of this but, as you'll discover, Provenza is a bit of an enigma. The longer you know him the more you realize you actually know nothing about him.

Previously Provenza was best known for directing *The Aristocrats*, a comedy documentary where some really famous and not so famous comedians tell the same very funny and very filthy joke with exactly the same punchline, 'The Aristocrats'. When I rang him the movie was being picked up everywhere. He had the hottest documentary film of all time. Mr Almost was in the middle of finally getting his biggest ever break, yet still our conversation went exactly like this:

'Provenza, it's Burnsy.'

'Burnsy! What's up? YOU FUCK'N LA CUNT! I HOPE YOU FUCK'N DIE! LEARN TO FUCK'N DRIVE YOU ASSHOLE!'

He was obviously driving. Either that or I'd really misread our relationship.

'Fuuu-uuuck, I hate this town!' he screamed, confirming my suspicions. Provenza's a New York Italian born and bred, and like all New Yorkers in LA he fucken *hates* the place.

'Sorry, Burnsy. What's up?'

'Provenz, you know Barry Castagnola?'

'Yeah, met him in Edinburgh. Good guy. Why?'

'Well, he just split up with his missus and I wanna hire a convertible, drive him across the desert to Vegas, take mush-rooms and watch the sunset.'

'When?'

'Second week of November.'

'Unbelievable. That's the only time I have free. I'm in.' *Click.*

Provenza can wear leather trousers, and that was our conversation. A grown man, at his age, at that point in his career.

'Do you want to come to Vegas and take mushrooms?'

'I'm in.'

Click.

A broken heart will make men do many a mad impulsive thing. I still have no idea what Provenza's motivation in all of this was. Like I said, the longer you know him . . .

2

When Burnsy Met Jerry

ONE NIGHT IN January 2002, nearly three years earlier, I found myself rushing to the London Palladium. I'd managed to drive there from Stratford in less than half an hour. No small feat in London, even at ten thirty on a Sunday night. The reason for my rush was that my childhood hero, the American actor and comedian Jerry Lewis, was closing a benefit gig for 'Turning Point Scotland', a drug and alcohol rehabilitation charity based in, of course, Italy.

In 1978 Perth had only two commercial channels and the negligible ABC (Australian Broadcasting Commission) which only seemed to broadcast church services, lawn bowls and *Doctor Who*. The commercial channels, Channel 7 and Channel 9, took it in turns of a Sunday afternoon to show sport, Elvis movies or Dean Martin and Jerry Lewis movies. This constricted programming was unfaltering for about three years. Dumbfounding to me now is the fact that 7 and 9 clearly never paid any attention to each other's Sunday line-up as it was not uncommon for them both to be showing cricket (the same match, I might add), an Elvis flick or a Dino and Jerry. If it were cricket or Elvis I would have to entertain myself by going to the beach or something equally criminal.

Pretend to like cricket, and Elvis? Pah! He usually threw only one punch in the entire film and spent the rest of the time singing and wobbling like a drunken knickerless Welsh chick. But if it were Dino and Jerry my afternoon was set.

I approached the stage door where either the man knew who I was (which was highly unlikely as I was not in one of the three places in the UK where I might be considered well-known: the Edinburgh Festival, the Glastonbury Festival, or my flat) or security was extremely lax. I had rung ahead and asked to have my name put on the door, but when I said 'I'm Brendon Burns' I could just as easily have said 'I'm the guy who flew the second plane' for all the notice he took. Hardly the kind of security one might expect to be surrounding a comedy god. Or maybe it's just a testament to the British sense of civility. Perhaps no one has ever dared to gatecrash the hallowed sanctuary that is the backstage area of the London Palladium. Then again, I'm Australian, so such matters of etiquette are as important to me as who wins *Britain's Got Pop Idol Factor Brother*. I'm sure someone cares but I just can't, no matter how hard I try.

If you've ever been backstage at the Palladium you will know that it is a bewildering maze. Everywhere you turn there are two signs pointing in opposite directions, one signalling the exit, the other the stage. I followed the sign to the stage around two corners only to be confronted by two more arrows that contradicted the last. After about fifteen minutes of wandering aimlessly I finally found my way to the wings. Bobcat Goldthwaite (the screeching guy from the *Police Academy* films) was onstage not getting much of a response and everyone was milling around in quite a panic. Peering out into the crowd, I realized Bobcat was actually storming. The reason for the lack of noise was that the theatre was only a quarter to a third full.

After Bobcat the compère introduced the star of *Eight Legged Freaks*. I looked around for David Arquette but instead saw comedian Rick Overton make his way to the stage. I hadn't known he was in *Eight Legged Freaks* before then. Neither had the crowd: they too were expecting David Arquette to make a surprise appearance. I like Rick, but I haven't been around him enough to tell him that listing one's CV, while par for the course in the States, is a big no-no in Britain. Particularly if you're not the actual star of the movie or TV show being referenced. In fact it's a bit of a private joke we play on visiting Yanks. Stating the upcoming comedian's credentials before he's proved them is a bit of a nod to the crowd that 'this next guy is a bit of a wanker'.

'Hey, mate, anything you want me to tell them before I bring you on?' I've often asked an American act who has rubbed me up the wrong way.

'Yeah, tell 'em I've done Leno,' comes the inevitable reply.

'Sure I will, and good luck with them knowing or caring who the fuck Leno is,' I'd mutter under my breath before announcing, 'OK, ladies and gentlemen, you've seen this next act on *The Tonight Show with Jay Leno* . . .'

To which British audiences would respond with mumblings like 'No we haven't', 'Who's Jay Leno?', 'What's *The Tonight Show*?', 'Must be a Yank', 'Must be a wanker', 'Let's boo him off'.

The act would then walk on to borderline animosity while I and every other comic on the bill rushed to the back of the room to watch them die on their arse.

Anyway, once Rick was done it was time for a montage of Jerry's work. I was slightly apprehensive about squeegeeing the beery goggles of nostalgia. When one was seven, Benny

Hill was hilarious, now his work is beyond contempt (although it has to be said that slapping a tiny frail old man's head will always conjure a wry smile from my stoniest of faces). But I needn't have worried. It was brilliant. Does his work stand the test of time? Buggered if I know, but not since the trailers for *Star Wars Episode One* have I been so put in touch with my inner child. As I peered from the wings up at that screen I was seven again. Was I amused? I still couldn't tell you, as I gazed sheepishly with a stupid grin plastered all over my face.

Then suddenly there was a skirmish behind me. I turned and there was a really pockmarked swollen old purple guy behind me complaining in hushed but still very stern tones. I fixed my attention back on the screen. Then I nearly spun my own head off as I did the biggest double-take of my life. IT WAS HIM! Jerry fucken Lewis in the flesh (and, frankly, lots of it, mostly round the neck)! I spun my head back to the screen so as not to appear to be gawking, but I couldn't help myself. I turned sideways to grab a few more peeps. The dude did not look well or pleased. The night had been going since 7.30 and it was now about 11.30 and Jerry was not a happy bunny. I later learned that he had a lung condition and was on steroids as treatment, which in turn made him swell. No shit. The guy's head was translucent with a purple interior. He looked exactly like the bell end of a stonking hard-on.

'Holy fuck, he looks like balls,' I said to myself.

It was one of the rare occasions I managed an inner monologue. I have very little cut-off point between thought and speech. Which is handy for improvisation and put-downs. (Often I'll recall what I've said onstage without thinking on the way home in the car and muse, 'Phew, that was lucky. I'll remember that for next time.') Not so good for social situations. (Equally often, after a more civilized engagement, on the way home in the car I'll labour, 'Shit, that was awkward. Can't wait to retell it onstage though.')

Here, I was grateful for my uncharacteristic behaviour.

I averted my eyes from Jerry and turned back to the screen. I found it easy to refocus my attention mistily on the footage. So much so in fact that I did not react to the huge thud I heard behind me. At first I didn't make the connection between an irate seventy-five-year-old man with a lung disease about to go onstage and the dull splat of two hundred pounds of human flesh hitting wooden floorboards. Perhaps I was just determined not to rubberneck, but it wasn't until I heard the rasping that I put two and two together. Jerry had indeed hit the deck face first.

His bodyguards dealt with the situation with military precision and within seconds they had an oxygen mask clamped to his face. The noise emanating from him was disarming to say the least, something akin to a turkey being drowned in a tub of Vaseline. The compère was back onstage like the proverbial deer in headlights. Trying desperately to fill time. At one stage he said to the crowd, 'Hey, everybody, let's see how the band is doing. Give them a round of applause!' He turned to the band leader. 'Hey, how ya doin'?' The band leader just shrugged in response. Then the band followed suit, shrugging in unison. A whole row of men in tuxedos pulling the 'Meh! What're you gonna do?' face. It was painful.

The compère then claimed there was a technical hitch and that Jerry would be on in a minute. I put this down to shock. Surely he couldn't expect Jerry to recover and still go on. Luckily, Bobcat Goldthwaite stepped up and did some filler. More and more American acts appeared backstage not entirely unlike coyotes whose prey was stage time. At this point I saw my friends whom I'd arranged to meet there: Canadian comedian Glenn Wool, Puppetry of the Penis maestro David Friend and his girlfriend Janie Raney (her real name). An ambulance was on the way so Glenn suggested that we adjourn to the green room.

From the dressing-room monitor we could hear that another comedian called Tony V had been brought on. 'What, Jerry ain't goin' on? Sounds like a job for Wool!' said Glenn mockingly as he took off his jacket.

'Do you think they're in the mood for dick tricks?' enquired Friendy. Friendy is the world's most Aussie man. He and his buddy Simon Morley invented the Puppetry of the Penis, a worldwide franchise where well-endowed young men do impressions of people, objects and landmarks using only their cock and balls.

As the gauntlet for what would be the most inappropriate thing any one of us could do or say had been thrown down, I imagined the greatest indiscretion that could be committed. After it had been announced that Jerry had fallen ill, with no introduction or hint as to who he is or what he does, Friendy should walk out onstage fully clothed, pull out his penis and perform his most famous piece of genital origami. The stunned crowd would gape upon his groin as he lifted his testicles to one side and then stretched his penis across the middle of them, yelling, 'Look everyone, a hamburger!'

We fell about laughing, and all of a sudden I felt guilty. There was a man on the brink of death downstairs and here we were making jokes. 'No way,' Glenn retorted. 'If I was the king of comedy and I keeled over and died just before I was about to go on at *the fuck'n Palladium* I would hope, no, I would *expect*, that there were young comics upstairs making jokes about it.' Glenn has a fantastic gift for making immoral

17

humour seem not just ethical but downright mandatory.

I was swayed completely. 'Yeah, you're right, we *owe* it to Jerry to be making jokes right now.'

So we went downstairs to see if he was OK/gather more material. He was already in the ambulance and quite a crowd had assembled. I saw British comedian Daniel Kitson, who earlier in the night had made the rather premonitory comment 'Ladies and gentlemen, it has always been a secret ambition of mine to perform to a third-full Palladium in front of people who have paid sixty quid to see a dying man.'

As the comics and the paparazzi milled around the ambulance containing Mr Lewis, it was announced that he had come to in the back and was debating whether or not he would go to hospital. Immediately I remembered something that was said to me backstage by the compère after Jerry had collapsed.

'That fucking arsehole.'

'I beg your pardon?' I said, reeling.

'I've been dealing with that arsehole for three months,' he spat. 'He's faked it. He just didn't want to go on.'

'Mate, there was no way he faked it. I was right next to him. He hit the deck hard.'

'He's the king of the pratfall, Brendon!' he said, shaking his head patronizingly.

'He's seventy-five!' I retorted, gobsmacked.

But the rumours were already running rife. Apparently he had feigned illness because the whole thing was such a debacle and as it was being filmed for American television he didn't want to be seen to be a part of it. My belief was that all this was true – but then, he keeled over. A man of seventy-five with a lung disease cannot throw himself face first on the floor and go into the convulsions I witnessed. Even if he were faking it, the face planting and pretending to go into a fit alone would have prompted a genuine seizure in the man.

The paparazzi were trying to squeeze their way into the back of the ambulance and one photographer in particular was edging his way in past the comics blocking his view. I was just about to tell him to get fucked when some six-foot-four New York Italian in leather trousers piped up, 'Abdul, that ain't fuck'n cool, man.' He dragged deep and long on his cigarette.

'Why you care?' Abdul replied in a very Abdullian accent. 'You make your living, I make mine.'

'C'mon, man, the guy just had a seizure. That ain't even news. Leave him be. You're a better man than that.'

I was immediately impressed. This guy had predetermined why the other guy was there, introduced himself before the fact, then tried reasoning with him man to man when he inevitably whipped out his camera. Much better than the 'get fucked, cunt' plan I had in mind.

While this was going on, Jerry suddenly returned to full health. We could hear him yelling at his manager. His entourage started clearing a path. Then, like lightning, he was ushered from the ambulance and into his limo before anyone could photograph him. The limo sped off down the road, and just like that he was gone.

Once the hubbub had died down, Glenn, Friendy and Janey made their way over to me, pissing themselves laughing. Friendy was holding a flyer for the show.

'What?' I enquired.

He held up the flyer. 'High on Laughter' read the title.

I shrugged in response. 'So?'

Friendy pointed to the bottom of the flyer. 'Keep reading.'

Just underneath, in pink letters, were the words 'Recovery is the punchline'.

'He got us!' Friendy laughed. 'He got us good!'

Looking over my shoulder, the Italian American let out a loud singular 'HA!' like some sort of male witch but actually almost yelling the word, then another, even bolder 'HAAA!', then another longer 'HAAAAAAAA!' The other three looked at me, waiting for me to introduce them to our newfound friend.

I put out my hand. 'Hey, man, I'm Brendon Burns. My friends call me Burnsy.'

'I'm Paul Provenza . . . Provenz,' he offered economically, shaking my hand hard and drawing on a newly lit menthol.

'This is Glenn, Friendy and Janey.' I gestured at each of them in turn. 'You wanna come drinking?'

3

Big Trouble in Little Southend

OUR FLIGHTS WERE BOOKED, and as fate would have it Barry and I were booked on a number of dates together right after he'd agreed to come to Vegas. Life on the road is like that. You won't see someone for years then all of a sudden you're gigging with them every week. Barry, Provenza and I managing to find seven days we had free, and then Barry and I suddenly gigging together a lot, were big enough coincidences to feed my belief that we were truly on a holy journey of great spiritual worth. I could feel the universe bending to help me heal Barry's broken heart.

Two nights before we were due to fly to LA together, Barry and I were doing the last of these gigs, in Southend.

Southend is a rough seaside town on the south-east coast of England, and an irony bypass to boot. It's a comedy trouble spot. No one without the right accent really likes performing there and even those who do feel a bit dirty afterwards. Having a good gig in Southend is a bit like having great sex with a pensioner. I'd say fat chick, but with a fat chick you're happy that at least she enjoyed herself. With a pensioner, OK you may have been paid, but you just wish it hadn't gone so well. Southend was one of the few places in Britain that had a full slate of British National Party candidates for the 2008 local elections. When you hear of people throwing bricks through the windows of paediatricians because they read in the paper there was a paedophile 'operating' in the area . . . well, Southend is where said brick-throwers go on holiday.

I refer to it as the south-east 'coast' of England, adopting much of the local optimism. It's mud for most of the year. Yet they have boats, which they keep in said mud. In the summer, when the tide goes down, one can see these boats idling sideways like tin cans on the sea of shit that is Southend-on-Sea. The town's full name, incidentally. Another optimistic oversight on their part, one presumes to attract tourists who upon pulling off the A13 at the promise of sea views arrive at a pier eddied by bubbling diarrhoea and invariably go 'Where's the sea?', 'Why do these people keep boats in mud?', and 'Oh fuck, I've been stabbed.' Naturally such an extreme opinion is founded on ignorance and bigotry. Like all comics I'm basing my entire opinion on one gig in front of fifty people years ago. One mediocre gig can tarnish an entire town for years in a comic's eyes. I still won't play Liverpool to this day because 'They're allllll fooking cahmediahns in Liverpoooooll'. Sorry. I can't do the voice. Even in print.

'I fuckin' hate Southend,' geezered Barry as I drove, preparing his accent for the gig. 'I feel like a fuckin' minstrel down 'ere. "Orright, you cunts-on-sea. I'm one a you. I'm not though. You're all cunts. What's that, mate? Yeah, if you could all keep yelling throughout the gig that'd be great. Anyway, we've got a convict comin' up! Be lucky. You fuckin' cunts."' I laughed as he carried on. '"S'great bein' a cunt innit, you cunts. Ere luv, bet you don't get many of them to the pound. Although I do. I'm a right cunt and I know a cunt that knocks 'em off the back of a van. Be lucky! *Mmnnnnneeeeerrrrr.*'

That was Barry laughing his best cockney wanker laugh.

We'd decided earlier we were going to stay over to try and pull. Well, I decided and nagged Barry into it. I figured it would be good for him to get back on the horse. He figured the horse reference wouldn't turn out to be a metaphor.

'Beggars can't be choosers, Barry,' I opined.

'Thanks, that's given me a lift,' he said flatly as he stared out the window.

'Look, it's fucken Southend. If we can't pull there what chance have we got in LA? Get back in there, my son,' I enthused, jiggling his belly. He slapped my hand and insisted I concentrate on driving.

Most comics say in interviews that comedy isn't the aphrodisiac everyone thinks it is. The stock answer being that we don't really get groupies, just drunk guys telling us jokes. This is nonsense, told largely to put girlfriends at ease regarding the temptations of the road. The truth is, we don't get the rock star treatment. There are no girls waiting by the stage door for us afterwards. In fact, there is no stage door when you're a jobbing comic. That's why we don't have the mystique and subsequent level of fanny. But it's a foot in the door nonetheless. Of course it is. We just have to go to them. Not the other way round. The drunken guys do usually blow it for us, however, by butting in and telling us jokes. The most popular 'joke' being, 'So is she your groupie then? You must get loads of fanny. You gonna fuck him, love? Hahahahahaahhaha!' Either that or most comics are usually so socially inept that they blow it for themselves by making a slightly funnier version of the same joke.

The truest answer to journalists asking whether or not comedians get groupies would be, 'Nowhere near as many as rock stars but way more than you.'

However, I was right. We hung out at the bar after the gig and before long were approached by a few girls. Given, we weren't wearing Ben Sherman shirts nor had our hair been over-gelled back like we'd tucked our heads into a lazy horse's slack arsehole. We stood out as not your usual Southend stock-fodder males.

The very nature of going on the prowl is the best evidence of humans being just another animal. While no girl wants to get pregnant every time she has sex, she still wants to get the most alpha male she can. Unbeknown to her, her vagina is still thinking about giving birth. Hence, when it comes to courting a suitor, natural selection is evident in women. Contrary to popular belief this isn't the work of sophisticated human intellect. This is raw instinct at its most carnal. Women are attracted to the unknown in order to give their offspring a broader DNA strain. If this sounds patronizing and sexist I should stress that the human penis is even less sophisticated, never thinking anything beyond 'I've gotta find somewhere warm to be sick'. And 'I hope she's pretty enough to keep him distracted'. If one-hit-wonder courtship was just down to sex feeling nice, girls wouldn't be so picky, men would never aspire to anything, and society as we know it would collapse.

This was never truer for us than in Southend that night. These girls naturally longed to mate in a fashion other than being seagulled by a passing carload of boys. (I think that's how they procreate in Southend. Then the girl is sick in a puddle. Nine months later, yet another swamp thing rises out of the roads. Either that or they pour blue WKD on a haemorrhoid.)

Anyway, regardless of all that, it's nothing to be proud of, but it's easy to pull in Southend if you have an accent that hails from beyond their inner ring road. As we were capable of expressing ourselves beyond sliding our arses across the back dash of an Escort, the girls asked us to come to a party they were going to.

I was blatantly playing wingman as Barry was doing quite well. It was decided immediately which one he wanted.

'I like the blonde, is that all right?' he whispered out of the corner of his mouth.

'Hey man, go for it. Tonight's about you.'

As we walked along, I watched him work. He really was quite charming. For a man so recently on the rebound he possessed no air of desperation. I was impressed. It took me three months even to think about doing it with another woman. Even then it was largely me crying and whichever girl it was holding me. He also seemed genuinely interested in what the chav girl had to say. Something I'd not mastered. I've blown the coop many a time by blurting out something like, 'Hmmm, really, chav, that's quite interesting.'

For an Aussie I'm quite a snob. Not about Australians though. We call our chavs bogans, and at heart I am one. At the very least I share their taste in music, no matter how much I delude myself that I'm well travelled, learned and cultured. The moment I hear AC/DC's 'Back in Black' I regress into a little metal-headed bogan from Perth, Western Australia. Which is doubly odd as back in Oz I'm considered posh. I guess it might have something to do with the fact that my family's not old money. In Australia there's no such thing. So I guess the Burnses are just CUBs or Cashed Up Bogans as they're known. Which if you ask me is a fairly boggy way of saying it.

Before I was born my parents raised my brother and sister in a caravan in the Australian outback. My dad got his start when he discovered a big mulch-cum-peat deposit in the south-west and sold it to garden stores around the country. From there he became a world-renowned inventor and investor. You know those punctureless tyres you see on modern tractors and fork lifts? He invented them, among countless other things. Today he's working on wave energy technology. He's getting it done too. He's one of those big-brained people who sees something that needs doing in the world and goes, 'Wait! You've got it all wrong. Look. Oh get out of the way. You're bloody useless. I'll do it.' I happily imagine him shoving boffins aside as if shirking up his sleeves to tend to a car engine. Never finished school, started in the Aussie outback, has a full understanding of pretty much every science known to man, yet still says 'fuck' a lot when in the right company. I think the last bit is why I still like him. I'm proud of him for the other stuff obviously, but, as much as he'd deny it, he's still got a lot of the outback in him. My whole family does. My old neighbourhood friends and all my cousins are all dyed-in-the-wool working class too. My parents worked all of us kids to death on farms and mining excavations every school holiday to teach us the work ethic and abolish any of the snobbery our newfound wealth may have led us to.

Yet, despite growing up in this well-grounded environment, there's still something about the uneducated working classes of England I find unforgivable. When I moved to England I thought we'd all be sitting around wearing tweed and quoting Keats. Anyone else is just not what I had in mind.

We sauntered along, and Barry and his chav girl were chatting happily while I drowned out the drivel emanating from mine. Some gibberish about *Neighbours, Home and Away* and kangaroos being cute, I believe. As we made our way through a mall we nodded and went 'All right?' at a group of eight lads as they passed by. Well, not so much 'All right?' as 'Orrye?', like everyone does, almost unconsciously, walking along any given mall up and down parochial Britain on a Saturday night. A brief, barely audible 'All right' from two lads with two girls is unspoken code for 'Not going to beat us up then?' The return 'All right' or 'Orrye' from at least two of the gang of men is a return code meaning 'Nope, you're all right, we're just eight lads not eight cunts'. If only one of them says 'Orrye' that's code for 'Sorry if it kicks off but these other seven are cunts and I never know what they're gonna do. I can't control them. Run! Run!' Alternatively, if eight lads meet eight lads and they all say 'Orrye', that means 'Look, this is way too evenly matched and we could all get hurt'.

Before long the girls were joined by three guys they knew. They seemed friendly enough. There were plenty of 'Orrye's, and small-talk chatter and merriment ensued. I was talking to one perfectly amiable fellow when one of the girls told them we were comics and that they'd been to see us. One of the guys suddenly turned, in both senses of the word, and said, 'Fuck 'em, they're not coming to Terry's party.'

This can often happen. When guys find out you're a comedian they get intimidated. Usually the ones who consider their sense of humour their trump card. Which invariably it isn't. As this dickhead was proving.

'It's Terry's party,' he continued, 'and they're not fucking coming.'

'All right mate, calm down. I don't want to go where I'm not welcome.' My tone was calm and unaffected. I was wearing a bandana, pink sunglasses and a bright red leather jacket. I figured men found this hipster look soothing and women thought it sexy. I got punched a lot and fucked psychopaths mostly.

Barry continued, 'Yeah, all right mate, settle down.'

We had both obviously figured that this bloke was Terry's mate and Terry was obviously mates with cunts and no two guys on their own want to go to a cunt's party for cunts. No matter how many 'Orrye's you get all night, you're still out-numbered by cunts. And they're just too damn unpredictable.

'No worries, mate. We'll see you girls later,' Barry said, open-ended.

'Yeah, it's a man's house after all, ya gotta respect that,' I supported.

Barry and I were well in tune here. We weren't that desperate to go and these guys were obviously going to foil our attempts at pulling anyway. Getting the girls to go some-where else with us was a much more viable option. The high road was merely a detour. Sure enough our actions were rewarded with the desired response. This was nothing short of a revelation to the girls. Their eyes glazed over in creamy adulation. If we'd asked them to marry us then and there they would have. They'd never seen two men resolve a situation like this without glassing someone.

'We're really sorry,' my chav said to me.

I'm sorry. I can barely remember her face let alone her name.

Barry's chav, however, was a lot more taken with him. 'Maybe there's somewhere else we could go?' she said as she took Barry's hand.

'They're not coming to Terry's party,' said Dickhead as we walked off.

'We don't wanna go to Terry's fucking party,' we chimed.

As the three of us made our way past Dixons (or some-where equally obligatory), Barry turned to his chav and started to suggest a 'somewhere else', but then Dickhead yelled something unintelligible. To this day neither Barry nor I remember what he yelled at us, but it turned Barry bright red and he pelted off after the guy. I was gobsmacked. I honestly hadn't expected this. He literally just snapped and was gone.

Then I yelled the sentence I thought I never would: 'Leave it, Barry, it's not worth it!'

I practically puked out the second half of the sentence, such was my revulsion and disbelief. I was in a mall! In fucken Southend! On a Saturday fucken night! And I had just yelled 'Leave it, Barry, it's not worth it!' I was now a chav. I'd been in Southend for less than eight hours and the bunch of plastering, blue-WKD-drinking, statue-puking-on fuckers had got me.

'I can't believe I just uttered that sentence. I'm *so* above this.' I stamped almost in a tantrum. I shrugged at the chav girl. 'I gotta go after him.' She shrugged back knowingly – this was familiar to her – as I ran off after Barry.

I tore around the corner and to my surprise Barry was not fighting Dickhead but Dickhead's perfectly reasonable and amiable mate. Amiable Mate swung a punch at Barry and it just bounced off his skull, not even turning his face slightly. Barry stood staring back at him completely unfazed.

'Fucking shit punch, mate,' said Barry.

The guy looked worried, as Dickhead and his other friend had gone ahead. And here was Barry talking to him, almost nonplussed, after he'd taken his best shot at him. What's more, there was a certain quizzical sense of 'Hang on, you were "Orrye" a second ago, shouldn't Dickhead be involved in this?' between them as they stood still for a second with their heads tilted. Returning his attention to the fact that their fists were raised, Barry clocked the previously perfectly amiable fellow square in the head in response. As his heart wasn't really in it the blow just moved the guy's head sideways a bit with a dull thud.

Then Amiable Mate caught my eye. I started running again, tearing off my jacket and throwing my glasses to the ground. My regular speech, even written word for that matter, is coarse and profane. But when I'm truly outraged, for some reason I get comparatively lucid and eloquent.

'I can't believe this!' I yelled at the guy. 'It wasn't even you there was a disagreement with. It was that belligerent mate of yours. Why is this happening? What, just because we were talking to what you perceive to be *your* women? How primitive and parochial is that? Let me just clear something up for you.' I started to growl from my guts. 'We're two guys that just split up with our fiancées. It happened out of the blue. We've got a lot of pent-up anger that needs releasing and we'll be glad to take it out on someone. I can't guarantee if we start at what point we'll stop.' My voice then took on a tone that was deafening, and from somewhere very deep and disturbed came this: 'I'M FUCKEN BEGGING YA!' With this I had finally arrived at the scene and I squared up to the guy. My fists weren't even clenched, more like claws. I wasn't looking to throw a punch, I was looking to take strips of flesh.

The guy, realizing this, and obviously baffled by the extent of detail I'd gone into, did a double-take at Barry and I both nodding in unison, assuring him that everything I'd said was true. Spittle and snot steaming out of our noses like bullocks. Then his face changed. Perhaps himself knowing the lengths a broken heart will take a man to in a fight, he ran off so cartoonishly that I actually expected to see a puff-of-smoke effigy in his wake.

As he ran off to meet his friends further down the road I truly warmed to my theme. I yelled at them, 'You motherfuckers! You cowardly cunts!' My outrage had given way to gusto now. 'You can't even stand by your mate when there's three of you against two of us!'

Amiable Mate met with his friends in the distance. I could only vaguely make out what was happening as I didn't have my glasses (yes, the rose-coloured sunnies I was wearing were prescription).

'Brendon,' Barry murmured, tugging on my sleeve.

'What, you wanna go pee on 'em to mark your territory, you fucken gorillas?'

The three lads walked over to where the eight lads we had said 'Orrye' to earlier were now milling.

'Brendon,' Barry continued, louder this time.

'Fuck you and your town, you shit-football-team-having monkeys!'

All eleven lads were now staring in our direction.

'Brendon—'

'And where the *fuck* is the sea, you pricks?'

'Brendon!' Barry snapped. 'They're talking to those other eight lads.'

'Southend-on-Sea my hole. There is no sea!'

'Brendon, there's eleven of them now.'

'They're all right,' I said to Barry. 'We said "Orrye" to them earlier.'

'We said "Orrye" to those three earlier as well.'

. . .

We started to run.

'Fuck!' I yelled. 'Shit, my glasses!'

Barry and I stopped and quickly scoured the ground for them. I'd gone from puffed-up giant to blind geek in one humiliating move. After scaring off three guys with my tirade I then squinted geekily as we both floundered about in desperation.

31

'Got 'em,' I decreed, holding them up like Barry gave a fuck. To his credit, he did.

I planted them on my face and it was now our turn to pelt off cartoonishly leaving puff-of-smoke effigies in our wake.

When it was apparent that they weren't bothering to chase us we stopped and cracked up laughing.

'That was a shit fight,' said Barry, coughing and spitting as he laughed. 'Me and that bloke were just embarrassed by the punches we swung.'

'You all right?'

'Yeah. He threw the shittest punch.'

'Ha-ha-ha, yeah, I heard you telling him.'

'I know. And how funny was that when he ran off?'

'I know. Did you see the look on his face?'

'Jesus Christ, you talk a lot in a fight.'

'Yeah, it gets quite scary.'

We relayed the whole thing back to each other blow by blow, and lack thereof. Giggling stupidly on the adrenalin of it all. Afterwards we walked along in silence for a bit, snickering here and there. I felt a stinging tear in my throat from all the yelling.

'Thanks for coming after me, mate,' Barry offered genuinely.

'No worries. Didn't even have to think about it.' I honestly hadn't thought about it.

After thinking about it, I asked, 'Barry, what the fuck did that guy say to you to set you off?'

'I've absolutely no idea,' he replied.

We laughed until I clutched at my throat in agony.

4

Finger Rings

'SAY WHAT YOU LIKE about 9/11, you can sure get cheap flights to the US on United now,' I chirped happily to Barry as stewardesses angrily threw peanuts at people. My intent was chirpy, but it came out raspy and debauched because I'd strained my throat so severely screaming at the people of Southend, and also because recently I'd taken to gargling Drambuie in the morning. Several musicians had informed me that Drambuie was good for a strained voice. Admittedly two of these musicians were also keen heroin users. So they also swore by eating lots of crisps after a night on smack to replace body salts.

'Say what you like about cheap flights on United,' Barry chimed back, mimicking my rhythm. His volume, however, was barely above murmuring to himself. 'They sure have a shit attitude since 9/11.'

In an effort to get enough attention from one of the stewardesses to get us our third drink, he bobbed his head up, down and from left to right. Then tried the internationally accepted face and mime: eyebrows raised, thin friendly smile, jiggle the plastic cup between thumb and forefinger dignifiedly. Like he was declaring the jape of the season. After

33

catching one skybat's eye, unable to disguise recognizing this she rolled her eyes, visibly sneered at Barry and carried on ignoring him.

Giving up, Barry turned to me. 'And the quality of stewardess has gone way down. Look at this lot. Bunch of moody mutton munters, the lot of them,' he spat with strangely amiable mock outrage.

'That's why they're so bitter,' I replied.

Barry looked at me, waiting for elaboration.

'Well, think about it. Some of these women have been doing this since the sixties and seventies. Back when it was a glamorous job. They were seeing the world. Getting fucked by the bright and the beautiful. Pilots were sexy then, and they were too. They were balls deep in them every port of call. Now those days are gone. All the men are too, and they're stuck up here handing out peanuts to drunken reprobates like us. They're crusty, bitter old sky bouncers. If they could throw us out they would. No hot girl worth her salt would bother applying for this job now and you can't rely on the pleasant flirtations of the gay stewards any more cos they all fucked each other to death in the eighties.'

Barry's eyebrows and ears pricked at my homophobia.

'Nah mate, perving on a plane or even the promise of decent service is a thing of the past.' I folded my arms resolvedly. 'Add to that, since 9/11 they, like every other fucken American who's been given a set of handcuffs at work, are now operating under the delusion that they and they alone are the last barrier of national security.' I was to discover this again and again on our trip. From security guards to prostitutes, if they possessed a set of cuffs they thought they were the fucken cops.

What's more, if you're on an American airline and you have

more than three drinks you're somehow 'disturbing the peace'. And by that they mean making them move their fat arses (I refuse to write asses) from the kitchen and back.

Considering this, I'd had an idea. 'Look, the only way we'll continue to be served is if we're ridiculously polite and gay. They can't resist a couple of queers and they can't be rude to us for fear of discriminatory accusations.'

'How can you be that homophobic and yet be willing to be perceived as gay in the same train of thought?' Barry snickered.

He didn't actually say that. Nor was he offended or caught off guard by my earlier comment. But one of us has to be the sympathetic character, and I'm clearly an arse. So let's pretend he was upset on behalf of his gay friends. Even though all straight men make gay jokes at each other when they're alone. It's how we let other people (and each other) know we're not gay. No straight man has ever, *ever* been offended by a gay joke when there are no gay men or straight women about to hear it. It's like a tree falling in the forest. A great big gay tree obviously. Any man who pretends otherwise is a liar and a homo. (Lesbians don't mind. They tend to join in. The lesbians I know refer to gay men as narcissistic bitchy queers and the gay men I know call lesbians ugly dykes. For a community that wants the same things they sure do hate each other.)

In short, straight men fear loving their fellow man. And gay jokes are a good way of telling our mates that we actually love them. You know it. I know it. And that's obviously the subtext here and throughout. Now, let's never mention it again . . . Ahem, you big poof.

So apropos, let's just say my 'character' went on to say, 'How is saying they died of AIDS in the eighties homophobic? I didn't say there was anything wrong with buggery. I'm just talking about the outcome. I'm not glad it happened. I'm actually complaining about it. Consistent travel abroad and arse fucking do not mix. A passport should come with at least three extra-strong condoms, gay or straight. I don't care who you are.'

Barry frowned. (He didn't. He laughed.)

'Now, shut up and hold my hand,' I said as I moved my left hand over his forearm and my right hand underneath to interlock fingers with him. 'Watch this. Nothing pisses them off more than not being afforded the opportunity to be shitty.'

I smiled and winked at the stewardess, hating, for lack of a better verb, her way down the aisle towards us.

'Geddoff.' Barry tore away his hand as she loathed up next to us.

'Ha! He gets so testy,' I conspired to her in my best Melbourne accent. Which, as I'm from Perth, is gay.

Barry elbowed me off.

'Barry Castagnola, I will not have you ruin another trip!' I then continued my 'girls' talk with her. 'Mha! Men! What can you do? Anyway, can I get a double Bloody Mary, please?' I then wrinkled up my nose and whispered, 'Extra spicy!'

She nodded and asked Barry, 'And for you?'

'Three beers, please.'

'Why's he acting gay?' she asked, gesturing at me.

'Dunnothinksitsfunnyiguess.'

'Oh.'

With that, she obviously went to shit our drinks out. I sulked almost inaudibly 'You're not a cop, y'know' at her. Like an old dog having a final defiant half bark after being told to shut up.

Barry turned to me with a thin smile. 'Mur-hur! Enjoy your Bloody Mary. *Exsthra sthpithy!*' He laughed genuinely and generously. I sat silent. He went on, 'That's good. You might wanna save your voice, mate. You're starting to sound as raspy as that fat gay guy that always plays the fat gay guy.'

'Oh yeah, the curly-haired one. I know the one you mean. Italian, isn't he?'

'Nah, Jewish.'

'He was the fat gay in *Independence Day,* wun't he?'

'Yeah. Not as good as his fat Jewish gay in *Mrs Doubtfire.*'

We sat silent for a bit longer as I pondered what everyone ponders when talking about the fat gay Jewish guy with the raspy voice who always plays type.

'I wonder if too much cock actually does that to your voice.'

'Mwah-ha-ha-ha-haa!' Barry howled. See? Not remotely offended or upset. Never was, never will be. Neither are you. Unless of course you're gay. In which case you've still no right to get upset. I've heard what you have to say about lesbians.

'So, where you staying?' I croaked.

'With my sister, then my dad. He's set up a gig for us next Saturday in an English pub. The landlord's really into it. It could be quite a neat little set-up, and an ongoing thing. This could be quite a big deal for me, bringing acts over once a month. Dad's absolutely chuffed. He's so excited about it, which is nice cos he's been a bit down on his luck lately. He's injured his shoulder pretty badly and hasn't been able to get out much.'

'See? See? Seeeee? That's the spirit! This is going to be awesome! This is going to change our lives! I promise! See? Seeeee?'

I was fishing for credit that never came. It didn't matter. He'd come round. This was going to be the best road trip ever. A spiritual vigil. We could both move on as free men. Well, Barry could. I was obviously already sorted. Living through positive thinking and embracing the collective unconscious, thank you very much.

Slowly we got suitably sozzled and were subsequently denied service by the bulldog-faced stewardess. 'I think you gentlemen have had enough,' she stated coldly and cunted right off.

'With a fuckin' head like that you'd think she'd want all men to get drunk,' Barry slurred. 'It must be the only way she gets laid ever.'

'Hey—' I went to complain, but he cut me off.

'Mate, leave it. The last thing we want to do is get arrested on an American airline.'

Without booze we sat bored for a while, fidgeting about, watching movies, et cetera. I was reminded of a game I'd read about somewhere that wrestlers play when they're on the road. It involves trying to get your travelling partner to openly look at a ring shape you make with your thumb and fore-finger. The point of the game being to come up with new and inventive ways to get them to look at it. I guess it must be inspired by the film *The Ring*. Whatever you do, you're not supposed to look right at it.

'Hey, what time is it in LA? I need to change the time on my watch.'

Barry looked at my watch, guessing. Next to the face I made a ring shape with my fingers, touching my forefinger to my thumb. Like the old international symbol for 'A-OK'. He looked square at it.

'Ha, you looked!'

'What?'

'You looked at the ring.'

'What?'

'It's something wrestlers do when they're on the road.'

'Ahhhhh, riiiight. Sorry, what?'

'I read it somewhere. Wrestlers in the WWE spend more time on the road than even comics do. So they play pranks or "ribs" on each other all the time. One of their road games is you have to make each other look square at this.' I remade the ring shape with my fingers. 'The only rule being that the hand has to be below the neck when you make the shape. You have to come up with new ways of making each other look at the ring.'

Barry nodded. 'Ahhhhh, riiiight.' Then he said with a thin smile, 'What?'

Ignoring his sarcasm, I made the ring shape again, just below my shoulder. 'You have to avoid looking at *this*.'

He looked right at it.

'OK, that's two nil now. But I'll let you off. And you have to try and get me to look at your hand doing the same.'

'Ha! I love it,' he said.

'OK, for this entire trip we tally them up.'

'Brilliant. I'm in.'

'Kay.'

'So, what's in this then?' Barry lifted his can of beer up. Obviously pointing at it with a finger ring.

I looked past where he was gesturing with his hand and stared him dead in the face. 'That's pathetic, you arsehole.'

'Hur-hur-hur-murrhurrrrr-HA!' Barry giggled.

We sat in silence again for a bit.

'So, did you let her keep the ring?' I asked.

'Fuck that. Gonna hawk it off at some point. You?'

'Nah, I gave it back.'

'Why?'

'Didn't want it. Too painful to keep and she seemed to want it more.'

More silence.

By the time we landed at LAX I'd tricked Barry into looking at ten finger rings to nil.

5

Provenza's

'I CAN'T BELIEVE they let you reprobates in the country,'
Provenz cackled at us. Drawling and sucking in air. (He wasn't
smoking but somehow always gives the appearance he is.
Moving his hand away from his mouth in a swaggering, con-
spiratorial fashion, he looks like something between the
Marlboro man and Tony Soprano.) A waft of curly hair
bobbed atop his large frame as he stretched his arms to their
full massive span to support his declaration. The Cindy
Crawford mole on his top lip almost winked.

Presence. That's the thing about Provenz. He has presence.
He wasn't necessarily jumping up and down, drawing
attention to himself. Yet all and sundry were aware of him. I've
been in nightclubs with the guy before, where no one could
hear a thing. Yet given fifteen minutes a crowd of strangers
will have gathered around him. Women tell me he has
leading-man good looks despite being in his late forties. To me
he looks like one of Andrew Lloyd Webber's cats. He would've
been the one that sang about fucking the Pope or something.
A cat. That's it. The guy's a fucking cat – slinky and
voyeuristic. He reminds me of my schoolfriend's cat, Yang. It
used to saunter in and watch us smoke weed. Naturally we

could never tell if it understood how stoned we were but it always appeared when we did, looking right through us, so ever-watchful. Now that I think about it, Provenza only ever eats white meat and tuna fish too.

Just as you did with Barry, picture Brando saying 'What have you got?' in *The Wild One*.

Now make Garfield say it.

Bingo! I guarantee you've got him too.

We lumbered our suitcases into the back of Provenza's car – a sleek new BMW convertible. I was thrilled when I saw it.

'*My* convertible, my convertible!' I exclaimed, jumping for joy.

'*My* convertible, asshole.' Provenz, one eyebrow raised, seemingly lit up a menthol using only his lips and teeth.

'Fair enough,' I replied as I skipped over the rear of the car into the back seat. 'The one I've got in mind is an old Cadillac with leather bench seats anyway.'

'Never gonna happen,' he offered coolly as he turned the keys in the ignition.

After three loud revs he tore out of the car park and immediately into contraflow faster than I'd ever thought possible.

'So watcha wanna do?' he asked as he swerved in and out of the traffic from LAX, screaming and yelling at other drivers all the way. Sensing his anger, I figured he was going to benefit immensely from this spiritual journey. Here was a man who required enlightening for sure.

'I need a beer,' I said.

'Relax, all in good time, buddy.' Provenz began to reel off a to-do list, swearing intermittently at pretty much everyone on the road. 'I've made a contact to get those mushrooms CUNT! you need for our trip to Vegas but we need to FUCK'N

ASSHOLE CUNT! get back to mine to settle in FUCK'N COCKSUCKER CUNT ASSHOLE FUCK! and make plans. Plus I've got a few EAT SHIT YOU FUCK AND DIE ASSHOLE FUCKSHIT! calls I need to make.'

'I need to take a shit,' said Barry calmly behind sunglasses. Staring off into the middle distance. His nose high in the air as the warm LA air washed over him in the front seat of the roofless car.

'My place is good for that,' Provenz fired back at him, ever smirking, his cigarette wiggling in his mouth. 'Also I've contacted the Laugh Factory and Comedy Store to see if we can get you guys some stage time while you're here.'

We both jumped at this. Holiday or not, comedians are stage whores. More so if it's LA or New York.

'I keep getting the strangest feeling that while we're here I'm going to bump into someone I haven't seen for ten years,' I said.

The guys ignored me.

We pulled up at his apartment building on Venice Beach. For November the place was still hot. On the corner opposite was a Blockbuster with the 'ter' smashed in. I made an impromptu suggestion for our gig. 'Ha! We should get up and make banal observations that no one could possibly have noticed.' I gestured at the sign and pretended to hold a fake mike. 'Hey, what's the deal with "Blockbus"? In Australia we call it "Blockbuster". Huh? Huh? Hey?' I tapped the imaginary mike. 'Fuck you people. You're dead inside. C'mon! "Blockbus"? There's a sign in Venice with the T-E-R smashed in.' I tapped the fake mike again. 'You LA cunts, don't you even know your own town? "BLOCKBUS"!' I gestured emphatically.

Provenz and Barry were howling as we unloaded our bags out of the boot.

'Yeah, then I could get up and make out like I haven't heard you do it,' Barry said. '"Hello, Laugh Factory, I'm from England . . . What's the deal with "Blockbus"?' He gestured at his own imaginary mike. 'This thing's fucked . . .'

I know in print this sucks. In comedy, things that are actively unfunny make comedians laugh. It's kind of an anti-comedy. After years on the job you learn the rhythms and machinations of humour so well that actively ignoring them is very much an in-joke among comics. Funny is a language involving redirection and misdirection. Any deviations from this become in-jokes among funny people. One such dividing litmus test between unfunny and funny people is 'the orange for a head' joke.

A man walks into a pub with an orange for a head and sidles up to the bar. The barman says, 'I'm terribly sorry but I can't help but notice your head. How'd that happen?'

The man replies, 'No no, it's OK, this happens all the time. I was stranded on a desert island when I came upon a lamp. I rubbed it and out popped a genie granting me three wishes. For the first wish I asked if I could have sex with Elle McPherson. She appeared and we had a lovely time. Then I asked to be transported off the island back here. Which is why I'm still a bit parched and need a drink.'

The barman says, 'And what was your third wish?'

'I asked for an orange for a head.'

If you tell that joke to someone who's never heard it and he or she doesn't get it, or worse, they reply, 'Well that's just stupid', then they're not funny and you'll have to find the good in them elsewhere. Desert island/genie jokes usually involve a pun regarding the storyteller's appearance. Here, instead, it does exactly what it says on the tin. But like all jokes, if you have to explain it, it spoils it.

Which is exactly what I've done here ... And here.

Anyway, the guys loved the anti-comedy of 'Blockbus' and Provenza laughed his hyena cackle: 'HAAA!' then a second prolonged 'HAAAAAAA!' Provenza's laugh was more like a statement. A pronouncement that something hilarious was happening and that anyone within earshot should flock to the scene and join the merriment.

Barry looked him up and down quizzically, checking for sarcasm. Realizing it was his genuine laugh, Barry giggled along with his own machine-gun-like titter. Beginning with a hard, startled 'Murwahahahaha!', like a thigh-slapping whoop. As if someone had given him a pleasant surprise. Like he'd literally just seen a pig flying. Then settling into a goofy, warm rat-tat of 'M'hur-hur-hur-hurhurhurhur'.

Ironically, as stated before, a lot of guys in my industry don't like laughing quite so much. Because, let's face it, if you're laughing, then someone else is clearly the centre of attention. They almost view it as a weakness. To me, that's like preferring masturbation to sex. Comics can be a bitter, envious and insecure bunch. But guys who won't laugh at someone else's joke are the worst culprits. Like every laugh ever gained by another human being is somehow a personal affront to them, almost stolen. Barry and Provenz were the exact opposite. Their laughter came easily and generously. For all my faults I'm not one of those comics who thinks, 'Fuck! Why didn't I write that?' I'm just chuffed to be in the world of funny people. It took a lot to get here and I'm honoured to be so. There and then I could tell Barry and Provenz were the same. I'd definitely picked the right guys for my mission.

'C'mon in.' Provenz led the way, slinging one of our bags, I'm not sure whose, over his shoulder. We took the elevator up to his place on the second floor. Inside a full-figured red-haired girl was waiting in his flat.

'Hey baby.' Provenz walked up and kissed her on the cheek.

'Hey. I let myself in. There was some shit I needed to borrow.'

She looked us up and down, waiting to be introduced. Eventually Provenz caught on: 'Oh! Shit, sorry. Ali, this is Barry.'

''ello,' Barry offered genially.

'And . . .'

Provenz paused and pondered, trying to decide which side of my ego he should introduce.* I made his decision easier for him by swaggering over to her, grinning, kissing her hello on the cheek and gently moving her hair out of her face. Finding an immediate excuse for a subtle point of contact being paramount here – her hair covering her face, a loose hair on her top, or an eyelash on her cheek. A boob askew would've been too far at that stage. And camel-toe realignment is an invasion no matter how long you've known a woman.

'This . . . is . . . Burnsy,' Provenz said. Acknowledging the

---

*I should try to explain this as briefly as I can. That year I'd performed part one in a trilogy of stage shows at the Edinburgh Festival called 'Brendon versus Burnsy' in which I separated my onstage and offstage personas. Brendon being me when I'm 'off', Burnsy being me when I'm 'on'. For nearly ten years I'd been acting out a role on- and offstage on purpose in what I was convinced was a comedic masterstroke called the 'ten-year joke' in which I would behave in a fashion so boorish that no one would be able to see the man behind the character. Then one day I would pen a show unveiling the 'real' sensitive, intellectual and thoughtful me onstage. Resulting in my receiving the Edinburgh main award, book and movie deals, etc. What's more, no one would see me coming because they'd always figured I was just some loud-mouthed bigoted buffoon. I'd show them. I'd show them all. Exactly what I'm still not sure of.

decision-making process as he looked at me out of the corner of his eye.

Later that day I would confide in him that I'd noticed this and I'd figured Burnsy was going to be a lot more fun on this trip than Brendon ever could.

'I can do a week with Burnsy,' Provenz added with a chaotic look in his eyes.

'Well hello, Burnsy,' Ali purred. Her voice upwardly inflected, responding to the gentle but blatant flirtation.

'Ali's one of my oldest and best friends,' Provenz interjected.

Friend! Good to note.

'Barry and Burnsy are the dudes from England I was telling you about,' he continued.

'Although I'm Australian,' I added.

'Oooooh, an Aussie,' she purred. 'I thought I noticed the sexy accent.'

God bless America.

I threw myself into it so much that originally it was the 'five-year joke', but after a while I found I couldn't control myself and had no idea when I was or wasn't doing it. Whenever my friends asked me why I was behaving in such a fashion (having an inkling of the 'real me' as they did) I would always reply in a super-thick Aussie accent, 'Five-year joke, mate. Five-year joke.' By the time 'Brendon versus Burnsy' came round it took me nearly three years of hindsight to even realize that it'd been ten years of behaving in this fashion. I'd done the whole thing on purpose, eventually unknowingly, but on purpose nonetheless.

Needless to say, the 'ten-year joke' didn't work, I didn't win anything, I didn't show anyone anything, it wasn't worth it, I wasn't as smart or deep as I thought I was, and it led to a complete and utter mental break-down. But again, that's an entirely different book altogether. I'm sorry to keep threatening you with this 'other book'. Let's just hope the threats are idle and we'll end it here.

If I seem removed from this now, it's simply because it isn't me any more. Hell, while I'm at it, I'll blame all the sexism, racism, homophobia and poor grammar on Burnsy too.

Seriously.

It's the only country in the world where women feel that way. I would say possibly rural Ireland, but I think they're just craving a wider gene pool. Never in my travels have I heard a French woman utter, 'Now say somesing to me in your Auzzie aczent . . .' To any other nation Australian men sound like passing trucks honking on a motorway and our women sound like cats trying to bark.

'OK, I gotta go,' Ali said, interrupting my train of thought and kissing Provenz gently on the cheek. He kissed back. 'I'll catch up with you later.'

'Kay, catch up with you later. I gotta work out what I'm gonna do with these reprobates.'

'See you later, boys. Nice to meet you, Burnsy,' she breathed, and with a light pat on my chest she was gone.

Barry stood there smirking at me. I squatted, patted my chest then straightened my legs, standing up, spreading my arms out wide. My left arm was in the two o'clock position, my right arm at eight. Grinning the big wide grin like I had in my vision. As if my grin had brought the sun out. It was a move I would do onstage if a joke had gone down particularly well or I was just particularly proud of myself for no real apparent reason. Like I said, I was a bit of a wanker.

Barry tittered. 'That didn't take you long.'

I did the same cabaret move with my arms again, grinning broadly.

'Mur-hur-hur-hur-hur. Hey Brendon, I think we should get you some coke,' he added sarcastically, 'you look like you need some more confidence.'

Provenz and I cackled.

'How do you know her?' I asked Provenz.

'She used to live next door. Now she's one of my best friends.

Man, I love that girl so much. I didn't know what it was to love someone completely until I met her.' Without skipping a beat he turned to me. 'You should definitely fuck her.'

'What? Didn't you guys go out? Won't that fuck with your head?' I spluttered.

'What, so we fucked a few times and now I own her? That's not true love. That's owning someone. I think she'd like to fuck you and I love both of you. Fucking go for it! Fuck her brains out. True love is complete acceptance of another person and placing no boundaries *whatsoever*. Complete acceptance.'

Barry shrugged compromisingly. You had to give it to Provenz. He could make anything sound like sense.

We stood there in his kitchen considering it for a while until ADHD intervened.

'Cool poster,' Barry said, squinting up at a print of Jesus on Provenz's wall.

I thought this weird as both Provenz and Barry were atheists. I stared back and forth from Provenz to Barry to the poster.

'Take a closer look,' Provenz offered, reading the quizzical look on my face.

I walked up alongside Barry and started squinting at it too. 'Ahhhh, that makes more sense.' The picture was actually a composite of hundreds and hundreds of hardcore pornographic images.

Earlier that year I'd had what alcoholics refer to as a moment of clarity, an experience where at my darkest and most desperate hour, after just finding out that *she* had gone back to *him*, I really properly contemplated killing myself. Instead I dropped to my knees and prayed. Really prayed, begged even, for someone, anyone, to help me. Then some sort of deep-seeded psychological sense of self-preservation kicked in and a voice began talking to me in my head. And thank God it did. The voice made me realize all the things I had to be thankful for and showed me how I would recover:

Now you know what you are. You're a preacher. Get up. You've got work to do.

I know it sounds like total wank, but I think we should be grateful that the voice didn't say 'Kill everything in sight' because it was incredibly convincing. It was the voices that had given me my vision of us. It was also the same voice that kept making wild predictions.

Reminded of this, I said, as I stared deeper into the Jesus-shaped fuck pictures, 'I've still got the feeling I'm going to bump into someone I haven't seen for ten years.'

As the disciple I now saw myself as, I couldn't decide whether the picture bothered me or not. Would Jesus have been OK with this? Pondering this, I figured he must have been knee-deep in pussy. Think about it . . .

1. Good-looking guy, according to the pictures (although paler and more blue-eyed than expected, given his clime).
2. Charismatic performer.
3. Powerful Dad.
4. Not remotely interested.

All this considered, I figured Jesus was a funny hipster swinger and would've been cool with his image being a sum total of butt-fucking, cumshots and blowjobs.

'You are Satan,' I joked to Provenz.

He smiled, raising his eyebrows up and down *à la* Groucho Marx. 'Thank you very much. Now, c'mere, I gotta show you this.' He led us into the lounge area. Up on the wall was another massive photographic print. This time it was a Jewish guy with a thin smile leaning against a piano. 'Guess who that is without his make-up. It's one of the few photos of him not done up.'

I stared closely for a while at the print. 'Groucho Marx?' Well, he was already on my mind.

'Nope,' Provenz replied confidently. 'No one ever guesses.'

That was a red flag to a bull. 'No one ever?'

'Never.'

'I will,' I insisted.

'I give up,' said Barry, instantly taking Provenz at his word that no one ever got it.

I tried for ages to place the face. The guy looked the way a young Shelley Berman should've looked. The guy in the photo had his nose, lips and mouth, but without the wrinkles. The real young Shelley Berman looks nothing like the old one. This was way more what I expected.

The guys were out on the balcony smoking and had finished two cigarettes by the time I conceded. 'I dunno, I give up.'

'S'fuck'n Chaplin,' Provenz murmured, lighting yet another menthol behind a cupped hand.

'No way,' Barry and I spluttered in unison.

'Yeah. Look how Jewey he looks. S'fuck'n awesome picture, man. No one ever guesses it's him.'

'Was he?'

'Yup. Why'd you think he had it in for Hitler so much?'

'But wasn't Hitler a fan?'

'Yup. Didn't get the joke I guess. You guys wanna smoke some weed?' he added, gesturing towards his outside balcony. 'Wait. Lemme show you where you're sleeping first. Probably best to get some of the formalities out of the way before getting too fucked up.'

His flat was gorgeous. Everything a modern bachelor would have in mind. An open-plan kitchen led directly into the lounge where the windows went all the way to the ceiling, about twenty feet high. Everything was space. An open staircase led to a mezzanine bedroom, all white walls and sandy carpets. No doors or walls, just his bed and closets.

'This is you,' he said, helping me lug my stuff up to the main bedroom.

There was no clutter anywhere other than a bench-pressing bench with a good seventy to eighty kilos on the bar. Up against the rear wall was a huge white double bed facing the bay windows. The view of Venice Beach outside was only partially obstructed by the building in front.

'Holy shit!' I exclaimed. 'This place is gorgeous! What a view!'

'Yeah. It used to be all the way along but then they put up that fuck'n block. My whole building fought it tooth and nail. Can you believe I used to wake up to that view every day and still get depressed?'

'Dude, it's awesome. How can you people see that building as completely fucking up your world?'

'It knocked about half a million dollars off our motherfuck'n property value.'

'Oh . . . well, still, it's amazing. I can't sleep here though. This is obviously your room.' I meant it, too.

'You can and you will, I insist,' he insisted, and he meant it too. 'It's a rule I have. My guests sleep here. I sleep in the study. Besides, I got work to do and I don't need you cluttering up my office with your bullshit.'

I gestured concession. He smirked as he made his way downstairs to Barry on the outside balcony.

'Oh yeah, my other rule,' he continued. 'You have to fuck Ali in my bed.'

'Done.'

6

Merchant of Venice

'HA . . . HAAAAAAAAA!' Provenz bellowed.

'That's like thirteen nil now, you spastic!' I yelled at Barry mockingly. I'd tricked him into looking at another finger ring as we smoked joints and dry bongs on Provenza's balcony.

'I don't care. I love it.' Barry giggled, surrendering good-naturedly. Speaking in weed-smoking snippets. Each sentence like a short burst of air from an inflated balloon with the rim stretched wide in order to get the mouthpiece to make a squeaking noise. Puffing out his cheeks, filled with smoke, swallowing rather than inhaling, until his inevitable coughing fit and tears came.

Provenz looked on bemused yet quizzical at us both. 'Sorry, what the fuck?' he begged.

'I gotta take that shit I was talking about,' said Barry, exiting.

'S'upstairs, enjoy,' Provenz responded ambivalently.

While Barry shat, I explained to Provenz the rules of finger rings.

He smirked. 'Cool. You know what you should do?'

Provenz outlined his plan to me while Barry was on the bog.

'Good shit?' we asked nonchalantly when Barry returned.

'Yeah, showeditwhowasboss,' he replied under his breath.

'Hey Barry, help us out will you?' I asked, changing the subject, as I fidgeted with my phone. He looked over my shoulder at the phone in response. 'I can't seem to change the wallpaper on my phone. Can you have a go for me?'

He rolled his eyes patronizingly and snatched the phone off me with a 'What are you like?'

While he was shitting we'd changed the wallpaper of my phone to a picture of my hand in the finger ring position. It took a while to register. Then his eyes lit up and he burst out laughing: 'Mwurrhurhurhurur-hur-hur! Brilliant! Brilliant! I love it! *Love* it!'

'Fourteen nil, you arsehole!' I gloated. 'You'll never be able to keep up with the ways I'm gonna get you.'

'Hey, you fuck'n asshole, that was my idea,' Provenz protested dejectedly.

'I don't care if you gang up,' said Barry. 'Get me as many ways as you can. I'm loving it. I love surprises.'

Provenz rubbed his hands together. 'Game on. It's get Barry week.'

At the time, neither of us knew how far he was going to take this.

'So what you wanna do now?'

'I could eat,' I replied.

'Yeah, I could eat,' Barry concurred.

'Cool. Let's head down the boulevard.'

Venice Beach Boulevard is one of the few places in the world that looks just like it does in the movies, only with more homeless people. As we walked past the market stalls I saw something that made me trip a little. If you've done a lot of psychedelics in the past, sometimes the knowledge that you're going to trip again kick-starts it all over again. The weed wasn't just giving me a weed buzz. I felt mushrooms and LSD definitely rearing their heads too. The trigger was a white Jamaican dude with dreadlocks in an all-white outfit, roller-skating by. He was playing a homemade self-amplifying electric guitar. Everything started getting warm and wavy and I had an undeniable sense of déjà vu.

I'd seen the guy in movies before. In the background, when-ever someone shot anything on Venice Beach, he'd be there. Like a permanent fixture. He smiled and nodded knowingly at me as he passed by. His grin like mine in my vision. This was my movie. I hoped my ending was mapped out and we'd all learn and grow in a nice neat little bundle. But I definitely had the shapes of a beginning: a suburban kid from Perth, WA on Venice Beach Boulevard. One of the three major cinema story arcs: stranger comes to town; I forget the other two. I didn't know what I'd achieved by getting here but it had to be some-thing. I figured the Jamaican was nodding at me because he knew the secrets I did. We were both free spirits. Not a care in the world, unencumbered by what society felt we should be. What I hoped Barry and Provenz would become too if they helped me pursue my photo. Yeah, that was it.

'We write our lives, gentlemen,' I muttered unintentionally to Barry and Provenz.

'Wha?' they replied in unison.

'Oh, nothing. Although I keep getting the feeling that I'm going to bump into someone I haven't seen for ten years. I just know it.'

This was still not the last time I would say this. I caught myself nearly revealing everything and dismissed it. Admitting to anyone that you were where you were because some voices had told you to do so really requires timing and a major omen as evidence.

'What you wanna eat?' Provenz asked, cutting through my musings.

'I could do Mexican?' I offered.

'Yeah, burritos and shit,' said Barry.

Provenz stared at us flatly again.

'Mexican food sucks in England,' we explained in response.

'Well, I'll be sure to make you take me to get chips and curry sauce when I next land in London,' Provenz protested.

'Aw c'mon, that's not the same,' we moaned.

'No it ain't. I'm fucking with you. I could do a taco. Let's head up here, I know a place.' Provenz gestured further up the Boulevard. The strains of the Jamaican's guitar were still in the distance.

The self-proclaimed world-famous Venice Beach markets that line the Boulevard (which is very LA: even non-cognitive concepts presume they're globally renowned) are not really markets per se. Most markets sell stuff. Venice Beach seems to be littered with people selling what they reckon. Tarot card readers, atheists, spiritual gurus, sometimes just a guy with a white board writing down his thoughts in marker pen. The atheists just sat there in deckchairs with a sign behind them saying 'American Atheist Society'. While everyone else was flogging pseudo-enlightening bullshit, they were offering the most deliciously tongue-in-cheek counterpoint. Just sitting there not reckoning anything other than . . . well, not that anyway. Nothing to sell. Not even yelling, 'This is all bullshit!' I felt the urge to buy them a crystal from the stall next door.

Further along I noted a henna tattoo stand. I immediately had an idea. 'I'm gonna get a tattoo later,' I said, with the intent of planting a seed.

'All right,' came the noncommittal replies.

Over several plates of flour tortillas, avocado, salsa, sour cream, mince, kidney beans and a few jugs of margarita, we started another one of our trip's many running anti-humour jokes. Any time one of us made a your-mum joke or said anything mildly innuendous (I'm aware that's not a word but it really should be), the others would take it completely literally and reply 'Why would you say that?' and 'That doesn't even make any sense'.

For example:

'Whoa, it stinks a bit here.'

'Your mum stinks.'

'Why would you say that?'

'That doesn't even make any sense.'

'My mum's got no problem with personal hygiene.'

'You've never even met her.'

'I think you're making that up.'

'I don't think you even know what you're saying.'

Et cetera.

We tuned into the background music. Barry announced, 'I know this tune. I had the album when I lived out here. I used to play it all the time. I can't remember the name of the band but they used to be one of my favourites.'

He said this in the same tone I'd used when I was certain I was going to bump into someone I hadn't seen in ten years, yet I paid it no heed.

When Barry left our table briefly to go to the toilet, I told Provenz my idea for tricking him again. I was going to get a tattoo of a finger ring on my left shoulder.

As always, Provenz had a more elaborate plan. 'You know what else you should do? On your wrist you should have another tattoo of the tattoo. Then when you point it out to him, you can point at it with yet another finger ring and get him with three in one.'

'Brilliant!' You had to give it to him. For a man approaching fifty he was fantastically immature.

After paying our bill we made our way back down the promenade.

'I'm gonna stop here and get my tattoo,' I said to the guys as we passed the henna tattoo stand.

'OK, me and Barry will head back,' Provenz conspired.

'Yeah, I gotta give my dad and sister a call,' came Barry's reply. 'Probably should have an argument with them or summink. That'dbegood.' He giggled.

Once they were gone I turned to the guy at the stand. 'Can you do a tattoo of anything?'

'My wife can do a tattoo of anything, she's really talented,' came the reply from the hippy.

'OK. I need a tattoo of this.' I made the ring shape with my thumb and forefinger.

'Sure, she can do that.'

'Then on the wrist of the hand I need a tattoo of another hand making the ring shape.'

'You want another tattoo of the tattoo?'

'Yeah.' Salvador Dalí would've been proud.

'My wife can do that, she's really talented,' he reiterated.

Everyone in LA is talented apparently. They let everyone know too. It's like they're under the constant misapprehension that everyone is a casting director of some sort waiting to discover them. Which in turn makes most people act like they're a casting director.

'My wife won't be long,' he said, and ushered me to a chair under their canopy. I wanted to ask if she was off being talented somewhere. 'So where's that accent from? You from Ireland?'

I felt my Irish friends bristle at the prospect. I was just

pleased he hadn't said South African. 'I'm Australian but I live in London,' I replied.

Normally the next question is 'So what did you move there for?' But again, this was LA. He clearly presumed it was something to do with entertainment. The predictable list of questions that usually allowed me to announce that I was a comic were, surprisingly to my chagrin, cut short.

Before long his talented wife returned from spawning whatever creative miracle had struck her fancy and she sat down next to me. I explained to her what I needed, she got me to make the shape with my fingers as a model, and she got started.

7

Hangin' with the Homeless

'So what did you get?' Barry asked, once I'd made my way back to Provenza's. They were on the balcony smoking more weed.

I pulled up my sleeve and gestured at the henna tattoo, simultaneously making a finger ring. He peered in, eye level, at all three ring images at once. Squinting directly at them with his mouth open. Then his face lit up in recognition. He burst into more fits of gleeful laughter. Ecstatic at the effort on his behalf.

I giggled too. 'That's seventeen-one now!' He'd got one in over dinner while passing me a jug of margarita. I was chuffed he was digging the game so much. Pleased that my efforts were appreciated and that the extent of work and thought going into cheering Barry up was doing the job.

'Three in one! Brilliant!' Barry tittered and sighed.

'I sat still for an hour for you.'

'Brilliant!'

'And I had to listen to a cunt.'

'S'evenbetter!'

'I'll still think of more ways to thrash you, you know.'

'Hey! Fuck'n asshole,' Provenz protested.

'Sorry, *we'll* think of ways. The extra tattoo on the wrist was Provenz's idea.' Provenz folded his arms contentedly. 'I came up with the henna idea though,' I said quickly, taking credit back.

'Brilliant!' Barry was unperturbed as to who came up with what.

'So what did we decide was on the cards tonight?' I asked.

'Well, I rang Doug Stanhope earlier and we're waiting for him to call back. I'm also waiting to see who's on at the Comedy Store and Laugh Factory over the next few nights to try and get you guys some stage time.'

I was thrilled on both counts. Doug and I had been in contact via the internet, swapped albums and had become fans of each other's work (I think), but we had yet to meet face to face. He, like me, was another filthy comic with a small cult following. However, as a cult comic in America Doug was doing a lot better for himself than I, the cult comic in England. I should stress here that claiming I'm a cult comedian is not necessarily bragging. It simply means a small, devoted fan base. Cult status in England is not really a good thing. It means I'm rarely allowed on TV and have to work extra hard for very little financial return. Whereas a cult comedian in America has a big enough marketplace to make him a million-aire, even without TV. I make a living, but I have to have a high turnover of material. Only a certain amount of people will ever be bothered to see it and it's pretty easy to reach all of them in a year. Which suits me fine . . . kind of. It takes a very special routine for me to not get bored shitless delivering it after a year or so. A great deal of my sense of humour is irritatingly repetitive and after a while I even start to bug the shit out of me. Comedian Matt Kirshen, whom I've written with and for, once remarked of me that if there was no audience and comedy was entirely left up to my sense of humour, I'd just be up there yelling a sentence I was amused by that day. As always, Matt was bang on the money. I got up that night and yelled what he'd said several times just to prove it. It killed at first, but after a while even fans started to look at me as if to say, 'OK Brendon, seriously, we get it. Move on.'

Doug and I swapped albums when we discovered there was a lot of overlap in our material. Not always in punchlines, but we'd certainly shared a lot of premises. Originally we heard of each other through a mutual comedian friend, Dave Fulton. Dave was forever quoting a titfuck joke of Doug's to me: 'So I asked my girlfriend for a titfuck. She asked, "What's in it for me?" I said, "When I come I'll stop punching you in the head."'

I guess you had to be there. I've never quite understood it either.

Then, on his first trip to the Edinburgh Festival, Doug and I had a very similar routine about fucking a melon on ecstasy. Dave brought it to our attention. My routine ended in my partner asking me, 'What kind of melon was it?' His ended with a fan approaching him, excited that he'd found another melon fucker, querying what type of melon he used. It would've been suspicious if not for the fact that Doug and I were the kind of guys who would fuck a melon on ecstasy and, given such a lifestyle, would also appeal to and attract fellow melon fucker lovers.

I contacted him via email, assuring him that stealing just wasn't how I worked. What's more, if I was a joke thief surely I'd steal clean. And, I didn't want to speak for him, but for me the routine wasn't exactly a 'keeper'. I could never see myself in a fistfight outside a club screaming, 'You motherfucker! Melon fucking is my territory!'

Thwack!

'Man, *I* own the melon!'

Crash!

'No, *I'm* the melon man! Everybody knows it!'

Anyway, since then Doug and I had been in touch every now and then and I'd always been dying to meet him. To be honest I looked up to him quite a bit. Not for any melon-related prowess, but if comics on the British circuit were to be honest, we all crave American recognition and acceptance.

To me, him being in contact now and us having artistic visions in common was definitely another sign that we were tapping into the collective unconscious. Perhaps a melon-fucking collective, but a collective nonetheless.

'That's awesome!' I exclaimed. 'I love Doug. He and I have never been in the same room before. And I swear I'm going to bump into someone I haven't seen for ten years.'

'Yeah, he's a great guy,' Provenz said, ignoring my premonition. 'He did some great stuff on *The Aristocrats* for me. He told the joke to his baby nephew. It was one of the biggest reactions the film got. He utilized the phrases "analingus", "blort of wet acrid shit" and "her vagina looks like a callused dockworker's heel" in the set-up. The baby started crying with immaculate timing.' Provenz smirked, his cigarette ever wiggling.

I wondered if he'd ever been a newborn, or if he just shot out of the womb a fully grown adult pervert.

I turned to Barry. 'You get a hold of your dad?'

'Yeah, he's gonna meet us later.'

We sat and watched the sun set on Provenza's balcony, shooting the shit, drinking and smoking more weed. The November evening air still as acrid and warm as Stanhope's aforementioned blort. After a while, almost as soon as the sun had gone down, we heard drums and revelry in the distance.

'Is that a beach party?' Barry asked.

'Yeah,' Provenz replied. 'They do it every night.'

'That's fucking awesome,' I said. 'We gotta go.'

Provenz wiggled his cigarette and shrugged his shoulders again. 'Sure, why not? I've lived here for years and never once checked it out.'

We stopped at the corner store, bought two six-packs, then made our way to the shore where the drums were emanating from. There was a good twenty- to thirty-strong party happening. We sat down with them and I offered the guy next to me a beer.

'You have beer!' he exclaimed. 'This guy has beer!'

Immediately, three guys sidled up next to me. I gave them a beer each and they in turn handed over several pipes stashed with weed. I took one for myself and passed on one each to Barry and Provenz. We were hailed at the party as the kings who brought beer. If I'd known it'd elicit this response I would've forked out for a carton. It seemed odd. A beach party without beer.

'Why the fuck are they so excited about a six-pack?' I whispered/yelled into Provenza's ear over the sound of the drums.

'They're fuck'n homeless, dude,' he hollered back in my ear. 'They don't have any money.'

Barry and I did a double-take at each other. Simultaneously our eyes lit up as we raced to say, 'That's not homeless, that's just never going home from the party.' Barry laughed, having got there first.

It had to be said they were nothing like English homeless people. Not smelly, drunk or cantankerous. I imagined the warm weather, beach and weed lent itself to that. But to not even smell homeless? It was weird. They pretty much reminded me of every beach bum I knew growing up in Perth. I guessed the difference was in England a lot of homeless people just don't want to live in society. These guys just hadn't made it in show business. Partying on the beach every night probably didn't help. I'd never been to a party that was self-perpetuating before.

We sat about chatting with them happily, telling them where we were from etc. Then suddenly the drums kicked in extra loud. Everyone stood up and started whooping, cheering and dancing. Forming a circle and dancing round it like some sort of stereotypical pow-wow. People around the circle took turns jumping in the middle and dancing about while everyone on the outside cheered them on.

It came to Barry's turn, and to be honest I was worried about him. He may have been having a laugh but he was still a man on the rebound. I figured he'd decline bashfully. To the contrary: he jumped at his turn. Flinging himself in the middle, he totally went for it. Like I said before, he's fit and fast for a big fella. And he totally went ballistic. Skipping his knees high in the air on the spot. He got the loudest cheers of all as his manic moves really revved up the circle to new heights. Provenz started a chant: 'Go Barry, go Barry, go Barry!' Everyone joined in. 'Go Barry, go Barry, go Barry, go Barry!' This spurred him on, and he made his way round the circle high-fiving everyone one by one and jigging his arms about like a man possessed. He pushed it until eventually he retired from the centre of the circle, prompting a hysterical reaction from the crowd. More people gathered to the circle as he bent over out of breath with his hands on his knees.

'Whooo Barry!' Provenz and I cheered as we slapped him on the back.

He huffed and puffed then uttered breathily, 'I'm' – *puff, pant* – 'fucked.'

He wasn't though. He had a great big grin on his face. He wasn't a man on the rebound at all. Here was a man on the mend.

'So how was my dancing, boys?' he asked.

'It wasn't just great, Barry, it was sublime,' I said.

'Sublime,' said Provenz, nodding softly. 'Good word. I think that's what we should call this trip.'

On the way home we saw the Jamaican guy on roller skates again. He was playing something Barry recognized. 'There's that song again,' he announced. The Jamaican smiled and winked at us.

Yeah, I was definitely on to something. The world was talking to us, letting me know that I'd done the right thing by Barry, bringing him here. You could see the signs. You just had to keep your eyes open.

8

Doug

BACK AT PROVENZA'S FLAT, Doug and Barry's dad, Keith, returned our calls and we agreed to meet in a bar somewhere near Doug's place. It was the rarest of LA bars in that it had a beer garden where you could smoke. Keith arrived first. Naturally he looked like an older, greyer Barry but with the hair of Kenny Loggins. Like a lot of men, he'd reached an age where he picked a decade and stuck with it.

I'd met him before. Earlier that year during the Edinburgh Festival Barry was struggling for numbers. He asked me to plug his show at the end of mine because he had his mum in the audience. I went one better than that. At the end of my show I explained Barry's predicament to my audience and commandeered them through the Pleasance theatre courtyard directly from my show into his. When I met Keith later that week, he'd already heard about this and was openly grateful for my helping out his son in this fashion. It wasn't that big a deal. It was a good show and we'd all got in free. Barry said it was the best night he'd had. Naturally I was happy to take credit. It was this act that had brought me close enough to him for him to call me in the middle of my vision. If kismet could exist between men, this was ours.

Keith, like Barry, was an unassuming man but with an incredibly dry wit. Barry talked about him often as he was more like a best mate to him than anything. Although something bothered me about him being so willing to party with us. I didn't think it was any sort of a way for a dad to behave. At least I'd had the decency to leave my boy at home while I was getting hammered. Hypocritical I know, but it's easier to project one's bullshit on to someone else than it is to change. But it was a small niggle, and besides, Keith loved me for everything I was doing for his son. So who gave a fuck so long as I was being complimented? Besides, he really was good fun. Not like anyone else's dad I've ever known.

Once when Barry was being heckled by a drunk woman Keith piped up, 'Why don't you go get a proper stiff one up you, you proper cunt?' Then turned back to the stage and yelled to Barry, 'Carry on, son.' For that and countless moments like it, Keith was a bit of a legend on the comedy circuit.

We were all happily shooting the breeze when I heard Doug's whiskey- and cigarette-induced growly voice making its way round the corner. We saw each other through the clear plastic lining surrounding the beer garden and our faces lit up as our eyes met.

'Finally!' I bellowed at Doug over the top of everyone's happy conversation, dropping everything to greet Doug as soon as he got into the beer garden. I was already pretty hammered. Having swigged a shot at the bar for myself every time I went to get a round.

'Burnsy!' Doug exclaimed, arms open wide, just as happy to finally meet face to face.

I picked him up and hugged him. 'Finally!' I said again.

With him was Scottish comedian and promoter Brian

Hennigan. I nodded and hugged him hello for the first time too. Provenz stood up and hugged Doug hello and shook Brian's hand. Introductions were made all round and we all sat down.

'My round,' I exclaimed, immediately wanting to hold court any way I could. Everyone ordered beer except Provenz, who was driving.

I made my way into the bar more sizzled than anyone in my party knew. There were three black guys standing at the bar and I sidled up next to them.

'G'day fellas.'

'Hey man. S'up.'

'You from England, man?' one of them asked. Black Americans are always intrigued by white foreigners, I find. As long as you're not South African they figure you're less racist than 90 per cent of white America. Also, if we're to be honest, the rest of the world's white population loves black Americans and are just as intrigued by them. Hence a white Aussie approaches black strangers fearlessly in a bar. Even if they think he's English, both parties are like a twelve-year-old with a new watch. We don't break it open but we want to venture within to see what makes it tick nonetheless.

'Get fucked, I'm Australian,' I responded jovially. Pushing him playfully.

They all laughed. This was definitely not a response from a white guy they were used to.

'Cool, man, cool,' the questioner responded, enjoying my gall. 'What you doing in the US?'

'My friend just got dumped by his fiancée so we're going to hire a convertible, drive to Vegas, take mushrooms and watch the sunset.'

I felt cool saying it, and it invoked the desired response.

They howled and went in wide to shake my hand. They started slapping my hand with the black guy's elaborate handshake. To their surprise I reciprocated effortlessly.

'Hey man,' the guy said, 'he knows how to do the handshake. He's got some brother in him.'

I don't care who you are, white guys love it when black guys think they're cool. I've got black friends in South Africa who call me their nigger. And I have to admit I'm chuffed when they do.

Again, having gigged in South Africa I knew the full African shake, which is even more elaborate than the average black American one. It has all the traditional shakes and wristlocks but it also winds up with a brief pushing and sliding of thumbs. When the guy failed to do this I brazenly corrected him: 'What the fuck? Call yourself a black fella? What're you doing?'

They howled even louder at my elevating chutzpah. 'Man, what the fuck you talking about?'

'You ever been to Africa, mate?' My voice was raspy like Doug's from all the booze and fags. It matched my audacity perfectly. I think in America you're not even allowed to say 'Africa' in front of black people unless you follow it up immediately with '-n American'. I think the sensitivity could be due to the fact that only decades earlier 'Africa' was always preceded by the words 'go back to'.

I would never try and pull this shit with any English black people, however. Let's face it, you know white Australia too well.

'In Africa they do it like this,' I said, and guided him through the handshake again with the thumb press this time.

Here I was, a white Australian, showing a black American how to shake hands like a 'proper' African. My newfound friends found it hilarious. They were literally slapping their thighs.

The laughter wore down to a natural chorus of sighs.

'What's your name, man?'

'Burnsy.'

'Hey Burnsy. This is Bob, Darryl, and I'm Zanthor.'

'Fucken what? Zanthor? That name is awesome! What, do you fucken fight crime or something? Please tell me that if you tear your shirt open there's a big "Z" underneath.' I was genuinely thrilled that I'd met a dude called Zanthor. 'Show me your licence. Is it a rap thing? *Zanthor!* Fuck! Did your parents hate you?' I was like a dog with a bone.

As their laughter died down again, Zanthor slapped me on the shoulder. 'Hey Burnsy, what you drinkin'?'

'Well that's very kind of you fucken Zanthor but I got a big round to get. Thanks, mate.'

The barman, who'd been enjoying the show, piped up, 'What'll it be then?'

'Can I get five beers, a squash, five Jaigermeisters and a double whiskey while I'm waiting.'

'Whoa, you ain't fuckin' around!' came the chorus from Zanthor and the Zanthites.

'I got a broken heart to heal, gentlemen.' I knocked back the whiskey in one and through a shiver rasped, 'I'm on a mission from God.'

'I heard that', 'Amen' came the various replies through the nods, raised tumblers and high fives from the Zanthites.

I took the tray with my drinks and nodded my goodbyes. 'Gentlemen! Good to meet you. Behave yourselves.'

'Yeah, Burnsy, you too.'

I made my way out into the beer garden to Doug and the guys. Immediately I made my presence known there too.

'What took you so fucking long?' they nagged.

'I met a guy called Zanthor,' I replied ecstatically. They deferred. It seemed as good a reason as any. 'How cool is that?' I set the drinks down on the table and handed them out.

Spontaneously, an opportunity struck me. 'Hey, check it out, he gave me this.' I placed my open palm in the middle of the table. It was empty, but I made a finger ring in Barry's direction. He stared straight at it. He and Provenza howled while the others looked on baffled. 'That's like twenty to four now, you twat!' Barry was still loving it. I'd got him a few times earlier and Provenza had started helping him out to even the score somewhat. Not that Barry couldn't get me, he just enjoyed being got so much more.

Doug, Keith and Brian continued to look on quizzically, awaiting an explanation. We all explained the rules of the game to them. When we were done I showed them my henna tattoo. 'Look,' I slurred, 'I got this done to get him. I pointed at it with another ring finger to make it three in one.'

'Er, um, great fuggen . . . I dunno.' Doug looked a little more worried and apprehensive than necessary. His attention was soon diverted to the tray of drinks though. 'Whoa, Jaigermeister on a Monday evening. It's a little too early for shots. I'll be out by twelve. I haven't eaten yet.' Doug looked me up and down, then continued, 'I thought you were a straight-edge guy. I heard you were sober on one of your albums.'

'Yeah, well I'm back.' I grinned a big grin, raising my shot glass at him.

'Yeah, when I heard you were sober I was thinking, this guy and me can't hang out. Cos, er, I dunno fuggen . . .' More of Doug's boozy logic. For a guy so gifted with such a genius turn of phrase onstage he sure did express himself a lot in real life with 'fuggen', 'I dunno' or 'I dunno fuggen' a lot. I didn't care. I was just stoked he'd been listening to my album.

'I took a break for a bit,' I explained, raising my bottle of beer and swigging it to wash down the Jaigermeister.

Admittedly on the album he was referring to the material in question which began with my saying 'So I haven't had a drink or any drugs in [however many days or months].' Then I'd wait for the crowd to say nothing and deliver the punchline. 'You see, anywhere else in the world that would get me a gut-wrenching sweeping round of applause. Here in [whichever town I was in] it just gets a room full of bitter people asking, "Why?" [Pause for laugh.] Surely you didn't have to drive every night?' No matter which town I was in they'd always gain a sense of civic pride that they were the only ones who didn't clap because their town was so hard-drinking.

However, as I gradually fell off the wagon the set-up to the gag went from 'Not had a drink or any drugs' to 'Not had a drink or a class A drug' to 'A night on the piss' as the goalposts of what I considered to be sobriety got shifted further and further apart.

The conversation made its way round the table organically. I waited impatiently for an opportunity to steal the focus again. Doug mentioned something about bombing onstage at a gig somewhere, which gave me the opening I needed to tell my favourite ever comedy death story. It's actually my favourite story of all time. Comedians love to share their death stories the most. It gives us a sense of camaraderie. We've all had to go through bad gigs to get to the professional stage and I guess the fact that we've died and are still standing is something we're all a little proud of. Statistically speaking, people's two greatest fears in life are speaking in public and death. Death is number two. Number two. I think that's why comedians call going down badly 'dying' onstage. When a comedian bombs everyone in the room feels like they've just witnessed death. That's why we're so shunned afterwards. As far as they're concerned we're walking zombies. It's like no one understands how we're still standing.

What doesn't kill you makes you stronger, goes the saying, and in stand-up a metaphorical death makes one stronger too. That's why we describe having a great gig as 'killing'.

Comedians can have a certain amount of disdain for an audience, as so much of our vernacular involves the crowd suffering. Our ultimate aim, of course, being to make people laugh until it hurts. The better we went over, the more vile our description of the audience's devotion to us:

Dude, I killed! I made them piss and shit themselves. I think someone may have lost an eye.

Man, I killed so much the landlord snapped his daughter's pelvis so I didn't have to when he gave her to me as a token of his esteem.

Mate, the gig was that good, everyone in the audience followed me home, watched me take a shit, then stayed while I froze the turd overnight. Then in the morning I drilled a hole through each and every one of their heads and skull-fucked them with my frozen-solid shit.

Dude, I'm pretty sure bits of them are still in my teeth.

It is a dark art after all.

Now, Doug had afforded me the opportunity to tell a story I knew would be appreciated.

About ten years ago, two Australian comedians were booked to do a gig in a remote outback pub. When I say remote, I mean remote. This was rural Australia, the Australia depicted in Castlemaine XXXX adverts and the *Crocodile*

Dundee films (though I should point out that real Australians have far bigger beer bellies and a lot less teeth than the actors playing them). An outback pub is the only place for literally hundreds of miles where desert dwellers can congregate. To put things in perspective, an outback farmer would think nothing of driving the equivalent of London to Newcastle for a cold beer.

So it came to pass that after a harrowing four-hour flight in a beaten-up twelve-seater airplane and a ten-hour drive in an even more dilapidated truck (in which our heroes had to take it in turns to sit on the back tray with the obligatory salivating blue heeler dog) they found themselves outside the architectural cliché that is the Aussie outback pub. I can picture this particular pub even though I've never been there. I guarantee there were four paint-stripped wooden posts on the porch supporting a wide towel-laden balcony upstairs, all sweltering under a corrugated tin roof.

Upon entering the pub/hotel they were greeted by the man/woman who poured beer/owned the hotel. The she-man took them up to their rooms that were clearly maintained at a level of humidity flies found most comfortable. The sheets were filthy and torn.

After a heavy night's drinking they woke the next day and wandered downstairs. The place was heaving. Entire families had come from far and wide, bringing their own deckchairs and wine coolers. All the men and their sons were dressed in blue wife-beater singlets and football shorts arranged in order of height, the women and girls in floral dresses. Next to each man was his own wine cooler filled with beer and ice. The stage was the only uninhabited corner of the function hall with a two-foot-high PA. Attached to the PA was a three-foot-long mike lead with a tiny pen microphone at its end.

On first was comedian number one whose act consisted mostly of sound effects. He blew the speaker within the first twenty seconds. Looking around at the stony-faced crowd, he realized he wouldn't be paid unless he did his allocated time. Consequently he had to press on for twenty minutes making dog, engine and drum machine noises with no amplification whatsoever. It goes without saying that the crowd were less than impressed as he barked and whooshed like a child doing a puppet show to disgruntled relatives. However, no one was booing, or for that matter giving any reaction. They just sat there dumbfounded, occasionally looking at each other and shrugging. Finally his time was up and he walked off to the sound of his own feet.

Enter comedian number two, who was not exactly known for the originality of his material. One has to wonder whether, at this particular gig, he probably wished he'd stolen from acts less cerebral than, say, Steven Wright. Said material may well have proved bankable in Sydney, where people's taste in comedy was more sophisticated, just not that well researched. Out in the country, however, Mr Wright's stuff died a death.

'Sponges grow in the ocean. That kills me. Ever wonder how big the ocean would be if that didn't happen?'

Again, the eerie thing was that even though they weren't laughing, none of the people were booing or heckling either. Until one adventurous lone punter stuck up his hand, humbly, as if in school.

Comedian number two by now was willing to accept any interaction. 'Yes, can I help you, mate?' he asked hopefully.

The punter rose slowly to his feet and nervously gave a quick look around to check that he wasn't stepping on anyone else's toes. Once he had confirmed to himself that there were no objections he pronounced unsurely, 'Ummmm, not quite sure what you're doing. I'm sure it's very good . . . but, well, the thing is . . . we've all come a long way to be entertained.' With this he looked around again for support. The other punters nodded and murmured in agreement. He continued, 'Anyway, you've probably figured this out for yourself, but . . . it's just not working out. So maybe it would be best if you just left?'

When I was done telling the tale I almost took a bow.

'That's fuggen hilarious,' Doug howled appreciatively.

'What the fuck do you say to that?' chimed Provenz.

'Brilliant!' concurred Barry. Bless him. We'd shared a few car journeys over the years and he'd listened to the whole thing for what must have been about the third time, patiently.

'My favourite bit has to be "Not quite sure what you're doing",' I said as a follow-up. The way I always do when I tell that story. 'As if to say, "Look, it's not you, it's us."'

'Fucken fantastic,' said Keith.

'Sublime,' said Provenz.

'Yes,' said Barry, arching his eyebrows as they chinked glasses.

'Right,' Doug announced, wrapping things up, 'we're going back to mine. I'll go get some booze to take home.'

'I'll help.' I stood up to leave with him.

'Cool. I'd better ring my wife first. She's already shitty with me for some reason or other. I dunno fuggen.'

9

Provenza and Keith's Big Adventure

WE GOT BACK TO Doug's after I'd insisted on paying for a mountain of booze. A few more friends of his joined us, including Fahey Younger, a Melbourne comic I hadn't seen for years. Now relocated in LA under the name Trinny. I didn't quite understand why anyone would come all the way to America just to redefine themselves. But as I said before, it's easier to project than change.

I hadn't seen her in years and she was one of the people I knew on the Melbourne circuit I could relate to and got on well with. Being young new upstarts we were kind of loners in an older man's game. I was chuffed that she knew Doug and was here now. I rabbited on and on about the parallels between him and me both personally and professionally. Pretty hammered now, I divulged part of what I saw to be our travels into the collective unconscious.

'You see, Doug, you and I are spiritual brothers,' I blathered at him and Trinny. 'You see, Fahey or Trinny, whatever you wanna call yourself. You moved all the way here and you found your own little version of Burnsy for a friend.'

'I guess Doug is a little bit like my baby, the way you were,'

Trinny offered noncommittally. Not wishing to upset the boozy love-in.

'Don't you get it, Doug?' I continued. 'We're from miles apart yet we're thinking and expressing the exact same things. I mean, look at us. We could be brothers. We even look the same.'

Doug did a double-take at me.

'I wish,' piped up Doug's wife Renee. She had joined us somewhere between the bar and their house. I remembered, in his act somewhere, Doug referring to the fact that they had an open relationship. Seeing as Renee was utterly gorgeous, my loyalty to my newfound soul brother went out the window at this offer of pussy.

'Oh really?' I responded, with upward intonation.

'Yeah. Doug and I are splitting up anyway. We should get together.'

Doug just looked on and laughed. I couldn't tell at whose disloyalty, hers or mine. Doug is an utterly remarkable man like that. I've never met anyone more committed to not giving a fuck. His middle name should be 'Meh', delivered with a shrug and a swig.

'Doug's an asshole,' Renee went on. 'And a loser.'

'Whoa! Whoa, whoa! You don't do that,' I responded, indignant.

'What?' she drawled.

'You don't ever call a man a loser in front of another man.' I meant it. My code of ethics, however shaky and misplaced, had been clearly challenged. You can hit on me in front of your man but don't ever call him a loser while you're doing it. Particularly if he's a buddy of mine. 'That's bang out of order, Renee.' I was proud of the standards I had set for myself. I really was.

'Yeah Renee, you fuggen cunt. Now go fuck this guy before I lose my temper.'

Doug was giggling, and we all cracked up laughing. In my hysterics I accidentally bumped the table and spilled beer on my henna tattoo. I rubbed away the smearing on the edges.

'Holy fuck, your tattoo's running,' Doug exclaimed.

'Yeah,' I replied.

'I thought it was real.'

'You thought it was real? That I'd do that just to win the finger-ring game with Barry?'

'Yeah. I thought it was a bit scary.'

I considered how nuts I'd have to be to scar myself for life just to trick Barry. Then I thought about everything I'd said to Doug, and laughed. 'I might be nuts but I'm not crazy.'

'That remains to be seen,' interjected Provenz.

The rest of that night is a total and utter blur of images to me. Between booze and jetlag I remember sucking on Trinny's finger and reassuring her husband it was nothing for him to worry about. I remember one of Doug's bigger older friends eyeing me up suspiciously and clearly thinking I was the biggest loud-mouthed dickhead ever. I remember not being sure what I'd said to prompt this but wishing I hadn't. The last thing I can recall is Provenza yelling at me, 'Brendon, please! Shut the fuck up! We're trying to get to know Keith!', everyone laughing, and Keith replying humbly, 'Really? Me?'

It occurred to me at that point that I hadn't heard a word anyone had said for at least forty minutes. Which meant chances were I'd been talking for forty minutes straight. And if I'd been talking for forty minutes straight, chances were I was being an arsehole. We still had six days of partying to go, and thankfully self-preservation kicked in. 'I'm gonna pass out just there,' I said, pointing at a bed just inside Doug's balcony. I stumbled over to it and crashed out, face down, into total blackout.

Obviously I have no idea what was said after I passed out but I *believe* it went something like this:

Ext. Doug's balcony – night. Brendon has passed out on Doug's spare bed. There is much revelry at this.

PROVENZA

Now Keith, you were saying . . .

Everybody laughs. Keith is holding a bong.

KEITH

I don't know if I should smoke this. I've been on Vicodin for my shoulder. I was in a pretty bad car accident.

ANGRY MAN
(gesturing at Brendon in bed)

Who the fuck is that asshole?

DOUG

That's Burnsy. He's a funny fuck.

BRIAN

He's on ma fucken bed, the cunt.

81

DOUG

C'mon, he's jetlagged and was scooting back
Jaigermeisters at eight. Besides, he bought all this booze.

ANGRY MAN

He's still an asshole.

TRINNY

No, he's sweet really, you just got to get to know him.

BRIAN

Fine, I'll take the couch.

BARRY

He's been caning it since we flew out yesterday.

ANGRY MAN

That guy just flew in?

PROVENZA

He hasn't stopped since we got here. Anyway, fuck him.
I'm still trying to get to know Keith.

Everyone toasts their glasses.

EVERYONE

To Keith! Keith, Keith, Keith, Keith, Keith!

Keith shrugs and pulls on the bong. He pulls too hard and bong water goes flying out his nose.

Montage – everyone is drinking, smoking weed and laughing. They move on to shots and get progressively drunker and higher.

Keith, after a shot and a toke on a pipe, coughs, splutters and pukes over Doug's balcony. Everyone is howling and laughing except Barry.

Doug pisses on to Keith's puke while everyone cheers.

Provenza yells at Keith in hysterics.

PROVENZA

You're fuck'n awesome! You're coming to Vegas with us and I'm gonna buy you a hooker!

KEITH

What?

PROVENZA

Yes! You're coming to Vegas!

KEITH

You're the fucking man, Paul! You are the fucking man!

Barry listens in. Not taking any of it too seriously.

Scene.

10

Breakfast at Doug's

I AWOKE, SEEMINGLY coughing up a pillow, as there was one actually in my mouth and smothering my face. Had I been so annoying that someone had attempted to suffocate me? I pulled my face away from it with a start. I'd not budged all night and had left a definitive indent in the bed. Surveying my surroundings, it took me a while to retrace my path over the past few days. Systematically ticking off exactly where I *wasn't*:

1. My flat in London.
2. London.
3. A Bed and Breakfast in Southend.
4. Southend.
5. England.

A plane . . . yes, a plane. That was it. Now that things were slowly coming back to me I started the process anew. Systematically ticking off exactly where I *was*:

1. America.
2. Los Angeles.

3. Not at Provenza's.

4. Doug's place. Bingo!

I looked at the clock next to Doug's computer. It was 6.25 a.m. The house was decidedly still. I looked out through the glass doors of his spare room/study to the balcony. The sun was only recently up and the smells in the air told me we were near the ocean. Outside, the place was a tip. Empty beer cans and cigarettes everywhere. They'd also managed to drain the few bottles of spirits I'd bought. Judging by the sheer volume of empty cans I figured that more people had turned up after I'd passed out. Then I remembered passing out. Then I remembered doing so because chances were I was being an arsehole. Then I remembered being an arsehole.

I looked back at the bed where I'd passed out then back to the balcony. I must've been really wiped out to have slept through the festivities within a few feet of them. I hatched a plan to redeem myself in front of Doug and his wife. They'd been such fantastic hosts and I'd clearly blown it.

I wandered downstairs and saw Brian asleep on the couch. It occurred to me that I must've stolen his bed. I woke him up to apologize. 'Brian,' I whispered. I don't know why. If you're trying to wake someone up you may as well yell. I think the whisper is so you don't get caught. So when the person eventually stirs you can say, 'Oh, sorry, did I wake you?'

'Brian . . . Brian,' I continued.

Eventually I gave him a shake and in my normal (booming) speaking voice said, 'Brian.'

He came to with a start.

'Oh, sorry, did I wake you?' I asked, covering my bases.

Brian blinked, slowly coming to, and did his own beery systematic checklist. Retracing events in reverse:

1. Who the fuck just woke me up?
2. Oh, Brendon.
3. Where am I?
4. Oh, I'm on a couch.
5. Why the fuck am I on a couch? I was supposed to be sleeping upstairs.
6. Oh, Brendon.
7. Fuck.

'Fuck, dude, I'm so sorry,' I lied. 'I so didn't mean to wake you. Do you know where there are garbage bags?'

Brian rubbed his eyes. 'Wha?'

'Never mind, I'll find them.'

I made my way into the kitchen and checked under the sink.

'Never mind, dude, I got 'em.' I held up the bags in triumph.

Back in the lounge, Brian sat up and started rubbing his face. I genuinely felt awful.

'Dude, I'm so sorry I passed out on your bed last night.'

'S'all right. It happens.' He genuinely seemed unfazed by it. He was, after all, Scottish, and, to top it off, a mate of Doug's. This can't have been the first time someone had passed out where he was supposed to sleep.

'Look, please, go back to sleep. I'm jetlagged and wide awake. I seem to remember being an arsehole last night and want to make it up to everyone. I'm gonna clean up upstairs. So please, go back to sleep.'

'Nah, you're all right,' he replied. He really was a good guy.

With that I made my way upstairs and started clearing up all the cans. You may remember earlier that I stated I'm incapable of doing anything quietly. As gingerly as I tried I obviously was still making an unholy racket. It wasn't long before Brian made his way upstairs to the messy remnants of the night before. He stood and watched me for a while before guilt set in and he too set about clearing the debris. As we did so I filled him in on what I remembered and how Provenza telling me to shut up was the trigger for my moment of self-awareness. He nodded empathetically, giving me the impression that he understood.

Between us we made short work of the mess and afterwards stood surveying our good work. Both of us feeling proud of what good house guests we made. By now the sun was fully up and it was looking like another beautiful day in LA.

'Right,' I announced, sweeping my hands clean, 'I think I might get some breakfast together. Where's the nearest shop?'

'Just go out the front, turn right and it's across the way. I'm gonna shower.'

'Nae bother,' I responded in my worst Scottish accent.

I went out, turned right and crossed the way. I picked up enough eggs and fillings to make omelettes for everyone. To my surprise, when I returned Barry and Provenz were there to pick me up. We said our hellos and then Provenz announced we should get out and get some breakfast.

'No need,' I declared, 'I've already got enough to make everyone omelettes.'

Both Barry and Provenz were visibly impressed. 'All right,' they said.

'You see, last night, Provenz, when you said "Brendon, shut the fuck up, we're trying to get to know Keith", it occurred to me that I hadn't heard another person's voice for at least forty minutes. So chances were I was being an arsehole. I figured I should get to bed. I kind of want to make it up to everyone. So I cleaned up as well.' I waited to be congratulated, but it never came. So I got on with cooking for everyone.

I made Brian's first. Filled with everything: ham, cheese, tomato, garlic, avocado and onion.

'Awesome,' he remarked as I laid his plate on his lap. It was enough recognition for me.

'No tomato in mine, please,' Barry asked. I bristled at the idea that he wouldn't want it exactly the way I was making it.

'Yeah, no ham in mine,' Provenz ordered.

Suddenly I felt quite offended. I couldn't understand why they weren't more grateful. I'd just acknowledged that I knew I had been a prick and now here they were barking at me like I was some sort of waitress. I snapped out of it and got on with their breakfasts.

Before long the smell and sounds from the kitchen and lounge room stirred Doug and Renee. In their dressing gowns they sleepily ventured their way into the lounge after having checked out upstairs. They were both openly pleasantly surprised at what I had done.

'Hey.' They nodded at everyone in unison.

'I cleaned up upstairs,' I butted in.

'Yeah, we saw. Thanks. Thanks a lot.' Doug tugged on his hangdog jowls. 'And breakfast too! Hey, Renee. Burnsy's doing breakfast.'

'I can see that,' she chirped. Clearly they'd made up. Either that or they'd had an argument about me and I had now redeemed myself.

'That's fantastic! What a guy, huh honey?' he added as Renee wrapped her arms around him underneath his dressing gown.

'What a guy,' she beamed.

This was more like it. People who appreciated and understood my amends.

But then Doug blew it when he saw the avocado. 'But I don't want any of that fuggen . . . fuggen guacamole shit on mine.' And with that he wandered off into the lounge.

Cunt! Cunts! All of them cunts!

Renee joined me in the kitchen as I cooked and washed up plates. 'So you doing dishes too?' she asked. 'You really don't have to do that.'

'Yeah I do. I hate people who don't clean when they cook. It's like taking all the glory with none of the work.'

I looked at her. Her breasts were nearly poking out of her pyjamas. My dick shifted.

'So, have you apologized to your man for last night?'

'What the fuck for?'

'You called him a loser in front of me.'

'Oh fuck off! You're a comic. You guys should be able to handle that.' She pushed me playfully. 'Y'know, Doug really respects you as a comic.'

'Does he?' I replied, excited.

'Yeah. We listen to your album all the time. Most guys give us their albums and they're shitty, but he thinks you're really funny.'

I was ecstatic inside. Like I said, I kind of looked up to Doug and his approval was why I was there at their house.

Doug came into the kitchen, joining the conversation midway. 'Yeah, at first I was hearing some of the topics and premises going "Hey fuggen?"' He pulled a suspicious face. Implying that at first he'd thought I was stealing from him. 'But then I knew that it went in a different direction each time and I loved it. It's fuggen funny shit.'

'I love the presumption in America that it's always us stealing from you no matter what the time frame,' I said. 'Seeing as my album was recorded and produced before yours.

When I heard yours I just figured we had some similar ideas.'

'Yeah fuggen . . . I get that . . . fuggen . . .'

I handed him his omelette.

'Lemme get some fuggen hot sauce on that.'

He produced some hot sauce from a cabinet and to my dismay absolutely doused the omelette in it.

'Holy fuck! How much hot sauce are you putting on my cooking? You know that's a real alcoholic's thing to do?'

Doug grinned, nodded in acknowledgement and took his food into the lounge.

I made Renee and myself an omelette each and we made our way in after them.

'So, what're you guys gonna do this week?' Doug asked.

'We're gonna get a convertible and drive to Vegas, take mushrooms and watch the sunset,' I replied proudly.

'Fuck! I wish I could come. I gotta go on the road.'

I was relieved. As much as I liked Doug, he wasn't in the vision. There were only three of us, of that I was sure.

'Fuck, I wish I could get out of it. Provenz, lemme give you directions.'

Doug got out a map and showed Provenz an alternative route. At one point during this, Provenz stared over Doug's shoulder and announced to me, 'Oh, Burnsy, we might have to forgo that convertible. Keith's coming so we might need his four-wheel-drive.'

'What?' This bothered the hell out of me. I liked Keith, but him being there was completely throwing a spanner in the works. 'I still feel like I'm going to bump into someone I haven't seen for ten years,' I insisted again. Why, I'm not sure.

'Kay,' said Barry dismissively before returning to the original theme. 'Anyway, like Provenz says, my dad wants to come so we should get a bigger car.'

'How funny was it when Keith threw up last night?' said Doug, laughing. 'Your dad's a king, Barry.'

'What happened?' I asked.

Doug attempted to relay the story. Giggling all the way through it. 'Fuggen Keith thought he'd try mixing Vicodin, booze and weed. He was like, "Oh, I don't know if I should toke on this. I'm on Vicodin for my arm." He pulled on a bong. Turned fuggen white and puked over the balcony.' Doug went into fits of hysterics.

'That's my dad. S'great innit,' Barry chipped in, embarrassed.

Now I was even angrier at Keith and them. Not only for fucking with my vision but for fucking with my magnanimous mission of cheering up my disciple, Barry.

'It was at that point that I decided I was bringing him to Vegas and buying him a hooker,' Provenz offered while Barry looked at me ashamedly.

'What?' I spluttered, even more flustered now.

'Yup,' Barry fired out sarcastically. 'Apparently I've got that to look forward to. My dad. Coming to Vegas. Gonna fuck a hooker. Awesome.' He clapped his hands then rubbed them together.

'What?' I spluttered again, glaring at Provenza.

'C'mon, let's get our shit together and let these good people get on with their fuck'n lives.' He jangled his keys as he made his way to the door.

'What hooker? When? I need my convertible,' I stammered indignantly.

This was getting out of hand. Exactly how much had gone on while I was asleep? First Keith was coming. Then my convertible was dispensed with. Things were slipping out of my control fast.

'Fuck, I wish I could come to Vegas with you guys,' Doug repeated as he stood up and hugged me. 'Burnsy.'

'Finally!' I said, forgetting the mission for a split second to hug him back.

'Finally,' Doug fired back in return.

Everyone said their goodbyes and gave out hugs as we made our way to the door.

'We are getting my fucken convertible,' I said, 'I'm convinced. I'm going to bump into someone I haven't seen for ten years.' I don't know why I linked the two, but I did.

11

Dude! Where's My Convertible?

'I NEED MY CONVERTIBLE,' I insisted again, having pestered Barry and Provenz the entire way home.

'You might have to let go of that, Burnsy,' Provenz said as he ushered us into his study.

'I need a convertible.'

'OK, OK.' Provenz resignedly switched on his computer. 'I'm trying to accommodate you here. I'm just saying it might not happen.'

'It *has* to happen. I really need this, guys.'

There was desperation in my voice. They both stared at me.

'Why?' Barry asked.

'Yeah, what the fuck?' Provenz concurred.

I took a deep breath and decided now was the time to tell them.

'OK. Before Barry rang me I had a vision. In that vision I was happy. It was me and two other guys. I couldn't tell who. But that's when Barry rang me. I decided that I wanted to pursue the man in the photograph. To prove to myself that anything in this life is possible. That our lives are a movie and we're the directors. I promise you something's up, fellas. There is a God and he loves us all so much and everything in this stream of consciousness we call life is somehow inter-linked. I've seen and felt proof. Not a judgemental primitive biblical God, mind. Rather a marvellous inexplicable one. There's been hints and signs everywhere on my way here. We are tapped into the collective unconscious here. If we take the shrooms we'll see it. I know. I promise you that if you help me none of our lives will ever be the same again. Please, I need this. I need to be the guy in the photo. Even for only an instant. I need to take shrooms, become one with the desert and find my answers.'

After I'd poured it all out there was a long silence. I sat there and waited for the revelation to sink in.

'What? And God really likes convertibles?' Barry asked, deadpan.

'I guess you're closer to him with the roof down,' Provenza added.

'All right,' Barry said with a shrug. 'Couldn't hurt.'

'Yeah OK,' agreed Provenz. 'Could be funny.'

I didn't care that they'd responded so flatly. So long as they agreed to go along with it. 'Yes, fellas, yes! I promise you, Barry, something miraculous will happen to heal your broken heart. You can achieve anything with positive thinking and belief.' I took another look at Provenza's composite porno picture of Christ on the wall. It was another sign. 'We can bend the universe around us if we want. Our lives will never be the same again. Something will happen to change us all for ever. I just know it.'

'Yeah, but your life also changes for ever every time you eat a Mars bar and take a shit,' Provenz pointed out with a shrug as he stared at his computer screen, searching for car hire companies.

'Yeah, some holy mission? Have you met Brendon? He

might look and sound like Jesus but he does a lot more drinking, drugs and fucking,' Barry snickered sarcastically.

At the time I detected no irony and went along with it at face value. I presumed in a way I was like Jesus.

I remembered something from earlier. 'There's something else I need to do. I'll be back in a sec.'

'Righto,' Barry said. 'I've gotta call my sister.'

'I got some shit to do too,' Provenz muttered.

I made my way back down to the Venice Beach markets. I'd remembered that in my vision we were wearing cowboy hats and I'd seen a bunch of them outside one of the shops. I'm not sure if I remembered it that way after seeing the hats or not. But facts get in the way of belief. Unless of course they support the belief, then they're cited as insurmountable proof.

I got us a hat each, Provenza's bright red with a sheriff's star on it. Barry's was tanned with some sort of fake teeth in it, and mine was a thatched light brown with opaque blue gemstones around the edges. I didn't bother haggling with the stall owner as I had no idea what I was supposed to pay for them. I asked him for a price for all three and accepted it.

I returned to the flat, where Provenz was trying to tap numbers into his touch-tone phone, swearing at it like he was driving: 'Fucking *cunting* thing!' He was obviously trying to use an automated touch-tone service. An experience made even more annoying by a phone keypad that wouldn't work properly. I could vaguely hear the computerized voice on the other end: 'Please enter the extension number now.' Clearly well practised yet unsuccessful at this, Provenz thumbed his keypad in response. It bleeped as he typed in the four-digit number slowly and determinedly. When he got to the fourth digit there was no bleep in response. He tried again delicately.

No beep. Again. No beep. Fed up, he pressed harder with his thumb. The phone gave two longer beeps. 'I'm sorry, you have entered too many numbers. Please select from the following options.'

'CUUUUUUUUNNNNNNTTTTT!' Provenza screamed. He started banging his phone against the counter. 'CUNT, *cunt,* CUNT, *cunt,* CUNT!'

'I'm sorry, can you repeat that?' the voice responded.

'FUCK!'

'I'm sorry, I'll have to reconnect you to the switchboard.'

'Fuck'n *cunt!* Answer your fuck'n phone! Give me a human!'

It was infuriating just watching the process. 'Man, do all your business calls begin with you this frustrated? Get a new phone, dude. You're starting everything in a bad mood.'

Provenz looked at me like an ape that had just had a man fed to him, breathing heavily over the carcass. His chest heaving in and out as he clasped the phone loosely, like a thighbone. Trying not to smash it over anything, he let out one final 'FUCK!' and hung up the phone.

I stood there for a while. Then offered, 'If it's any consolation I bought us hats for the journey and the photograph,' I said as I produced the hats from a bag.

'What photograph?' he quizzed. 'Oh that,' he added as Barry entered the room.

'Brilliant! Hats!' Barry enthused as I handed him his.

'Hey Barry, check out the teeth on yours.'

I put the hat up to his face, making a ring finger in an attempt to trick him again.

'Getfuckednotlookingatit.' He batted my hand away, popping the hat on his head.

'Hey, suits you, dude,' Provenz said.

'Very nice,' I agreed. 'Put yours on, Provenz.'

'I think it only fitting that I play sheriff on this journey,' he mused. 'Oh, by the way, I spoke to the Laugh Factory on Sunset. They're putting you and Barry in guest spots tonight.'

'Cool.' I nodded at Barry.

'Yeah. My sister's gonna come get us in Dad's Jeep.' He looked me up and down in my hat. 'Don't fuck her.'

'I ain't promising anything,' replied Provenz, lifting his hat in a most sheriff-like fashion.

'I need that convertible, boys, if I'm going to see this through,' I reiterated, steering their attention back to my holy mission.

'And I need Keith there if I'm going to see my mission through,' Provenz responded.

'Why do you *need* to buy Keith a hooker, for fuck's sake?' I queried.

'Why d'you need a convertible and cowboy hats?' he fired back.

'I've still got the strangest feeling I'm going to bump into someone I haven't seen for ten years,' I said.

This was the last time I would have to say that.

12

Body of Evidence

'I STILL THINK you've got to let go of the whole convertible idea,' Provenz yelled at me from the front seat of Keith's Jeep as we made our way to the Laugh Factory.

'No way. I need it. It's crucial for the photo.'

'Look, I'm all for it, Brendon,' said Barry, who was driving. 'And I appreciate you paying for me to come out here and all. But we need to fit Dad in and he's really in a lot of pain with his arm and all.'

'What are you guys on about?' asked Barry's sister. She looked like Barry, only with a valley girl accent. As with Barry, I imagined a similar scene with a police sketch artist:

'She was blonde and everything was in the right place.'

'Sounds like a Barry or a Kevin.'

'No, it was a girl.'

'Fine – Sally then.'

She was really quite patronizing to him. Like a lot of valley girls are to foreigners. Constantly saying things like 'Oh listen to your accent, Barry. It's so cuuuute.'

He told her to shut up a lot.

'Look, I need that convertible if we're going to see through my vision.'

'What vision?' Barry's sister asked.

'Nothing,' Barry said, cutting the conversation short, not wanting to involve her in our consumption of psychedelics.

Then, like a bolt from above, the Jeep's engine completely packed in and started pumping thick black smoke out of the bonnet.

'Fuck!' we all cried in unison.

The engine ground to a halt, pumping out smoke with such vigour we feared it would burst into flames.

'Quick, pull into that garage.' Provenz was pointing at a service station, rather fortuitously immediately to our right.

'Fuck,' repeated Barry as he pulled up, switching off the engine before he'd even stopped.

We all clambered out of the Jeep coughing and spluttering.

'Don't open the bonnet,' I warned, 'it might be on fire.'

'I know, I know,' said Barry. 'Fuck.'

'This is a sign for sure,' I announced, capitalizing on the moment.

'Fuck off!' Barry and Provenz fired back in unison.

'Fine. I'm going to go over there and smoke.' And I wandered off. Pleased that the universe had stepped in to aid my cause.

'I gotta call Dad, see if he's with the AA or whatever it is here,' I heard Barry say to his sister.

I leant against a pole far away enough from the pumps to light up a cigarette. I could hear Barry and his sister bickering in the distance while Provenz played diplomat. Before long I saw a guy with his girlfriend. As they got closer I could hear snippets of their conversation. The guy's Irish accent became more obvious as they drew nearer. It was warm, friendly and chirpy but with a more upward intonation at the end of sentences than most. It was hard to place which county he was from as the lilt was something of a hybrid between Irish and Aussie. It reminded me of someone I couldn't quite place.

As they walked by me my eyes refocused on him in the evening half-light. He had a big chimpy face and grin that again reminded me of someone. Casually chatting away with his girlfriend, somewhere in their conversation he said the word 'three' yet pronounced it 'tree'. The Guess Who? board game in my mind flipped slowly as I narrowed this individual down to the Irish guy who lived in Oz and said 'tree'. The following sentence popped into my head: *Instead of thirty-three we say 'tirty-tree'. That means when Prince Charles becomes king he'll be King Charles the Turd.*

'King Charles the Turd!' I bellowed at the Irish guy and his girlfriend.

'I'm sorry, what?' came the startled reply from the worried couple. I'm sure all they were seeing was some sort of beardy biker hippy with red sunglasses and a bandanna yelling 'turd' at them.

'King Charles the Turd?' I reiterated enthusiastically. 'You're a comedian. You used to do a joke ending "King Charles the Turd". You used to work in Melbourne. So did I.'

He stared at me blankly. Trying to place my face. It couldn't have been easy. It'd been a long time and I'd changed my appearance dramatically.

'What's your name?' I asked.

'Owen Cavanagh,' the Irishman replied.

'Owen Cavanagh! Fuck, yeah! That's it!'

The moment I said 'fuck' his eyes lit up as the growl of my voice got him past the beard, sunglasses and bandanna disguise.

'Burnsy!' he beamed.

'How long's it been since I saw you?'

'Must be ten years.'

'Fucken oath! I fucken *knew* I was going to bump into you today. You have no idea what this means!'

I literally jumped up and down while he introduced me to his now even more alarmed girlfriend. 'You used to do comedy?' she asked him. Given the King Charles the Turd line one can imagine why he'd never brought it up with her.

We carried on with a little more small talk. I told him we were on our way to the Laugh Factory. He was visibly impressed. I then bragged a bit about how well things were going in the UK and how much I'd improved since leaving Melbourne. I was still barely above open spot stage when he'd last seen me and felt compelled to validate myself. Out of politeness I asked him what he was up to. He told me details but I didn't really give a fuck. All I cared about was that he was there. He was my living, breathing, bona fide proof, and that's all I needed him for.

Owen and his girlfriend looked past me to the guys and the Jeep, steam still pumping out of it. My jumping up and down had obviously piqued their interest because they were sauntering over, rubbing off grease and still spluttering smoke.

'Guys, come here. This is Owen Cavanagh.'

They nodded.

'Owen, how long has it been since we last saw each other?'

'About ten years,' he offered genially, still unsure of the impact what he was saying would have.

'No way!' exclaimed Barry.

Provenza didn't react much at all except for an acquiescent New York Italian downturn of his mouth as he popped yet another menthol into it. 'Fuck'n cool.'

'We are getting my fucken convertible,' I announced firmly, my eyes wide and brows raised.

They both looked back at Keith's steaming Jeep. 'I guess we are.'

13

Laugh Factory

'SO HOW'D YOU know that guy?' Barry asked as we clambered out of our cab outside the Laugh Factory. We'd left Barry's sister with the Jeep for Keith to come pick up lest we be late for the gig.

'Owen? He used to do stand-up in Melbourne. He's a nice guy.' I laughed at my own comment.

They stared at me, waiting to be filled in.

'Sorry, I just realized that that's what comics say when they don't rate someone's act – "He's a nice guy".'

They both laughed in recognition.

'True though innit?' Barry elaborated. '"So what do you think of Owen?" "Yeah, he's a nice guy,"' he mimicked, rubbing the back of his hair uncomfortably.

'No, what do you think of his act?' I said, joining in the charade.

'Lovely bloke,' Barry replied, staring at his shoes.

'Great guy,' Provenz added, covering his mouth.

'Yeah, great guy, great guy,' we exclaimed in unison.

'Calls his mum and everyfink,' quipped Barry.

'So you gonna book him for your gig in Kingston then, Barry?' I enquired mockingly.

'Lovely bloke ... sorry, what?' Barry replied facetiously with a thin smile, cracking us up once again.

'Yeah, check out the queue outside the nice-guy club,' Provenz added.

'He used to do this thing about Irish people pronouncing "th" as "t",' I said, 'so therefore Prince Charles would be King Charles the Turd.'

'Sounds like a great bloke,' snickered Barry as we all howled viciously. 'Hang on, then surely it'd be King Charles t'Turd?'

'Yeah, that always bothered me too,' I replied dismissively.

My attention was redirected to a woman approaching Provenz. She was about my age with big curly hair, a slim build and great tits for a woman my age. Not that I've ever been a woman my age but I'm hoping I'd look good for it. If not I'd definitely get my tits done. Not expansion but a lift. I hate having saggy boobs enough as a man. If I were a girl I'd be doubly pissed off. Tits seem to be the only physical upshot to me.

This is getting weird so I should stop.

Nice Tits hugged Provenz, simultaneously slipping a clear plastic bag of dried shrooms into his pocket. Provenz introduced her to us, but her name escaped me. I was way too busy checking out her arse. She had a nice arse for my age too. I'm not saying any more, but it was nice and round yet she had slim athletic legs.

I was snapped out of my trance by Barry saying goodbye to her. 'Lovely to meet you,' he ushered in his higher-pitched nice-guy voice.

The moment she was out of earshot I turned to Provenz. 'Who was that?'

Provenz told me her name again but again it escaped me as the information was immediately pushed out of my head by his follow-up sentence: 'You should definitely fuck her in my bed.'

'You think she'd fuck me?'

'She'd totally fuck you.'

'But what about Barry? We're supposed to be getting Barry laid.'

'I am in earshot you know,' Barry protested.

'Yeah?' we queried.

'I can fucking pull on my own you know.'

'Of course you can,' I said. 'You're a nice guy.'

'Great guy,' Provenz added.

'Lovely chap,' I continued.

'Fuck off,' Barry said, and shoved us towards the club.

'There's a whole room full of paying customers inside just waiting for you to be a great bloke,' I snickered. 'Barry Castagnolaughs.'

'Don't call me that.'

'HA!' Provenz cackled. '"Castagnolaughs". HAAAAAA!'*

---

*I should qualify this with Barry being the exception to the rule. In the beginning I made reference to him being the guy who prompts an automatic 'lovely bloke' response from everyone. His is without an 'awwww' noise and a tilted head. He really is just a lovely bloke and is still hilarious on-and offstage. The two are rarely married because to be a complete all-rounder in stand-up one has to be able to summon one's inner cunt. The inner cunt varies from person to person, but one has to find it and harness it in order to be whole onstage. My inner cunt has ideas above his station. That pretty much covers everything. Once I let it be known that I'm aware of that and take the piss out of myself frequently enough for it, I can pretty much go anywhere and say anything I want in front of an audience. Because we all have the understanding 'I know – I'm preposterous'. No matter what I write about Barry he won't be bothered by anything except any insinuation that he's one of the guys that are 'lovely'. Even though it's painfully apparent in my descriptions and quoting of him that he's thoughtful, erudite yet succinct, and extremely talented. But Barry's inner cunt won't hear any of that. But he's also fully aware of that. Which is why he's a funny guy.

'No, seriously,' I said, 'go onstage and be lovely. Tell 'em all about "Blockbus". I'm sure you'll be knee deep in pussy.'

'Shuddup.'

Provenz sidled up to the big Italian bouncer at the door, who stopped us. He was gruff from the outset. Something that always riles me at a comedy club. Why piss punters off when they've come specifically to laugh?

'Can I help you guys?' the bouncer growled.

'Yeah, this is Brendon Burns and that's Barry Castagnola and they're the guest spots tonight,' Provenz replied.

'Yeah, OK, they can come in when they're called up to go on. Right now we got the open spots on.'

'Yeah, but these guys are two of the top guys over in England and they wanted to check out the local stuff before they go on.'

'Like I said, they can come in the club when they're on.'

'Mate, our names are on the door,' I said. 'Literally on the door outside this club. Up on the fucken wall.'

While I pointed, Provenz made calming palms at me and ushered us away. He made one phone call, then the bouncer, obviously having had his arse chewed out a bit, let us in begrudgingly, still committing to his shitty attitude: 'OK, I guess you can go in.'

'How about an apology, mate?' I snapped.

He didn't even look at me as he clicked his number counter. Provenz nodded – 'I know, I know' – at us again.

Inside, Barry and I turned to each other and said, 'What the fuck's up with that?' Simultaneously the comedian onstage said, 'What's up with that?' It would have been a massive co-incidence but it turned out that they all said 'What's up with that?' They also said 'Mexicans' and 'stealing' or 'mowing' at some point during their act. 'Mowing' being US speak for lawnmowing. Only a year or so later the owner banned even black comics from using the word 'nigger' at the Laugh Factory. It was a token gesture after a huge worldwide controversy when a video of *Seinfeld* star Michael Richards yelling it in genuine anger at a black heckler appeared on YouTube. But there was no similar furore regarding Mexicans then and there. Black and white acts just went on and on about Mexicans and maids. We could have paraphrased the whole section of the show into the single sentence 'So Mexicans steal – what's up with that?'

Barry and I looked at each other with raised eyebrows. Barry tapped his imaginary mike. 'What's up with "Blockbus", you pack of thieving Mexicans?' We snickered.

'So what're you gonna do?' Provenz asked. ·

'Dunno, be funny I guess. Barry, I'll go on first to get them used to foreigners being on. I'm going to do something about our journey into the desert and you should get the compère to mention that you're the guy coming across the desert with me. Provenz, are you doing anything?'

'Nah man, I just wanna see how you guys handle this.'

The compère came over and did the traditional American 'Anything you want me to say about you?'

Barry seemed nervous about the gig, so I took charge. 'Yeah, tell 'em I was the host of the British version of *The Daily Show*.'*

He was visibly impressed.†

'And Barry was the star of his own sitcom called *Cyderdelic*

* If you're British this may come as a surprise to you. That'll be because it was called *The 11 O'Clock Show* and I only hosted for two weeks before getting the sack. Sorry – 'came to a mutual decision with the network'.
† When in Rome, after all . . .

on the BBC. I'm also going to talk about crossing the desert in a convertible so if you could back-ref it before bringing Barry on . . .'

'A word of advice,' Provenz interjected as the compère went back onstage to introduce us. 'Don't say anything threatening or violent about Bush. It's illegal.'

'It's fucken *illegal*?'

'Yeah.'

'Are you fucken kidding me?'

'No. Post-9/11 it's high treason.'

'What is he, Henry the fucken eighth? Are people not aware of how fucken Orwellian that is?'

Provenz raised his eyebrows. 'Brand new world, baby.'

We could hear the compère doing his intro to me: 'Tonight we've got a very special act doing the guest spot. He's Australian yet he's based in the UK where he was the host of the UK version of *The Daily Show* . . .'

'Oh, and don't say cunt,' Provenz called out after me as I made my way to the stage.

'Please welcome, Brendon Burns!'

The crowd clapped half as loud as they had all night for the open spots just because the compère had said they were local.

'Fuck you, you cunts,' I blurted out indignantly by accident.

My voice immediately cracked, and for the rest of my set (and the trip for that matter) I spoke with a whiskey rasp way beyond my years. Provenz had his head in his hands. The crowd laughed in shock. No one really says 'cunt' in America. Whereas in certain parts of the UK and Australia it's more an audible punctuating full stop. Spurred on by the laughs I went further, growling, 'What the fuck kind of welcome is that? You've gone nuts for everyone else just because the compère said something like, "He's from your flat, please welcome . . ."

107

Yet here I come with proper credentials behind me and you're staring at me blankly the same way cows look at cars. As if you're saying, "Fuck him, he's foreign." Fuck you, that was awful. Do it again.'

I stormed off the stage and bellowed at the compère, 'Do it again, mate.'

'What are you doing?' he whispered.

'I'm being funny,' I whispered back in my offstage voice out of the side of my mouth. 'They didn't clap enough. Do you mind bringing me on again?'

'Cool,' he snickered, and got back up onstage.

The crowd were laughing more now as he hammed up his surprise at the audacity.

'Well, what can I say about this next act, ladies and gentlemen?'

The crowd continued to laugh.

'He's from Australia . . .'

They started whooping and cheering.

'He's based in the UK . . .'

They whooped louder.

'He used to host their *Daily Show* . . .'

The noise reached fever pitch.

'Please welcome, BRENDON BURNS!'

When I walked on this time the crowd were practically standing on their chairs. The Laugh Factory is usually frequented by open spots looking to get discovered or stars running in new stuff. The crowd were genuinely appreciative of the lack of polish.

'Oh you're too kind, I had no idea,' I gushed sarcastically as they howled and whooped. 'That's the odd thing about America. You really don't give a fuck about the rest of the world, do you? The compère could have said "This guy is an actual king who can literally shit fire" and you'd still go, "I wish he was from Kansas. They've got good ribs in Kansas."'

It was going well. I figured I'd better do a joke.

'So I was up in New York in the village . . .' I hadn't been. I was lying. That's how jokes work. 'A lot of gay guys in the village, but very few lesbians. Very few lezzas,' I reiterated to a bloke in the front row. 'And I felt ripped off, mate. But then I figured it out. It's because lesbians can't afford to live in the village. Whereas gay guys can. Because gay guys tend to be quite well off. And that's because gay guys DON'T HAVE A FUCKEN GIRLFRIEND.'

I appreciate the gag translates to page awfully, as do most stand-up gags. Admittedly, that's largely due to the fact that the timing in the reader's head is shit. It's one of my oldest openers and a guaranteed laugh followed by a round of applause. It's a basic redirecting line, a comedy staple. The comedian takes the audience in one direction for a while then switches them somewhere else at the last second. I always liked to make the build-up slow on this one. Pausing after each sentence. Until the punchline arrives the crowd are left hanging for quite some time, wondering whether I'm funny or not. It's something that always makes the room more nervous than me, and that's where a comedian wants them. They're easier to control that way. Sometimes I let them know I'm doing it just to make the stud buck a bit more. Just to keep things interesting. 'Yes, I know at first it appeared I was about to be homophobic . . . turns out I was being sexist.'

The crowd started to whoop in their American way.

'Don't whoop,' I told them, 'you sound like idiots. I'm funny – laugh at me.'

They laughed, but it was a mistake. I'd set a boundary on how much they could express their appreciation to me. No one ever does that in America. I hadn't worked much there at that stage and it put everyone's guards up. It was a rookie error on my part. They now had too much of an inner mono-logue at the end of every line to focus on the next one: *That was funny. Ha-ha. I want to clap. No, wait, he might yell at me again. What's he saying now? Fuck, missed it.* Thereby fucking up the flow in the room. Which is crucial in a ten-minute appearance. Everything's about momentum.

I needed to come up with something to make me the guy they remembered. Which was always my aim in those days. Sometimes I would forgo laughs to achieve that. These days I just try and make them laugh as often and as loud as I can from start to finish. It's a lot easier and less mentally taxing.

In order to set someone up, I said the word 'wanker' on purpose while making the accompanying hand gesture. If I'd just said 'wanker' they'd have the right not to know what I was talking about.

A black girl two rows back obligingly took my bait. 'What does "wanker" mean?' she whispered loudly.

'What, does *this*' – I made the wanking mime again – 'not give you a clue?' I continued with mock indignance as she and the crowd came back to where I wanted them. 'Jerk off, miss, it means jerk off. Goddammit, how foreign am I? Am I speaking fucken German? You see, miss, that's what I said while doing *this*.' I made the hand gesture again. 'You see, miss, it's not that you can't understand me. It's that you *won't* under-stand me. And that's because you are a racist, madame. Racist! Racist!' I pointed at her as she howled in shock. Then she laughed loudly with her mouth open wide. Then she covered her face in shame.

The crowd whooped and hollered. 'I've changed my mind,' I said, 'you people are right to whoop. I'm very good at this.

Carry on.' They whooped some more. 'You see, America, I'm not up here to be discovered tonight. I'm doing fine in England, thank you. I came here tonight for two things. I'm here to drink your country in, the way you should. Tomorrow, my friends and I are going to hire a convertible and we're going to drive across the Nevada desert to Vegas, take mushrooms and watch the sun set.' The place went ballistic. 'Yes! Yes!' I concurred, still stirring them up as they cheered. 'Yes! That's *my* America, dammit!'

The applause died down, and I saw the red light at the back of the room flashing for me to get off. But I was spurred on now. The preacher in me took over (either that or the ego-driven comic who wanted to make sure that everyone was talking about me all night). 'Fuck you, don't give me the light! I'm not trying to get a part in a shit sitcom here. I'm making tons of money. That's why I can afford to be here on holiday, dammit!' I lied. I'd actually put myself in quite a bit of debt to be there. 'I came here for one more reason. I came here tonight to suggest this to you: "Kill your President!"'

The place erupted. Absolutely went nuts. People were aghast. I should stress that this was when Bush was in and America was still afraid to criticize him after seeing what happened to the Dixie Chicks.

I didn't think it was that big a deal. The bouncer at the back started flashing the house lights at me. I figured that ought to do it and wrapped it up.

'You could do that – I'm just planting seeds,' I yelled over the top of their cheers, nodding and waving in a mock campaigning fashion. 'Kill him! Thank you and good night!'

The place lit up. I walked back, waiting to be chastised by Provenza. Instead he was clapping his hands off. 'Man, you are such a fucking inspiration to me. Fuck! What balls!'

'Really?' My surprise was genuine. When he'd told me not to be threatening towards Bush or use the word cunt I thought he just meant that the crowd might not go for it. I didn't think it was because you *reeeeeally* shouldn't. I honestly was just being playful and didn't get what the fuss was all about.

'Fuck, I gotta follow that,' said Barry.

'Nah man, you've got nothing to worry about,' I told him. 'Just ride the wave. Say you're the guy that's crossing the desert with me. They'll love you for it.'

Barry was nervous. I wished he wasn't. He was supposed to be having a good time. I was in his ear telling him what to do. Feeling bad that I'd left the room in such disarray for him, I said, 'Look, I'm sorry I went on first. I just wanted them to be used to a foreigner being on before you. I thought I was making life easier.'

'It's fine, mate,' he responded, trying to get his head together.

The compère onstage was still talking about me. Which was the desired effect. At the end of every gag he was shaking his head and snickering, 'Man! Kill your President! I can't believe he did that!' while the crowd continued to clap and laugh. 'Anyway, the next act is the man Brendon mentioned was going to be crossing the desert with him tomorrow. He had his own sitcom on the BBC. Please welcome – Barry Castagnola!'

The crowd gave him nothing. I'd also worked him up into a bit of a nervous frenzy talking him through baby steps for the gig. I should've just let him do his thing. In the US, because there're no intervals there's no momentum, and if someone does well it's really hard to get the crowd to refocus.

Barry made the mistake of opening with a bit about

hijacking a plane with nail clippers, which was beyond hack in the States at the time. Thankfully Barry had his compèring skills behind him. Being a seasoned worker who had gigged on every continent, it occurred to him immediately. He switched directions and started talking about our trip together. I made my way to the corridor where the comics waited to go on to talk to Provenz more about my gig. By the end of Barry's ten we could hear in the distance he had the crowd onside.

'All right?' he asked ambiguously as he made his way back to the corridor where I was still talking about my gig to Provenz.

'Yeah, you're a great bloke,' I joked.

'Lovely guy,' Provenz joined in.

'Why would you say that?' he replied. 'My mum's not even here.'

After the interval came what is known in LA as paid feature acts, professionals who are given longer slots of fifteen minutes, then Tony Rock (Chris's brother) was supposed to close. When I made my way outside the act onstage was back-referencing my set. He was a black guy just saying, 'Man, kill your President!' The crowd laughed as he shook his head incredulously. *'Kill your President? That boy crazy ...* Although he can say that. A white boy foreigner? He got nothing to worry about.' He was killing with this. I was glad everyone was still talking about me. 'Cos y'know, if I got up here and said, "Kill the President"' – big laugh – 'a motherfuck'n helicopter would fly in overhead and marines and shit would be sliding down on ropes to take my black ass to jail.' The crowd clapped.

The helicopter line struck a chord with me. I figured at the time he was exaggerating about the American police state. I had no idea that a police chopper would be appearing in my immediate future to prove me wrong.

As I neared the exit the comic onstage veered back to the catch-all topic of Mexicans stealing.

I made my way outside and lit up a smoke. Pacing up and down outside was another black guy.

'Nice set, man. That true about the convertible and the shrooms?'

'There were no punchlines so it had to be true. You on?'

'Yeah man, I'm Tony Rock.'

'Oh, you're headlining. What they paying you for that?'

He told me the money. It was an insult. 'That's fucken shit! Man, you guys are getting screwed here.' This coming from a man who had just got onstage for free so that he could say he had.

'You guys do OK in England?' Tony asked.

'You bet. Everyone makes a living at it so they don't really have the sense of desperation they do here. People can afford to be themselves and polish their craft. Rather than having to get a deal to survive.' This is true. A lot of British guys don't know how good they've got it.

'So what do you guys make in the clubs there?'

I told him. It wasn't shit.

'Fuck no!' he replied while I nodded. 'Man, I'm goin'.'

'When're you on?'

'Man, I was supposed to be on by eleven o'clock but they running long.' It was already eleven.

'You got another gig?'

'Nope.'

'All right. Look forward to it, mate. Good to meet you.'

I went back inside and the compère was riffing more. He

was really good. Didn't have too much polish like most of LA. Just being himself and talking to the crowd for real. He also stood out because he didn't mention Mexicans stealing once. I'm not exaggerating when I say every professional act said something along those lines as often as the open spots did. I rejoined Provenz and Barry at their table.

'Anyone any good been on?' I asked.

'I dunno, but I gotta ask, what's up with Mexicans stealing?' Barry giggled.

'Yeah, what's up with that?' Provenz added, laughing.

The compère onstage was killing. Having a blast really playing around with the crowd. Then he made a move to bring up the last act. 'You guys have been a great crowd. Are you ready for the last act?' They whooped again. 'OK, you've seen him on . . .'

A bunch of shit that I've never seen.

'Ladies and gentlemen, please welcome – Tony Rock!'

The compère stood there for a while waiting for him to get onstage. The applause died down. No Tony. The compère made his way to the back of the room where the bouncer whispered something aggressively in his ear. He looked exasperated in response. Pointing at himself inquisitively, he shook his head and made his way back onstage while everyone looked on bewildered. The compère took the mike back out of the stand. 'Erm, sorry, ladies and gentlemen, but Tony Rock has left the building. Apparently he felt that the show was going on too long and that I was hogging too much stage time.'

This was unbelievable. The compère was the best guy on the bill and had kept several hours of comedy rolling along nicely. He can't have gone more than a few minutes over in the last section, maximum.

'What?' I yelled out.

Everyone turned to look at me.

'Yeah,' he called back at me from the stage. 'He complained that I ran over and left.'

'That's bullshit. I was just outside with him. You must've been over by, what, two minutes?'

'Yeah. He got pissed.'

The crowd were digging the spontaneity.

'But he just said he was due on at eleven. What time is it now?'

'Eleven oh five,' the compère replied.

'What the fuck is that?'

'Yeah, what's up with that?' He shrugged.

'Fucking Mexicans,' Barry heckled.

The place erupted.

'Hey, do you want me and Barry to tell you the story of how I lost my voice?' I yelled back at him. My voice was really strained and raspy now.

The crowd cheered.

'Dude, I don't know if people can understand you,' he replied.

The crowd laughed.

'Why don't you translate then?'

'Yeah, OK. Ladies and gentlemen, please welcome back Barry Castagnola and Brendon Burns!'

I looked at Barry to see if he was up for it. He nodded and shrugged. Provenz stood up and pushed him out of his chair, whooping and clapping.

'You sure you're cool with this?' I asked him out of the side of my mouth.

'Yeah. Course. It'll be funny.'

We got onstage and slapped hands with the compère. I

turned to the crowd and was really rasping and went full speed with my vernacular and accent.

'So, me and Barry were gigging in Southend which is a really rough area of England. It's full of cunts.'

I nodded at the compère and he supplied a translation.

'Yeah, Southend is a bad neighbourhood in England. It's full of assholes.'

Seeing what we were doing, the place erupted and continued to do so every time the compère translated successfully.

'I'd pulled some girl,' Barry started, but the compère was looking at him quizzically.

'Pulled?' he whispered.

'Picked up,' Barry whispered back.

'I picked up some chick,' the compère said.

'And one of the blokes—'

'Blokes?'

'Dudes.'

'Oh, and one of the dudes . . .'

'He snapped and went mental,' Barry continued. 'It all kicked off and I sped off after him.'

'There was an argument and a fight,' the compère chanced without any prompting from us. We nodded that he'd guessed right and he punched the air in triumph.

'Anyway, I looked at the chav girl . . .'

I looked at the compère. There wasn't time to explain.

'Slapper?' Barry offered.

The compère and the crowd continued to look at us blankly.

'Never mind,' we said in unison.

'So I go off tearing after Barry round the corner, screaming my head off,' I said.

The compère fired back, 'So I chase after him screaming my head off.'

'The guy swings a punch at Barry and he just stares straight back at him and says, "Fucking shit punch, mate".'

'The guy swings a punch at Barry and he just stares straight back at him and says, "Fucking shit punch, mate".'

We all nodded empathetically at this agreement. 'Is it the same?' 'Yeah, it's the same.' Each of us reading one another's feigned ignorance. The place erupted again.

Just then the mikes were turned off. We all tapped them and started yelling, 'What the fuck?'

'Fucking Mexicans,' Barry reiterated, again to big laughs.

'Zere must be rules to ze fun,' I croaked in a German accent.

We started on the story again but the bouncer turned on the house lights and made an announcement over the PA: 'Ladies and gentlemen, thank you for coming down to the Laugh Factory tonight. We're open here seven nights a week. Please immediately exit out the emergency exit to your left.'

The exit door right next to the stage was opened. The crowd looked around incredulously, shrugged, and started to file out.

'What the fuck?' I yelled towards the back of the room. 'Mate, we're doing you a fucken favour here. We ain't getting paid and we're filling in for your headliner.'

Provenz made his way over and mimed 'let it go' at me.

'That's fucked,' I continued. 'Fuck 'em, we'll do it outside.'

The crowd cheered.

'Folks, you've been a great audience, and if you want to come party with us we'll be in the bar next door,' the compère bellowed over the heads of the departing audience. I figured him desperate for attention and pussy.

'Nah, the gig ain't over till we say it is,' I persisted. 'Let's finish the story in the car park!'

At that point my voice gave out completely. From a whiskey rasp to a completely high-pitched whisper. I felt my vocal cords stretch to a thin, bloody painful reed.

'. . .' I said, inaudibly.

Barry patted me on the back. 'Mate, leave it.'

'. . .' I replied.

It was not the last time I would say this.

14

The (Fucken) Mexican

AS WE PILED outside I was still trying to commandeer the crowd into the car park so we could finish our story.

'. . .' I screeched as loud as I could. Dogs near by gathered unwittingly in the car park at the rear of the club.

'Dude, let it go,' Barry tried again. 'You can't speak.'

'Have you lost your voice?' Provenz interjected, wide-eyed.

I nodded and clutched at my throat in pain.

'HA! HAAAAAAAA!' he cackled. 'That'll teach you, you fuck'n asshole.'

'Murhhhhhurrrhuuuuuurrrr,' Barry joined in.

'What's up?' the compère asked.

'He's lost his voice,' came the answer from them both.

'You mean that's not his real voice?'

'No, he's normally the loudest, maddest fucker you've ever heard,' Barry managed through his titters.

'That was him low volume?'

I nodded like Harpo.

'Yeah,' they concurred.

'We gotta get him a fuck'n horn.' Provenz cackled again. 'This is too good!'

I mimed splitting my sides sarcastically.

'Oh, you zinging me with fuck'n mime now? Oh that's too perfect! I'm fuck'n hard!'

'Hilarious,' came Barry's response.

I punched the compère in the arm and pointed frantically at some Latino-looking girls who'd been at the gig. They were milling about, clearly thinking of leaving.

'Oh right, I got this,' he said, reading my mind. 'Hey girls, you wanna come party next door with us?'

Provenz looked at Barry and me. 'What you wanna do?'

'Drambuie,' I whispered in their ears, clutching at my throat.

'Yeah, that oughta fix it. HA! HAAAAAA!' Provenz toked on his menthol and pulled it away from his mouth like an old vaudeville comic would with his cigar, adopting the voice: 'Yeah, then perhaps we can get some glass for you to chew, or maybe find you a homeless dude to make out with.' Then he returned to his normal tone and added, 'I could hang out. You?'

'What, and watch Rain Man here try and pull?' Barry snickered. 'Too right!'

The compère talked the girls into joining us and we made our way into the bar next door. The barman knew the compère and stayed open for us. I bought a round and an extra Drambuie for myself. The warm fluid temporarily soothed my throat and I was able to raise my volume to a barely audible croak.

'That was great fun tonight,' I offered.

'Dude, that was awesome,' the compère agreed.

The circle jerk continued.

'You were hilarious,' I told him.

'Thanks. You guys too.'

'You must have been the only act on that didn't say anything about Mexicans stealing,' Barry chipped in.

'Fuck that shit,' he returned.

I knew I only had a limited amount of voice left so I had to move quick.

'Any of you girls Mexican?' I asked.

'I'm half Mexican,' came the reply from the prettiest of them.

'Perfect. You're the only race I haven't slept with. We should go home together.'

Everyone howled. She was visibly turned on by the audacity.

'Sorry, I'm Australian, we don't fuck about,' I lied. 'Have you ever been with an Australian?'

'No.' She giggled.

'This guy's amazing. You're my fuck'n hero.' The compère looked at Barry and Provenz. 'Is he always like this?'

They both nodded.

'Unless it's not working,' Barry added. 'Then he pretends to be somebody else.'

'HA! HAAAAAAA!' Provenz howled.

'Shut up,' I snapped obnoxiously and returned my attention to the Mexican girl. 'How old are you?'

'Twenty-one,' came her blushing reply.

'That's OK. I can do that. C'mon, we can complete each other's sets. You can be my first Mexican and I'll be your first Aussie.'

We all laughed playfully and continued to drink and chat organically. Every ten minutes I would steer the conversation back to her with 'So it's on, right? Go on, live a little. Treat yourself.' The others egged me on.

Before long the barman wanted to go home and called time. As we made our way outside we walked the girls to their car. The Mexican girl was tempted to come home with me but her friends thought it a bit freaky for her to go with all three of us. The compère was milling around with some other girl we'd met and we said our goodbyes to him.

'Look,' I suggested, 'I know it's a bit dodgy jumping in a car with strangers so I'll go home with you and your friends.'

They eyed one another suspiciously.

'No, I've got college in the morning,' said one of her friends, cock-blocking me.

Fair enough too, I figured.

'You should come dancing with the homeless with us,' I blurted out inexplicably.

'What?'

'Last night we went dancing with the homeless. Barry kicked up a storm. Provenz lives on Venice Beach. They go all night.'

I'd started and couldn't seem to stop. Equally inexplicably, she actually found this intriguing. I sensed I was on to something and continued.

'That's why we're driving across the desert. You have to live like a free spirit sometimes.'

She went to leave with us when her friend yelled, 'Look, you can go if you want but I am leaving right now.' Which is girl-speak for 'If you fuck that guy I am disowning you and telling your mum/boyfriend/counsellor'.

She looked back and forth, then shrugged. 'Here's my number.' She scrawled it on a piece of paper for me. 'You will call me, won't you?'

She clambered into the car, and I regained some face with her friends by not pressuring. They all waved out the window at us.

'Promise you'll call?' she asked again out the window.

'I will.' I waved the piece of paper in the air.

When they exited the car park, the boys were staring at me mouths agape.

Barry shook his head. 'How the fuck did that happen?'

I shrugged in response. I couldn't believe it either. Half of me was just trying to be audaciously funny.

'You gonna call her?' Provenz asked as we slid into his BMW.

'Shit yeah. Did you not see her? Will I have time to when we get back from Vegas?'

'Sure.' Provenz stuffed his cigarette butt into his ever-filling ashtray bottle. It made a single *psss* and died a death.

'Awesome. I can't believe how easy that was. See, Barry, all you need is some chutzpah to get back on the horse.'

'Somehow I don't think "Go on, I'm a fat bloke from South London, I'll complete your set" carries quite the same mystique, Brendon.'

We howled.

Barry continued mocking me: 'Nah, nah, go on love. Treat yourself. I'm on the rebound and everything. Proper desperate, me.'

We were in stitches, and I mimicked padding at my pockets desperately.

'Fuck!' I spluttered.

'What?'

'That Mexican bitch stole my wallet.'

15

Speed

I CAME TO with the morning sun washing over me. Again, at first I thought I was back in the UK. Hence, not only was I surprised to be woken by *any* morning sun, I was even more surprised (pleasantly) that it was Venice Beach's.

I stretched out wide across Provenza's kingsize bed. Today was going to be a great day. We'd worked until the early hours of the morning finding my convertible online. Or I should say Provenza worked until the early hours of the morning while I nagged him.

'I thought you'd lost your fuck'n voice?' he'd snapped as I arched over him in his office the previous night.

'I've got enough to see that this is done. Look, the fucken Jeep broke down then Owen turned up. How much more proof do you need that we're on to something here?'

'Yeah, two entirely unrelated separate coincidences – what's up with that?' Barry interjected with the same mock American hack stand-up voice we'd been adopting all night. The whole way home, after I'd shown I was joking about the Mexican girl stealing my wallet, we'd been finishing every sentence with 'What's up with that?'

'Fuck'n Mexicans,' Provenz added.

'Look, take the piss all you want, boys, but if you help me do this I promise our lives will never be the same again. You'll even be glad that Chris split with you, Barry, and something will happen for you, Provenz, I just know it.'

I awoke with this sentiment still in my head. I rolled over, stood up, scratched my balls and walked over to the edge of the mezzanine to see Barry sleeping on the couch.

'BARRY!' I barked. My voice was raspy but still twice the volume and urgency of your average clock alarm. He awoke with a start. 'VEGAS, BABY, WHOOOOOO!'

'Vegas whoooo,' he replied flatly. The second half of his 'whoooo' muffled by planting his face into a cushion.

I bounded down the stairs and into the kitchen. Barry rolled over, attempting to signal that he wanted to go back to sleep.

'Coffee?' I asked.

'Please,' he muttered in reply. 'Goodlastnightwasn'tit?' he jabbered, half asleep. He wasn't really a 'glass is half awake' guy just yet.

I boiled the kettle as he performed the traditionally exact amount of ball scratching and face rubbing required.

'Yeah . . . fucken Mexicans,' I carried on, as if there'd been no sleep interval in our running gag.

'What *is* up with them?' Provenz said, making his way out of the study pushing down his morning boner.

'So, what's the plan today?' I asked, giving his dick a wide berth, which was more than it did for me. It could've made the coffee on its own.

'Well, we gotta get a move on if we're gonna pick up the rental and Keith. *And* take the route Doug suggested. Traffic out on the 405 freeway is going to suck and we gotta get him from Canyon Country, which is at least an hour north of here, and then we gotta get the 14 freeway North West.'

His need to get going filled me with optimism. I wanted us to travel with the roof down so we could see the Nevada sky-line and nothing but the road in front of us. By evening it would be too cold to do so.

I checked my watch. It was already eleven thirty.

'We're going to have to move then. How long is it going to take us?'

'Even after we get out of town, it's a good six-hour drive. Like I said, we can't fuck around otherwise the traffic's gonna kill us.' Again, I was pleased that Provenz shared my sense of immediacy.

I was then confused as to why he thought that meant he and Barry should start smoking weed from a pipe on the balcony. I'd never seen that in any situation before, or since: the words 'Quick! We need to . . .' followed by 'OK, let's smoke some weed'.

This man needs fifty milligrams of adrenalin. Stat. / Of course, doctor. But first, let's smoke some weed.

The deadline is six p.m. I need those photos developed now!/ For sure, Ed. Let's just smoke some weed first.

Cut to

Int. Pilot's cabin – Barry and Provenz are pilots flying a plane. They're in the middle of a thunderstorm. They are both sweating and panicking.

BARRY

Captain! It's no good. The tower's out and we've lost two engines.

PROVENZ

Calm down, Barry. We can do this. We just need to smoke some weed.

BARRY

But we're out of Rizlas, Captain!

PROVENZ

Shit! That is serious. OK, we'll just have to make a bong.

BARRY

For the love of God, man! We don't even have a fucking pipe!

'OK, fellas, I'm going to shower and get ready,' I announced, hinting that they should maybe do the same.

'OK', 'All right' came the nonchalant replies.

I was quietly miffed. Not only was Keith fucking with my vision, now here they were not fully appreciating the importance of what we were doing. What I, I mean *we*, were achieving here.

'All right. Well, do either of you want me to leave the shower running?'

'Nope.' They continued to pack the pipe.

When I was all cleaned up and out of the shower it was still an hour or two before we packed our bags, put on our hats and got in the car to pick up the rental. I was pissed in both senses of the word by the time we got to the rental company as I'd been swigging liberally from my Drambuie bottle every chance I got.

At the counter I paid for the car but only put Provenz and Barry down as drivers.

'Why don't you want to drive?' Provenz asked.

'Because he wants to get loaded,' the rental guy fired back. 'Look at him.'

'Besides, I can't drive on the other side of the road,' I said, changing the subject.

'When you're that loaded,' he chipped in again. 'You guys want insurance?'

'Oh hell yeah,' we all replied.

'I'm gonna kill this thing.' Provenz evilly waggled his mouth again. The Cindy Crawford mole on his top lip now had its tongue out.

We signed the papers and the guy took us round the back to show us round the car. Taking note of scratches. We pointed out some that he missed. Looking the three of us up and down, he bluntly replied, 'Oh don't worry about them. I'm not exactly expecting you guys to bring this back in pristine condition. You going to Vegas, huh?'

We nodded.

'I thought so. Happy trails, gentlemen. You're insured, just bring her back in one piece still driving.'

'Are you not just trying to get us to lose our deposit?' we asked.

'Boys.' He eased in conspiratorially. 'It's a rental.'

'I love this rental company,' Provenz said.

Barry took the lead in Provenz's car out to where Barry's dad was meeting us. If I'd thought Provenza drove maniacally in his car, I soon wished we were back in it. He hurtled along in full LA traffic doing nought to a hundred in several seconds. He thrashed through the gears even though it was an automatic. I lost count of the times I screamed as we fishtailed along. Every time I screamed he placated me with the same sentence: 'It's a rental.'

'Provenz, look out!'

'It's a rental.'

'Provenz, there's an old lady!'

'It's a rental.'

'Provenz, that was the sound barrier!'

'It's a rental.'

The final straw came when we slightly lost sight of Barry in front and Provenz undertook through two lanes to catch up with him. A car in the fast lane veered slowly back into the middle lane directly in front of us. Looking to our left and right we were boxed in as the traffic ahead had come to a halt. Provenz slammed on the brakes and the car swung hard from left to right, swinging back and forth like a theme park pirate ship. Burnt rubber and black smoke caught up with and engulfed us in the open-top vehicle. We slid for a good hundred yards more and then came to a merciful stop. Thankfully the cars in front had heard our screeching and had nervously moved forward as fast and as far as they could, allowing us the precious few feet we needed to avoid collision. We jolted forward and sat back hard out of reflex into our seats and headrests.

A stunned few seconds passed.

'Fuck, Provenza!' I punched him in the arm. 'You fucken cunt!'

'Relax, it's a rental.'

'That's not what I'm worried about. *I'm* not a rental!'

'You are to me,' he said with vaudeville shtick.

I couldn't help but laugh.

He started to drive like a maniac again.

'Look, Provenz, please. I lost two members of my family in

a car accident. This really makes me nervous. It's a thing of mine. I'm begging ya, take it easy.'

'OK, OK,' he replied.

Just then my hat blew off my head. Instinctively I jumped out of my seat to catch it in thin air, my stomach bent over the seat and my torso leaning over the back of the BMW convertible.

'Nice catch,' Provenz said with a smirk. 'Look, the only thing we have to fear is hat loss.'

'Fear of hat loss in Las Vegas!' I replied excitedly.

'HA! HAAAAAA! Whooooo! Yeah baby!' Provenz yelled as he tore into another tiny gap in front, beeping his horn at no one in particular.

16

Castablanca

IT TOOK SEVERAL hours to meet Keith where he'd parked his Jeep over in Canyon Country. He'd had it towed and it was barely functioning. Enough to get him to that point but certainly not reliable enough for the drive across the desert.

It was late in the afternoon when we parked up by a slip road off the North Western freeway. My dreams of hot desert sun and open roads were squashed as it was clear we'd be driving through the night.

Expressing this frustration for me, Provenz yelled at Keith as we pulled up next to his Jeep. 'You no-car-workin', livin'-in-the-middle-of-nowhere motherfucker! It's gonna take hours to get on the road to Vegas!' He wrenched up the handbrake, smothering Keith and Barry in a billowing cloud of dust. 'I need to piss.' He leapt out of the car, stuck his dick through a hole in the wire-mesh fence and started pissing openly in public. 'I ain't fuck'n drivin' no more!' he shouted over his shoulder.

'I can't drive because of my shoulder,' Keith voiced immediately.

'You no-drivin', livin'-fuck'n-nowhere, make-us-come-get-you prick!' Provenz howled into the dusk.

'Look, fuck it, I'll drive,' said Barry. 'Let's just get going, for fuck's sake.'

'Hats, gentlemen.' I popped mine on my head.

'What?' Keith piped up. 'I don't get a hat?'

'That's right, you no-hat-havin' motherfucker,' Provenz said.

We'd been ragging on one another for the past twenty-four hours and it was time for Keith to play catch up.

'You brown-Jeep-drivin' tight bastard,' Barry said, giving his two cents.

'Hey, I won't be the butt of everything this weekend,' Keith snapped back. 'You all take the piss out of me too much and I'll crack skulls.'

'What, with your bad shoulder?' I asked.

'It's giving me hell, Bren. I was in a car accident. I shouldn't be out here really, but when I heard my boy and his mates were in town, well, how could I not?'

'We're going to have to put the roof up,' said Provenz.

'What? But my vision . . .' I objected.

'You're going to have to let that go. It'll be freezing.'

'I'm sorry, boys, but my shoulder won't take the cold either,' Keith said apologetically.

'You bad-shoulder-havin', can't-take-the-cold, livin'-other-end-o'-town prick!'

We all laughed as Keith realized he might be owed a baptism of fire with this band of men.

'I mean it,' Keith returned with a giggle. 'I will crack skulls!'

'You skull-crackin',' I began.

'Convertible-roof-needin',' said Barry.

'Brown-Jeep-broken,' added Provenz.

'No-hat-havin',' I continued.

Keith rolled his eyes. 'Oh fuck. I give up.'

'Fuck-givin'-uppin',' Barry responded.

Everyone, including Keith, laughed.

'If you're not willing to have the piss taken you're in the wrong car, Keithy,' I said, slapping him on the shoulder. He visibly winced.

I hadn't meant to and I felt bad, but I should have felt worse. As much as we were enjoying taking the piss, I was still a bit pouty about my vision being spoiled. I swigged from my bottle of Jack Daniels. I'd moved on from my sickly sweet breakfast aperitif of Drambuie and on to the evening's hard liquor. It burned my throat. Actually it had gone from a burning sensation to something more akin to sharp claws scraping my vocal cords. I took another swig to numb the pain.

'Well I can't drive, I'm drunk.' I offered the bottle to Provenz.

'No thanks. I think this trip's going to require some pacing.' With that, he nudged his bright red sheriff's hat to one side, leaving it slightly askew. 'Ma'am.' He lifted his hat on and off his head.

'You red-hat-wearin' sheriffy cocksucker,' Keith said.

'Wahey! That's the spirit!' said Provenz as Barry and Keith smiled warmly and knowingly at each other.

I continued to pout into my bottle of Jack.

Barry beeped the horn. 'C'mon!' We all piled into the convertible in response.

By the time we reached the freeway to Vegas, the sun was beginning to set. The banter was coming thick and fast. The hack material of the acts the night before was still fresh in our minds. If our road trip had a catchphrase it would be 'What's up with that?' or 'Fucking Mexicans' as it was our response to every banal statement of fact for the whole six hours there.

'We need gas.'

'What's up with that?'

'I need a piss.'

'Fucking Mexican.'

'What's up with that?'

'I'm gonna buy your dad a hooker.'

'Will she be Mexican?'

'What's up with that?'

There's nothing like four guys, a car and an open road. It's like walking into a bar in Ireland and hearing the Pogues. One can't help but feel roguish and mischievous.

'We might be like mates, Barry and me, but there's still always respect,' Keith confided. 'Because he always knows I will kick his arse. Cos I'm the old man.' He gave himself the double thumbs.

'Not with that bad shoulder you won't,' Barry chimed in.

'I will crack skulls,' Keith insisted as he playfully cuffed his boy on the back of the head.

Their relationship was unconventional for sure. I decided to test the dynamic.

'Can we get any coke from anywhere?' I asked.

'It's Vegas,' said Provenz. 'We can get coke from anywhere.'

'I don't want to get ripped off though.'

'It's Vegas, we can get ripped off anywhere.'

'Do you know anyone, Provenz?'

'Uh-uh. I'm drawing the line at mushrooms, thanks.'

'Barry?'

Everyone knew where this was headed by process of elimination.

'Sorry dude, I don't live here.'

Hmmm. Provenz won't. Barry doesn't live here. Who might fit the criteria?

So then I asked my friend's dad to help score us some coke the only way I knew how, with a 'VEGAS, Keith! WHOOOOOOOOO-ooooooooo—!' My voice cracked out at the end.

'Don't Vegas-whoo my dad,' said Barry.

'?' said our faces.

'I dunno,' Barry answered. 'It just bothers me and I don't know why. Like Brendon and swans.'

'You don't like swans, Bren?' asked Keith.

'Fucken cunts,' I said. Then I launched into an impromptu uncontrollable ranting stream of consciousness, jumping from thought to thought mid-sentence, sometimes mid-word. 'Smug, protected by the Queen, fucken arseholes. I don't wanna kill one. But fuck me I want to punch one and hold it and let it know that the only reason it lives is just because I'm letting it. Not cos of some toffee-nosed aristocratic bullshit medieval rule. Treason? Treason? What the fuck is treason? Overthrowing the sovereign? What the shitting hell do swans have to do wi— And sovereign? What kind of primitive bullshit is that? For bothering a sw— And *bothering*? What the fuck constitutes bothering? Do I work for them? Am I a slave? When did we start pandering to a smug bird's mental st— Cunts!' I started to point angrily as I argued meanderingly with absolutely no one. 'I don't like animals that don't have some degree of fear around man. We're the top-of-the-food-chain bitches. Look at sharks. A shark will fuck you up yet you don't see them pulling that kind of shit. I'm Australian, mate. We eat sharks with chips. And some fucken swan is gonna give me 'tude? Fuck that. Not on my watch. Way more majestic beasts deserve that privilege. Stick 'em in Africa and watch that snooty look get torn, gnawed and clawed off their stupid blank faces. If ever a group of animals needed a natural predator it's those fucken cunts and their bull-shit sense of entitlement. Bunch of fucken unjustifiable ego-having posh cunts. Fuck 'em.' I sat back, feeling slightly dizzy, having not breathed for a while.

'Wow,' said Provenz, drawing long on a menthol and

grinning from ear to ear like a Cheshire cat. 'There's a dog with a bone. *That* was sublime.'

Keith looked at me with a newfound glee too. Like a child with a new toy.

Barry smiled as he'd heard it all before. 'Well, how you feel about swans—'

'Cunts,' I interjected.

'That's how I feel about you Vegas-whooing my dad. It bothers me. I know it's irrational, it's obviously founded in something else, I just haven't processed exactly what yet.'

'Fair enough,' I replied.

He made a fair point – swans *are* cunts.

'Lemme make a few calls,' said Keith.

'You sure, Dad?' asked Barry.

'Yeah, fuck it – it's Vegas. I'm not going to see you for a while, and some of the casinos have swans . . .'

'Cunts.' Another Pavlovian interruption.

'I want to see what happens when he's on coke and comes across one,' said Keith as he and I shared a knowing smile in the back.

'Yeah, Keithy, VEGAS! WH—' I stopped short out of respect for Barry.

'You can Vegas-whoo me if you want, Bren,' said Keith warmly.

I looked at Barry.

'OK, just one,' he said.

'VEGAS, KEITHY! WHOOOOOOOOOOOOOO!' I howled, and cuddled Keith, who winced.

'VEGAS! WHOOOOOOOOOOOOOOO!' Keith joined in, ignoring the pain.

Then the whole car howled like wolves at the moon.

17

The Getaway

'FUCKING HELL, DRIVE Paul, drive, DRIVE!' we yelled at Provenz, and he turned three corners seemingly at once. When we hit the main drag the traction changed dramatically on what little bitumen there was. We actually had to lean to rebalance, screaming various swearwords as we did.

'Fuck, Paul, be careful!' yelled Barry from the passenger seat, practically having to hold on to him to rebalance.

'IT'S A MOTHERFUCK'N RENTAL!' Provenz yelled back.

'Did we just get shot at?' asked Keith.

'EVERYBODY SHUT THE FUCK UP AND LET ME CONCENTRATE!' Provenz screamed.

We were doing about sixty miles an hour already and we weren't even back on a properly sealed and tarred road. It took about another half an hour of us all nearly snapping our fingers in half as we clutched at whatever was nearest in panic before we could even begin to process what had just gone down.

As our adrenalin faded to a near sane level I produced the large solid rock of chemicals from my pocket and asked the first question regarding what had just transpired: 'So, what does crystal meth do?'

'That,' replied Provenz.

18
Exit Wounds*

'ARE YOU SURE you're OK with this, Dad?' Barry repeated.

'Of course he's sure,' I said.

'Yeah, look, like I said, it's Vegas and we'll just do what guys do in Vegas. One day I hope you'll do this with your boy. Just forget I'm your dad for a few days. What happens in Vegas stays in Vegas, son. Them's the rules. I know someone there who might be able to help us.'

'Hear, hear,' I toasted.

'Who you gonna call?' Barry asked.

'Randy. He drinks at my local from time to time. He's a prison guard in Vegas.' We all looked at him quizzically. 'What? Who knows more dealers than him? Anyone got any better ideas?'

'So long as you're cool with it,' I said as Keith scrolled down the contacts list on his phone.

'Boys, it's Vegas,' Keith reiterated coolly.

'Put it on speaker, I gotta hear this,' Provenz salivated.

Keith thumbed the phone accordingly and held it out for all to hear.

---

* Steven Seagal movie that went straight to DVD. And no, I'm not running out of ideas this early.

A harsh gravelly voice answered: 'Hello?'

'Hey Randy, it's Keith. You OK to talk?'

'Sure Keith, what's up?'

'I hate to ask this but I'm on my way to Vegas with my boy and his mates and they were wondering where we could get some coke en route.'

'Hang on Keith, I'm at work.'

'Oh shit. Sorry, Randy, I had no idea. I'm sorry. Never mind.'

'What? HAHAHAHA. Oh no, fuck that. I mean wait a minute. Lemme ask someone.'

'You sure?' asked Keith.

'Keith, it's Vegas,' said Randy. 'Lemme call you back.'

We all looked at one another with what-are-ya-gonna-do? downward-turning fish lips and open palms.

'Fair enough,' Barry offered.

Within what could have been no more than ten minutes tops, Randy rang back. Keith answered him on speakerphone again.

'Kay Keith, I've got three locations. Whereabouts are you?'

'On the fifteen about three hundred miles outside LA. The last thing we went past was Beacon station.'

'OK, perfect. You got a pad and pen?'

I had both at the ready in case I lost my voice again. I nodded at Keith.

'Cool,' said Keith. 'Go.'

'In about five miles you're going to see a signposting for the Devil's Playground.'

'Holy shit, I see it,' said Keith.

'Weird,' I said.

'Yeah, what kind of omen do you think Devil's Playground is, Christ boy?' teased Barry.

'Is that your boy?' Randy asked.

'Yeah,' replied Barry.

'Hey Barry. Heard about you and the ex. Shitty. Hope this helps.'

'Thanks.'

'OK,' Randy continued, 'almost just before a tunnel there's a turning for the Devil's Playground on your right called Zzyx Road. That's Zee Zee Why Ex. On your left is the arrowhead trail.'

'Really?' Keith asked. 'Are we going to space?'

'Ha! Kinda. Anyway, it becomes a dirt track after a short while so follow that for about a few miles then peel off to the right and that becomes Zzyx Road again. Take that for about ten miles. It's in the middle of nowhere and you'll think you're going the wrong way but you're not. During that time you'll go past a crossroads where it becomes arrowhead trail again, although I doubt it's signposted. Then a turning on your right. After the turning on your right there is a left about two miles up the road. It'll be a dirt track and hard to spot. You'll go past it no doubt but that's not a problem as the road ends only about a mile and a half later. You really will be in the middle of buttfuck nowhere. If you make it to the old bluebell mines then you can backtrack about a mile and a half. This is where bodies get tossed and shit so make sure you got fuel. The guy's name is Exit, short for Exit Wound or some gangsta shit. He's actually a white guy. A chemist. Tell him G-Ron sent you. I'll call him in a bit and tell him you're coming and who exactly it is who's sending you.'

We sat in silence, stunned.

Keith spoke first. 'Er, Randy, exactly how did you get that much information in under ten minutes?'

'Keith, it's Vegas,' came the catch-all reply.

141

'The system at work,' said Provenz.

'Ha!' laughed Randy at the other end. 'Oh yeah. Apparently he's a little twitchy and subject to blackouts. So if he loses track of the conversation or forgets who the fuck you are in the middle of it, don't take it personally. Just keep reminding him G-Ron sent you and exactly where the fuck he's currently residing.'

He said his goodbyes and we all yelled, 'Thanks Randy.' The singsong fashion in which we said it seemed somewhat remiss given that we'd just asked a prison guard to give us the address of a coke dealer.

'No problem, but don't say my name again,' he said sternly.

Seemed fair enough.

We followed Randy's directions to the letter. We peeled off on to a thin track that came off the 15 just before a tunnel. He wasn't joking about a dirt track. It was actually difficult to tell we'd gone the right way. As the convertible bounced up and down, threatening to fall apart as soon as the correct resonance was struck, we worried aloud more and more, taking it in turns to say 'This can't be it', constantly thinking that the road had ended as it became ever thinner, dirtier and more remote. Yet Randy's landmarks appeared. We came to the crossroads and a makeshift sign on a gas barrel read *Arrowhead* and *Zzyx* in crayon.

But doubt hung over us the entire time; the journey seemed to last for ever. That and the added factors that the light was fading fast now and we had to stop on numerous occasions to clear the path of various debris including more than one abandoned vehicle. Actually 'abandoned' and 'vehicle' don't quite do it justice. More like 'entirely aborted rust shell that looked as if it had been sitting at the bottom of the sea rather than ever having been driven anywhere'. Each time we stopped we worried more and more until finally we arrived at a dead end.

Scavenging around, we came across holes in the hills lifted by ancient wooden partitions signifying the mines. We backtracked, our eyes heavily peeled, until we came across something resembling a track now on our right. If the road we had taken was remote, this was positively the bat cave.

'Er, boys, I got a bad feeling about this,' said Keith. 'I don't think this is just some guy dealing on the side. Lemme call Randy.' He checked his phone. 'Damn, no signal.'

'Ya think?' said Provenz.

We all checked our phones. None of us even had a single bar reading.

'Shit,' I said.

'Well, given that most vehicles don't seem to make it out of here, I'm guessing T-Mobile doesn't bother either,' said Barry.

With that we pulled into a clearing, parked and piled out of the car. It was dusk now but we could see well enough. There were restored mine shafts littered around the edges of the excavation. Some had plastic sheets covering them. In the centre there was a massive Winnebago. More like a tour bus. It looked expensive and unkempt but was still clearly in use. Littered everywhere were full, half-full and empty fifty-pound bags of rock salt. There were also manufacturer-sized bottles of drain cleaner discarded everywhere. The stench of pungent cat piss, rotten orange juice and burning plastic filled the air.

Provenz, Barry and I swapped glances as the penny slowly dropped.

'Er, fellas, I don't think this guy is gonna wanna do us a deal on a couple of grams,' I said.

'Dad, how well do you know Randy?' asked Barry.

'Well, we don't hang out,' Keith revealed. 'He drinks in my

local when he's in town. I saw him the other week and mentioned we were heading out to Vegas. He told me to drop him a line if we needed anything. You boys wanted some coke so he was all I could think of. I've seen him doing quite a bit before down the pub.'

'Keith, this is a meth distillery,' I said.

'What?' said Keith.

'Randy said the guy was a chemist. As in a fucken meth chemist. Smell that smell? That ain't poppies burning. That's fucken meth. I've never done meth but I sure as hell know you don't need draining fluid and salt to make coke.'

'HA! This is getting fuck'n interesting,' said Provenz.

We glowered at him, pondering exactly how on earth his head worked.

Before we could explain to Keith what the salt and drain cleaner were for, we heard an argument ensuing from inside one of the mines. One of the voices got louder and louder: 'You fuck'n asshole! What did I tell you about leaving shit on? You trying to fuck'n kill us?' The voice was not assertive, more panicked than anything else.

Out of one of the holes came a gawky emaciated dude with a surgical mask over his mouth. Over his shoulder, rather alarmingly, was a rifle. He took one look at us and, oddly, given his next decision, removed the mask, thereby making himself fully identifiable. And then he pointed the rifle right at us.

Now, I'd had a gun pointed at me twice in my life. Once was by the Egyptian military while I was attempting to climb one of the pyramids outside Cairo (unbeknown to me there were riots in the city that day and they were a little tetchy). The other was when a weird kid at school snapped and pulled a replica handgun right to my head. He was *that* kid you'd read

144

about going postal. The whole situation was very, very real for a few seconds, before he revealed it as a replica. (Upon discovering that, I dragged him to the toilets and stuffed him in the urinals. Last I heard he got a job with the Defence Department.)

However, this time, my third, was easily the scariest given our surroundings and suddenly remembering that the man in question was subject to blackouts.

'Whoa whoa whoa!' We all raised our palms at him in a calming fashion.

In the dusk it was difficult to make him out beyond that he was a bit like the kid I'd stuffed in the urinals: ginger, kind of tall and very in need of a gun.

'Who the fuck are you guys?' he asked twitchily.

'We're friends of Randy's,' said Keith.

'Who the fuck is Randy?' he asked, quivering.

'Are you Exit?' asked Provenz.

'Yeah.' He lowered his rifle a touch. 'Who the fuck are you?'

'G-Ron sent us,' said Barry.

'Oh right, G-Ron.' His demeanour changed completely. Obviously long-term memory was stronger than short-term. Either that or he had no signal out here either. 'I'll be right back.'

He wandered off into the Winnebago but continued talking to us as we moved closer and waited outside.

'Did you move my cars?'

'Sorry?' asked Keith.

'The cars on the track. Did you move them?'

'Yeah, we did. It was the only way we could get through. Is that a problem?' Provenz spoke as if this happened to him every day.

'No. No, it's no problem. Just put them back on your way

out.' He carried on talking as he returned with what must have been two ten-kilo bags of shiny rocks: 'You know, I just need it to look like there's no one out here—'

'Whoa whoa whoa!' We all raised our hands again.

'What's wrong? Not enough?' His voice was more whiny than threatening now. 'Are you fuck'n kidding me? Tell that fuck'n nigger that until he can come out here and risk life and limb smelling like fuck'n cat piss, that's all I got. He's not my only guy, you know. Look, it's fuck'n pure.'

He pulled out a rock and stuffed what must have been five solid grams into my hand.

'No, it's not that, it's just we were sent for coke,' I said, wishing immediately that I hadn't.

I could feel the boys burning holes in the back of my head. And rightfully so. This conversation, and situation in general, needed to be over about ten minutes before we pulled into the clearing.

'Coke? Coke? Where the fuck am I supposed to pull coke from? What am I, a motherfuck'n alchemist? How about some gold and plutonium? What am I, a fuck'n magician?'

'No, it's just that Randy said—'

'Who the fuck is Randy? As a matter of fact, who the fuck are you?'

It was hard to tell if he was reaching for his rifle again. But thankfully there was a small explosion in one of the mines.

'Fuck!' he spouted, storming off to the source of the sound. 'Tommy, what the fuck did I tell you?' he yelled at a man leaving the mine who was clearly just as startled to see us.

'Who the fuck are those guys?' the man called Tommy said, pointing back at us.

'Yeah, who the fuck are you guys?' Exit yelled. Clutching his rifle. The drama had clearly triggered another blackout.

Reading this, Barry said, 'G-Ron sent us. We're all sorted. Thanks, we'll be off.'

This was our out, and we took it.

'Right. Tell me he owes me money . . . I mean *him*. Tell *him* he owes me my fuck'n money!' he yelled as we backed away. Exit then turned to the man called Tommy. 'Get the fucking fire extinguisher before everything goes.'

They both ran around hurriedly looking for a fire extinguisher amid their rock salt and drain fluid debris. Meanwhile we rushed as fast as we could without openly running to the car.

'Jesus, nice one Barry,' said Keith out of the side of his mouth. 'Let's get the fuck out of here.'

We clambered into the convertible coolly and Provenz did a quick but indiscreet U-turn, bringing us back facing the entrance track and me looking out at the mess behind us.

KABAAM! There was another explosion sending both Exit and Tommy to the ground.

'Who the fuck are you guys?' I vaguely heard Exit yell as he got to his feet and pointed his rifle at us again.

'Fucken hell!' I yelped.

BANG KRAPOW!

It was impossible to tell whether he'd shot at us, or there'd been another explosion, or both.

'Did he just fuck'n shoot at us?' Provenz asked.

'Fucking hell, drive Paul, drive, DRIVE!' we yelled.

19

Bright Lights Big City

FOR ABOUT AN HOUR we resolved all the possibilities for how we could be in trouble:

1. We hadn't taken Exit's twenty kilos.
2. We had nothing to do with the explosion.
3. G-Ron was in prison.
4. We certainly weren't going to ask Randy for any other 'favours'.
5. Exit would most probably forget that we were even there.

Once all avenues had been dealt with I spat out excitedly, 'Holy fucken shit that was intense. I think that might be the single wildest thing that has ever happened to me. Keith, you are a fucken animal!'

We replayed the story for one another, rabbiting on like kids who had had a big day at the fair:

'And then he said . . .'

'Holy shit . . .'

'And then I said . . .'

'Fucking hell . . .'

'And then you said . . .'

'Can you fucking believe that shit?'

'And then he fucking shot at us!'

'I know!' we all said. 'Holy fuck!'

We actually didn't know for sure if we'd been shot at. But it sure as hell felt like it, and the adrenalin buzz of surviving was euphoric.

'Fuck, we should see if the car got shot,' I suggested.

'Top sentence,' said Barry.

'Sublime even,' said Provenz.

'He's right though, Paul, we probably should,' said Keith.

'It's a rental,' Provenz replied.

'Another top sentence,' said Barry.

'Sublime even,' repeated Provenz.

'Seriously though, Provenz, Dad's right. Police see gunshot wounds in cars. We should pull over and check it out.' Barry Castagnola – ever the voice of reason.

'All right, all right, all right,' said Provenz, replacing the 't's with 'd's, in the New Yorker's way of compromising against one's will.

Then he used the handbrake to stop just to teach us not to nag.

When the dust had cleared and we all stopped coughing, we checked out the car and agreed that even if it had been shot it was impossible to tell. It was covered in mud and torn up pretty bad just from travelling off-road.

'Right, the car doesn't look like it's been shot,' I concluded.

'Top sentence,' said Keith.

We all looked at one another, clapped our hands, like we'd seen so many bands of men do in so many movies, and said, 'VEGAS!' We scrummed back into the car and tore off down the open road.

Everyone else in the car had been to the city before. As we

drew closer their descriptions of the bright neon in the middle of the desert filled me with anticipation.

'It's amazing,' said Barry. 'There's just one hill you drive over and you can see the whole place lit up. It's one of the few places in the world that's exactly everything you might reckon it is.'

'Yeah, we lucked out, it's best witnessed at night first,' Provenz added, justifying our tardiness. Implying, too, that he had a plan that was unfolding simultaneously with mine.

Having heard this my expectations were high when, what seemed like hours later, I first saw the bright red neon peering over a hill in the distance. At first I was ecstatic just to have made it. 'Vegas, baby! Vegas! WHOOOOOOO!' I bayed like a wolf. But I was soon depressed to see it was only a few lights and casinos. I found it anti-climactic.

'What? Is that it? This is bullshit. That's fuck all,' I remarked, much to the delight and snickering of my co-passengers.

'Nope, that's not it,' Barry responded with a smirk. 'That's just the gas station on the state line. When we get there you'll be able to see it from miles away. It's fucking brilliant. Crass, garish and everything we're looking for.'

'That's just the gas depot? Jesus. Bring on the crass.' I rubbed my hands Pogueishly.

As we pulled closer the gas depot flashed and flickered. At least three massive bright red casinos surrounded it.

'Let's stop here,' I exclaimed, gasping for a beer.

'Nope, you don't want to do that,' said Barry. 'We're only forty minutes away. Don't shoot your bolt yet. Trust me. We go over one hill and then you'll see.'

The next forty minutes seemed like an eternity as I acted like a schoolkid waiting for his mum to pick him up from sports. Instead of 'OK, Mum's driving round the cornerrrrrrrrrrrr . . .

now! OK, nnnnnnnnnnnnow! OK, she's . . . gonna drive round
. . . the cornerrrrr . . . now!' I predicted the view from the hill-
top at every turn: 'OK, here comes Vegaaaaaaaas . . . now! No?
Okaaaaayyyy . . . now! Nope? Okaaaayyyyyy . . . NOW!'

After a while everyone joined in my childish game. Taking
it in turns to do the same.

'Okkkaaaaaaaayyyyy . . . here comes Vegaaaaaaaaaaaa-
aaaaaaaaas . . . NOW! Fuck!'

'No, you're all wrong because you see Vegas is actually
going to appear over this hillllllllllll . . . NOW! Shit!'

'Ahhh, now, you see, you've jumped the gun. Vegas is
actualllllllllyyyyyy . . . heeeeeeerrrrrre . . . NOW! Balls!'

Eventually Barry put us all to shame with a simple, snappy
'Here it is right NOW!' and like magic the blinding neon
appeared before us. We all screamed at the top of our lungs
'Go Barry, go Barry, go Barry!'

They were right. It appeared just like it did in movies and
dreams. Pumping up so much light into the night sky it almost
had a heartbeat.

'VEGAS! WHOOOOOOOOO!' Elated, I punched the back
of Barry's chair. I just could not sit still in my seat. 'VEGAS,
BARRY, VEGAS! WHOOOOOOOOO!' I yelped as loud as my
throat would let me.

'Oh good, that's back is it?' Barry quipped.

'YOU BET IT'S BACK! VEGAS, BARRY, WHOOooooooooo!'
My voice cracked and degenerated into a high-pitched girlish
whisper.

'Oh my God, don't tell me you've lost your voice again the
moment we get here? Hahahahahaha!' Barry cracked up and
the rest of the car joined him, mimicking my girly raspy
whisper:

'Ten on black, pretty please.'

'Go on, you horny Mexican. I'm Aussie. We'll complete each other's sets.'

I joined in. It was undeniably funny that I of all people should lose his voice on this my insisted-upon spiritual sojourn. I reached for the pad with the directions on it. I scribbled on it fast and handed the note to Provenz.

'Maybe I'm not supposed to talk,' he read out for me.

'Maybe you're not supposed to have Drambuie for break-fast, Jesus, or whatever the fuck you reckon you are,' Barry mocked in response.

I laughed along with the rest of them. I didn't care. I still had Owen Cavanagh as my proof.

I scribbled out another note. Provenz read it again: 'Maybe we should pull over and take the top down before we hit the strip.' I gave the thumbs up. Everyone gave me the thumbs up back with overly expressive miming faces. I scribbled a third note and handed it to Provenz, who snickered as he read it out: 'I can hear you, you dumb fucks. I've only lost my voice.'

20

Viva Las Vegas

WE PULLED OFF the top and made our way down Vegas's main drag. Provenz joined me in the back seat so Keith could keep his shoulder warm in the front. Lights blinded us from every angle. American landmarks are different from others. Having seen them so many times committed to celluloid, when you see them for real it really does feel like you're living out a fantasy. Like you're in the movies. Vegas is surreal like that. Garish, crass and gross, yet so inexplicably delicious. It's the junk food of scenery. KFC stuffed with Big Macs and nuggets. Each casino on the strip trying to outdo the other in a battle of the kitsch. I would have screamed 'Vegas! Whooooooo!' but Vegas seems to do that on its own, visually, just fine. My bellowing would've been drowned out by the lights and sheer Vivaness. I felt the same déjà vu I'd felt in Venice. I began to trip again. The pale-skinned Jamaican seemed to be riffing on my shoulder and in my ears now. Everywhere around me swam.

I slapped Barry on the back. He nodded enthusiastically over his shoulder at me. We'd made it, two bachelors in Vegas, baby. *Wheeeee dawgy!*

'Where we gonna stay?' I croaked.

'We should check in with my cousin,' Provenz said. He was picking through a bag of sunflower seeds, endlessly spitting and discarding the remnants over his shoulder. 'He's now the manager of the Hard Rock Casino. No doubt we could stay there for free.'

I nodded. 'Free is good. This place is disgusting. It's perfect.'

Checking out the people on the street, I couldn't help but feel that most people's Vegas experience involved sitting around staring at lights while fat Mid-Western Americans took pictures of themselves standing outside a replica of the Sphinx.

'What happens in Vegas stays in Vegas, huh?' Provenz offered sarcastically as he saw me watching a family gawping at a fountain and light show. There were some swans paddling around in the fountain.

'Yeah, don't tell the wife I saw some water turn pink,' I responded meekly.

'Hey Brendon.' Provenz nudged me, pointing at the swans.

The fat Mid-Western man, photographing his wife, looked on in envy at the four of us guys as he attempted to fit the fountain, the swan and her arse into frame.

'Cunts,' I croaked at the swans.

Mistaking me to mean him, the fat man's head sank into his chest as we drove by hollering.

'Not you, the swans!' I yelled back, to no avail.

Even though I was here for debauched purposes, I some-how felt I was above the other Vegas tourists. Healing Barry's broken heart was my end, which was the good Lord's work; they seemed bovine by comparison as they queued for Siegfried and Roy.

'You wanna hear something funny?' Provenz asked. He

pointed further down the road. 'You see that light shooting out the top of that pyramid?'

I looked to my left. There was a massive pyramid-shaped hotel and casino made entirely of jet-black glass. Beaming out the top was a white laser that went way beyond the night sky, seemingly into space.

'That's the only man-made landmark that can be seen from space,' he announced.

'What about the Great Wall of China?' I asked.

'It's a myth,' Barry interjected.

'You're fucken kidding me!'

They both shook their heads.

'Hahahaha! How fitting. So this is what aliens must think of humanity? That's perfect.'*

Provenz continued his tour guide. 'You see that spire up there?'

Ahead of us stood the tallest structure in Vegas. It must have been over fifty storeys high.

'Yeah. It's huge.'

'There's a fuck'n rollercoaster at the top of it.'

'No fucken way.'

He nodded.

'Oh I'm going. I'm going. All we need now is guns and pussy. Whoooooo!'

I went to sit up on the top of the back seat when some guy in black and bright yellow spandex on a bicycle pulled up next to us. He looked like a demented bee. 'Quit throwing your shit out of the car,' he snapped, and Provenz waved calmly and

---

* Boffins among you will know this is all bullshit. Loads of man-made things can be seen from space. 'Space' being a very loose term after all. However, absolutely no man-made structure can be seen from the moon with the naked eye.

compliantly. I saw that his face and pants were covered with Provenza's spittle-ridden sunflower seed husks. Judging by just how many were littered over his face and body he'd been riding behind us for some time. I couldn't believe the guy's balls, picking a fight with a car full of four guys.

'What the fuck's it to you, cunthead?' I snapped back.

The guy on the bike pulled ahead, revealing a gun and a sign across his back that read POLICE in bright yellow letters. Then he turned back in warning, fully aware that by now we'd seen his gun. Provenz put his hand on my wrist to calm me and waved even more compliantly at the cop. Thankfully, between my croaky voice and accent he hadn't been able to understand me.

'You look like a fucken bee,' I rasped after he'd ridden on. 'Look at him. He's dressed like he's four. That's fucken entrapment. Looking that stupid and throwing your weight around. How can anyone not take the piss? What are we supposed to do, just lie down and take it? Then later say, "Yeah, we got chastised by a fucken bee!" Fuck!' The guys cracked up at me going off on one. 'Man, you gotta warn me what the authority figures look like,' I said to Provenz, sticking to my theme to everyone's continued amusement. 'You know what I'm like. Some cunt dressed like a, I dunno, a bell, or some shit, is going to tell us to move along or we're going to jail? I think that's a perfectly viable defence case. "Mr Burns, can you tell us why you assaulted Officer Brown?" "Yeah. He looked like a fucken zebra, your honour."'

'I'll keep you posted if it's a cop or not,' Provenz replied, 'but keep a lid on it. We do have mushrooms, weed and a suspiciously large uncut rock of crystal meth on us.'

'Oh yeah,' I said.

'I need a beer,' remarked Barry.

'Pull over,' said Provenz. 'I got some in the trunk.'

'Won't the fucken bee have something to say about that?' I rasped again.

'Nevada state law. You can carry an open container on the street.'

'Finally something fucking sensible in this godforsaken country,' Barry observed.

'VEGAS, BABY! WHOOOOOOOOOO!'

21

The Stripper

WE PULLED OVER and cranked open the trunk. We would have opened the boot but we were in America now. Having sipped away at nothing but Jack Daniels and Drambuie all day my mouth and throat were dry and beer was all the rehydration they needed.

'What you wanna do?' Barry asked.

'Strip club! Strip club!' I answered, bouncing up and down.

'OK,' said Provenz, 'there's about ten down that way.' He pointed to a mall, burped, swished down the rest of his beer and discarded the can in a bin. The others followed suit.

We made our way to the mall. As we wandered in, the first thing we noticed was that everyone was looking up. On the roof there were plenty of flashing lights, but not much more than Blackpool at Christmas. It was hardly worth blocking our fucken way, I thought. Every one of these idiots standing there with their heads lolled back, assuming some sort of dentist's chair position, their mouths agape like end-of-the-pier arcade clowns.

'Look at these cunts,' I said. 'I wonder if we stuck a ping pong ball in their mouths would we win a stuffed toy?'

Provenz stared at me blankly.

'He's talking about seaside clown stalls,' Barry explained. 'They have metal clowns with mouths like this.' Barry made the mime, mechanically rotating his head from left to right and gesturing towards all the fucktards near by. 'And you pop a ping pong ball in their mouths and depending on where it lands you win a prize.'

'HA! HAAAAAAAA!' Provenz cackled as the analogy hit him.

Just then the opening chords of Beethoven's Fifth blared out in surround sound. The lights started flashing and doubled, then tripled, then quadrupled, then quintupled. In perfect synchronicity, they flashed and changed colour to the music.

We all cracked up.

'Now this is how Beethoven is meant to be enjoyed. It's fucking classy innit?' Barry offered in a chavvy accent as we all laughed into our knees.

The music went on and even more lights lit up. Blinding neon reds and blues somehow seemed to accompany the music with immaculate timing. Brighter, louder, BRIGHTER, LOUDER everything flashed and blared. I could feel the audiovisual overload in my bone marrow. The waves of light captured and directed our eyeline as they swept up and down the mall. Everyone in the mall had stopped and was cranking their heads back and forth, following them like a hypnotist's watch.

In a permanent crescendo, the audible and visual spectacle was soon threatening to deafen and blind us all. Mesmerized we were, all transfixed, tilting our heads back, mouths wide open, until the final strains almost slapped us in the face. And then it was done. The lights returned to their regular flashing intervals.

Along with everyone else in the mall we stood there stunned until someone started a single slow hand clap. We joined in until everyone in the mall was whooping. We waited for the cycle to start again, heads up, mouths agape, adopting the end-of-the-pier clown visage.

Some English lads wandered into the mall and pointed at us.

'Look at those cunts.'

'This is shit. It just looks like Blackpool.'

To their surprise we all cracked up at their piss-taking. And as we were snapped out of our trance, we caught one another's eyes and clapped in unison, shouting, 'Strip club!'

Admittedly I've never gone to strip clubs to be turned on. I've gone for the laddishness of them. I've never gone because I was lonely. I've gone specifically because I've got company. Again, we straight men are idiots and if we spend too much time together we have to do something to remind us all that we like girls. Objectifying women might seem a truly ironic way to do this. But again, we're idiots.

The number two reason I don't go to get turned on is this: comics and strippers are very much alike. We keep the same hours, we have a drug lifestyle, we share compatible social disorders, and it's pretty much the same level of prostitution. So any comic going to a strip club is more likely to have an awkward encounter with an ex than to get turned on.

Vegas, however, was different. The girls were stunning and obviously all failed actresses, or actresses trying to make names for themselves. I was used to strippers having c-scars, staring vacantly into the middle distance, bored out of their minds. These girls were gorgeous. And I mean gorgeous. But also truly gifted at putting on a happy face. The girl on the table in front of me gyrated her crotch expertly as if she had ten extra muscles in her groin. I was actually dumbfounded.

'Look how gorgeous this girl is,' I whispered to Barry.

'Yeah, she's fit,' he said dismissively.

'No, I mean she's proper gorgeous. Usually strippers are fit or the right side of minging. But she's properly beautiful. This is depressing.'

'Why?' Barry quizzed.

'I dunno. It just makes you wonder what's making her do this.'

'What?'

'Well, she's obviously a brilliant actress.'

'What?'

Almost as if to prove my point some guy on his own popped his head over us and yelled, 'Look at this fuck'n bitch, she fuck'n loves it. Look how horny she is.'

He may have been creepy, but I couldn't blame the guy for buying into it. She was truly convincing. Her smile was plastered wide and deep. Her eyes twinkled. Normally the eyes give it away, but this girl was staring straight into this guy's eyes and thrusting herself so orgasmically at him she deserved an Academy Award. I doubt Meryl Streep could hoodwink a room the way this girl was doing it. She was on a very hard glass table bending her pussy into impossible positions and doing it all like she was having the time of her life.

'Look at this fuck'n slut,' Creepy-On-His-Own Guy continued. 'Man, that bitch is fuck'n hot! She fuck'n loves it, the dirty little whore!' He spat out the words with such venom and conviction it made me uncomfortable. 'Where you guys from? England?'

'Nah, I'm from Australia, but Barry here's from England.'

'Cool. What do you guys do?'

'We're comedians.' I didn't need to point as Provenz and Keith were at the bar.

'Cool. Fuck, look at this bitch! She fuck'n loves it, the filthy little slut!'

We stared some more at her phenomenal performance. She continued to look deep into Creepy-On-His-Own Guy's eyes.

'I see your point about the acting,' Barry yelled in my ear.

'Look at this fuck'n bitch! She's such a dirty little whore. She's fuck'n hot for it.'

We nodded back at him.

I was intrigued by Creepy-On-His-Own Guy's demeanour. Normally there would be a modicum of shame attached to his solitude, but this guy was out there. I asked, 'So what the fuck does someone like you do for a living, Creepy-On-Your-Own Guy?' knowing full well that I wouldn't be understood between accent, struggling voice and disco music. Barry overheard and laughed.

'Sorry, what?'

'What do you do for a living?' I yelled over the club's all-encompassing tinny blare.

Without skipping a beat, Creepy-On-His-Own Guy replied, 'I'm an elementary school teacher.'

Barry and I stared at each other.

'I come here most evenings when she's on. Look at her! She's so fuck'n hot! The fuck'n slut. She wants it.'

Provenz and Keith rejoined us, without drinks. It turned out he'd skipped out to make a phone call.

'Guys, we gotta go,' he announced. 'I can't seem to get my cousin on the phone. I think he's out of town. I can get us a rate at the Delta though.'

As he spoke he looked back and forth from the girl to Creepy-On-His-Own Guy.

'Hey man, what's up?' Creepy-On-His-Own Guy yelled. 'Have you seen this girl?'

'Yeah, she's hot,' Provenz said dismissively, then turned to us. 'We gotta go.'

I yelled back, 'I think maybe we should warn a bouncer or something about Creepy-On-His-Own Guy. He's a bit of a stalker.' Like I said, I used to date strippers and the chivalrous part of me was concerned.

'Don't worry,' Provenz said, 'this is Vegas. If he was to try anything every bouncer in the place would take him out somewhere and bury him.' He looked back at the girl, who crinkled her nose at him cheekily. 'She's fuck'n cute though.'

Fuck Meryl Streep. That girl deserved an Academy Award.

22

Blue Lagoon

'WHAT THE FUCK are you looking at?' I yelled.

'Leave it, Bren, leave it,' Keith said, pulling me away from the swans swimming in the fountains that lined the mall leading up to the Delta.

We made our way into the hotel, checked in and dumped our stuff into our respective rooms. My suite was massive, all windows with a huge view of the city. I pictured banging the arse off some girl later as we both took in the panorama. My bed was a Superduper Fistingking, or something of equally hyperbolic American nomenclature, and took up half the room. I jumped in the power shower, nearly had my eyes blasted out of their sockets by the power-lunching face-raping nozzle, dried off with my towel (executive family fucking tree tepee size), stuck on a fresh set of clothes, slid on my red leather jacket (mine, bright red) and made my way next door to the guys' room.

Keith and Barry had gone to get something to eat so Provenz and I chatted about this and that and then stuck on the TV. There was some bizarre and obscure animation special on. We watched a few that were pretty funny but then out of nowhere a cartoon tree came on and yelled, 'So, er, I have sex with my cat. What's up with that?' Provenz and I looked at each other and then openly howled in mutual recognition. I know he didn't consider it a sign but he acknowledged that I did. I thought back to our car journey during which we'd made variation upon variation of the same joke. We cackled together.

He took back the joint and started pulling on it in short bursts. 'See! Don't worry, Burnsy. You'll still get your moment in the desert. Everything's going along exactly according to plan.'

I believed him.

The cartoon tree spoke up again: 'So I took a shit in the desert. What's up with that?'

Barry and Keith returned from downstairs. 'Heyyyy!' I welcomed them in. I was in the highest of spirits since the cartoon tree had reassured me we were on the right path.

'You guys hang here for a bit. There's some business I gotta get outta my way before I can completely open myself up for the insanity of the next few days.' Provenz bid us farewell and left.

'No worries, see you later,' we all replied.

We sat down and I handed out some beers.

'Man, I'm a bit fucked but I want to keep going,' I said, chugging away, belching and wiping my mouth with my sleeve. 'I wish we could get some coke somewhere.' From my pocket I produced the solid rock of crystal meth Exit had handed me. I'd never done crystal meth before. 'Anyone for a pick-me-up?'

Barry cracked up. 'Murrururhurrurhur! Crystal meth? A pick-me-up? What do you use for sleeping tablets? Heroin? Murhurhurhurhur.'

Keith joined in with the fit of giggles, with the exact same laugh: 'Mwurhurhurhurhur.'

'Haaaaaa-haa-ha!' I joined in excitedly. It was very in-fectious. 'Keith? Barry?' I asked, dangling the rock between my thumb and forefinger, making a ring shape.

Barry ignored it so I didn't even bother pointing out that I'd tried. He and Keith were busy considering the implications of a father and son trying meth together.

'Yeah, why not?' said Barry.

'Yeah, go on Bren.'

I cricked my neck at the second use of 'Bren'. I should've just told him, I know.

'So what's it do?' I asked.

'It keeps you awake for a day, I heard,' Barry said as I banged and crushed the rock with a glass. It had barely dis-persed and already there was more powder than all three of us had ever seen.

'Fucking hell,' said Keith. 'I've had my day in the sun, boys, but that's a lot of chemicals.'

'Will I be all right on this, you reckon, Barry?' I asked.

'Ha! You? Murwurhurrhurhur! How much coke you done in the past?'

'Fair enough. I won't go mental, will I?'

Barry stared at me blankly for a good thirty seconds with his arms folded, waiting for the penny to drop. When it didn't he spoke up. 'Mate, you've already whisked me off to Vegas to pursue a photograph on some fucking "holy" mission. I hate to break it to you. You *are* fucking mental.'

'Oh yeah. We'll see, my friend, we'll see.'

I thought of the sign from the cartoon tree on the television, rolled up a note and snorted back a fat line of meth in one. It shot up my nose without the sting of speed nor the numbing cold blue of coke. Then it hit me. 'errrrrrrAAAAAAAARRR GGGGGGHH! FUCK!' I slapped at my nose. It felt like I'd snorted a roll of Refreshers. A sensation I actually knew from experience.

Both Barry and Keith laughed. Then they took it in turns to snort a fat line each. And started patting away at their own noses in agony.

'Yeah, stings a bit dunnit?' Barry and Keith opined.

'Fucken oath it stings!' I screeched.

It did, but I liked it. No pain no gain, cough to get off and all that. It kicked in, and my mouth started going ten to the dozen before my brain could catch up.

'Nah it doesn't hurt too bad not as bad as Ecstasy anyway there's no chemical aftertaste too I reckon my nose must be used to the worst when I was a   kid we used to snort Refreshers although we called them Fruit Tingles every now and then you'd get one that was a factory mistake and it was loads of different colours they were treasured you remember Refreshers remember when you got a marble that was all different colours and Clearies remember Clearies the ones with no colour in them they must have been factory mistakes too really precious one time my ball got trapped on the roof and you weren't allowed to get them off the roof sorry it was a tennis ball not a marble what was I talking about oh yeah you weren't allowed to get the ball off the roof until Friday and I got caught and I told Mr Dickson who was about to give me the bats that I thought it was a stupid rule as it ruined your ball and that I shouldn't be punished and he said that he liked that I always spoke my mind and that it was something to be admired and he couldn't rightly spank that out of me and that's always stayed with me . . . So what does meth do?'

'That!' they replied, gesturing at me.

We all babbled at one another excitedly and good-naturedly

without any of us really taking in what the others had to say for about half an hour, until Provenz returned.

'Right, I'm all done, what's on the cards?' he said as he re-entered the twin suite.

'You want some meth? We should go out. Let's go out,' I blathered.

'Oh great, you guys gave *him* meth?'

'Yeah it's not as strong as coke I think I dunno you want some?' I fired back quickly.

He looked me up and down. 'No, I'm good thanks.'

'OK then let's go out. I need some beers and I promised this comic I know back in the UK I'd make a bet for him I never bet but I should make this one bet for Geoff I used to bet on two up in Australia it's where guys throw two coins in the air heads he wins tails he loses and you bet on two heads or two tails if it's one head and one tail everyone loses but he gets three throws of one heads and one tails before he loses there are guys that are that good that they can throw it in a particular way I know this cos one guy once dropped a chip and I picked it up for him and he thanked me for my honesty and told me to bet on tails which was weird because he's supposed to get heads but just before he threw the guy in the ring mouthed tails at him and he threw tails they stopped it because people knew it could be rigged but I always used to win because I'd wait for the house thrower to come in and I knew he'd throw tails.'

I only stopped when I needed to breathe. They stared at me for a while.

'Anyone catch any of that?' asked Barry.

'Something about a guy called Geoff and tails?' chanced Keith.

'Seriously, good call giving him meth, guys,' Provenz said to the others sarcastically. 'Now c'mon, Keith, let's go get you a hooker.'

'I need to make a bet on red just one bet though because I know with my personality I could easily get a gambling addiction luckily I know when to walk away I only bet what I can afford to lose in one go cos if you sit there all night the odds are stacked against you–'

'Fuck'n hell fellas. Meth? Burnsy?' Provenz said.

Keith and Barry shrugged their shoulders, giggling.

'You're not really going to buy him a hooker are you tell me you're just joking man I need to get laid can we go to a club where I can get laid how easy is it to get laid with my accent in Vegas . . .'

23

Passenger 57

DOWNSTAIRS WE HAD a few drinks in the Delta bar. It was hard to tell who was a hooker and who wasn't. Before long some girl very obviously on junk wandered up and slurred, 'You guys looking for company?'

We all gave an audible 'Yikes!' when we turned to look at her. She had huge bags under her eyes and was clearly an overweight man. Pretty much rougher than a Scottish stripper and twice as high.

'Don't fancy yours much, Keithy,' I quipped into my drink while we all giggled.

'Crack skulls! I tell you boys, I will crack skulls!' he fired back.

'Looks like hers is already cracked,' Provenz remarked.

'Or she'll skull-fuck you for crack,' Barry added.

Keith burst out laughing at his son's gag.

'Screw you, guys,' the hideous hooker slurred.

'Oh shit, sorry, you still here?' Barry replied innocently. We'd honestly thought she'd already left.

She turned on her heels and waved some sort of Vegas version of 'Bah!' at us.

'Let's move on to another bar,' Provenz said.

'Hold on lemme get you a round of drinks I've just got to make a bet for Geoff first I was gigging with him the other night and he gave me twenty quid to stick on black I figure that's about fifty bucks I often get the American dollar confused with the Australian is that how much it is I'll just make one bet and be right back what're we having?'

'OK, I caught the end of that,' said Barry. 'What's everyone drinking?'

Keith tried to decline, saying he didn't have any cash to buy back, but the other guys insisted he stop worrying. I concurred incomprehensibly.

I ordered their drinks and made my way over to a roulette table with a dollar minimum bet. A brunette and her friend wandered by and I waved. The croupier paid out bets, spun the wheel and threw in the ball. I threw a fifty on the table.

'How many chips?' he asked.

'One,' I replied.

All the dollar droppers round the table stared at me like I was from space.

I put the fifty-dollar chip on red instead.

All eyes turned to me like I had some sort of system going. My system of course being not sitting at a fucken dollar roulette table all night. All or nothing – my statistical non-anomaly.

'Red fourteen,' the croupier announced. Smiling openly at me.

He handed out my fifty first. I snapped it up, nodded and left the table immediately. Now the other gamblers looked at me like I really *was* from space and had dropped my pants and taken a shit. Behind me I could see them staring vacantly at the chair I'd occupied. One guy shuffled over into it and put a bunch of chips on red.

'I won,' I announced back at the bar. 'What we having?'

'What'd you win?' asked Barry.

'Fifty bucks. I guess our drink problems are sorted for tonight.'

'Wasn't it your friend's bet?' asked Keith.

'It stopped being his bet when I stuck it on red. Fuck it. I'll give him forty quid next time I see him.* For now we've got a free fifty bucks.'

We swigged back our drinks and made our way to another bar in another casino just across the way from the Delta. It was a Wednesday night/Thursday morning but it was still surprising the number of girls who solicited us from the moment we got in. With the exception of the fat junkie, in the Delta the girls were ushered off, but here they were positively encouraged. And all the girls who had hit us for tricks were so gorgeous, every time we were approached I was incredulous to discover they were working girls.

'Her?' I would ask incredulously.

'Yup,' Provenz would reply with a nod.

'What about her?'

'Oh for sure.'

'Well, what about her? She can't be. There's got to be enough modelling work around.'

'Dude, that's a guy.'

'Fuck off.'

'Look at the Adam's apple and the hands.'

'Shit, even the trannies here are hotter than any girl I've ever fucked.'

'You want some time with her? I brought enough with me

---

* If it puts you at ease, Geoff got his forty quid but had no recollection of asking me to place a bet for him. I didn't have the heart to tell him black would have lost.

to cover you and Keith.' Provenz pulled out a fold of notes from his pocket and waved them at me.

'Mate, I'm not getting tricked into copping off with a bloke for money again.'

'Again?' came the chorus.

'Long story. Lemme get some drinks in first.' With that I took myself off to the bar.

This place really wasn't anything like the Delta. After Provenz had pointed out the type to me, there seemed to be nothing but working girls there. I ordered a round, and in the distance behind the bar was one of the most breathtakingly gorgeous women I'd ever seen. She was blonde with full lips, ice-blue eyes and thin-rimmed glasses. I immediately made up a romantic back-story for her. She was obviously intellectual and above all this. Clearly paying her way through college.

I knocked back a shot while I was waiting. I could hear the guys murmuring in the background. I looked to my right and a stunning black girl was earmarking Keith. I continued to drink and stare at the blonde in the glasses. Behind me, Barry and Provenza's conversation was getting more and more animated. I couldn't hear them but later they pieced together the following for me:

Int. Casino – night. Brendon heads off to the bar leaving the guys milling near by. A black girl approaches Keith.

HOOKER

Hey honey. You lookin' for company tonight?

KEITH

Sure.

HOOKER

You wanna buy me a drink?

Keith pats his pockets.

KEITH

Erm . . .

Provenza pulls out a twenty and stuffs it in his hand.

KEITH

You're the man, Paul! The fucking man!

Keith and the hooker sidle up to the other side of the bar.

BARRY

Tell me you're not going to go through with this.

PROVENZ

What're you worried about?

BARRY

It's fucking gross.

PROVENZ

C'mon man. When's the next time your dad's going to get the chance to do something like this?

BARRY

That's just it, Paul! The key word here is 'Dad'!

Scene.

I got our drinks and returned to the fold. Keith was still at the bar chatting while the girl nodded, pretending to give a fuck.

'What's up?' I handed over their drinks. Still staring at the blonde out of the corner of my eye. I wondered how I could get her to look at me. I kept sending out psychic signals.

Look at me . . . I'm special . . . I'm different . . . We could be in love . . .

She didn't return my gaze once. Just kept looking fed up and worn out. There was still such an elegant beauty to her. I figured I'd had her pegged perfectly. Working night shifts to pursue the American dream. Studying law during the day.

God bless her, I thought.

Barry and Provenza's continuing discussion snapped me out of my trance.

'Look, Paul, I appreciate you paying for the room and everything but it's just a bit fucking weird,' Barry said, trying to keep it together. 'Actually, fuck that, it's downright bizarre.'

Just then Keith made his way over. 'Paul, she says it's five hundred. Is that too much?'

'Five hundred dollars? I've bought cars for that!' I exclaimed as Provenz reached into his pocket.

'I ain't no car, honey,' the hooker yelled at me.

'Sorry miss,' I replied.

'Tha's ai,' she purred in a thick Georgian accent.

'Five hundred?' said Provenz. 'No problem.' He pulled out a

175

wad of notes and counted out the money into Keith's open palm.

Barry watched each note passing from Provenz's hand to his dad's with increasing revulsion and disbelief. His eyes were transfixed by each note, back and forth, back and forth. Like a dog watching tennis. As if to add to his woes, his dad then announced proudly to the girl, 'This is my son and his friends.'

'Oh, that's yo son? How nice,' the girl responded.

Barry waved a sarcastic toodle-oo wave with his fingers. 'Hello, nice to meet you.' Then he shook his head in disbelief. 'Nope? Nothing?' he pleaded with everyone around him. 'No one else see the discomfort in this?' His question clearly open-ended, yet treated as rhetorical. He opened his palms as if awaiting an imaginary ball. The ball never came. 'Unbelievable, just fucking unbelievable,' he muttered to himself.

'You are the man, Paul, the fucking man!' Keith pumped his fist in the air as he and the hooker took off.

'Bye-bye hooker about to fuck my dad,' Barry said with another sarcastic wave.

Provenz stood there swigging back a beer, again smiling like a Cheshire cat. For once I was lost for words. Barry and I just stood there stunned for what seemed like an eternity. Waiting for his dad to return and both of them yelling, 'Ha! Gotcha! We were only fucking with you two!'

But his dad never returned; there was no sting.

Eventually Provenz broke the silence with a wounded, sarcastic, 'Ahem! You're welcome.' His hands were on his hips, his tone expectant and magnanimous.

This opened the floodgates for Barry. He spat and stuttered for a bit, trying to find the words. 'You're welcome? What?

You're fucking welcome? Why'd you do that? I thought you were joking. I was watching you count out the money and . . . what the fuck? Why'd you do that? What did I do to you? The pair of you? That's so fucking low! I just . . . I just . . . FUCK!'

'Barry, it's cool,' Provenz tried with a soothing tone, to no avail.

'Cool? Cool? *Cool?* How the fuck is buying my dad a fucking hooker cool? Did you have to do that right in front of me? Couldn't you two at least wait until . . . I dunno, until I'm fucking dead?'

'Look, you don't understand. I never knew my dad and it's so cool your dad being able to hang with us and be pals and get fucked up together. That's such an incredible bond—'

'Incredible bond?' I cut Provenz off. 'Don't fucken moralize about it. You just bought his dad a hooker and now he's fucken her on *his* fucken bed—'

I was about to go further but Barry calmed me down and cut me off. 'Brendon, Brendon, it's fine, mate, I've got this.' He turned back to Provenz and without skipping a beat tore into him, repeating what I'd said verbatim: 'Incredible bond? Don't fucking moralize about it. You just bought my dad a hooker and now he's fucking her on my fucking bed. Oh God! My bed? Ewwwwww . . .' Barry grabbed at his hair.

Provenz stood there nonplussed. 'OK, now you're making me regret doing it. Some fuck'n thanks that is.'

'Thanks? You fucking—'

Barry lunged at him. I stepped in, holding him back.

'Whoa whoa whoa!' went Provenz in his best Tony Soprano voice.

Luckily Barry composed himself immediately: his centre of gravity and strength were way more than I could handle. 'I'm cool, I'm cool,' he insisted.

'Jesus. Couple of fuck'n queers here. Jeez, if it means so much to you fuck'n fags we can go up and tell him to do it on my bed only. Fuck!' Provenz said with an exasperation that was both baffling and audacious.

We both glowered at him.

'Do you want to go up?' Provenz offered.

'Fuck no!' Barry replied. 'I might catch him mid-stride . . . AAARRRGGGHH! God, now that image is in my head. FUCK!' Barry slammed his head into the counter.

Provenz ordered more drinks. In the distance I could see the beautiful blonde girl being escorted by a bouncer. There went my shot of speaking to her. They both looked over at me as he ushered her out. I figured looking like that a lot of creepy guys must come here and freak her out.

24

The Marine

'OK, YOU NEED to calm down,' Provenz said in an attempt to bring us round. 'We're having a blast. You just need to change the way you're looking at it. Let's finish our drinks and find a club where there are single women.'

'Grrrrr,' growled Barry.

I'd never heard a man make such a noise, only having read it in comic books as a child. It was pretty much the same. My attention, however, was seized immediately by the promise of American girls.

'Girls,' I rasped. It was all my voice could muster given the recent shouting match.

'Ha! How you gonna pull with no voice there, Rain Man?' Provenz cackled.

I crouched down and stood up, making the sunshine motion with my arms again. Ever beckoning with a big wide grin.

'This I gotta see,' Barry said, shaking his head.

'You had to give him meth, didn't you?' Provenz said to Barry.

There was another pregnant pause. Barry stood there looking at Provenz with his arms folded.

'You had to buy my dad a hooker, didn't you?'

Provenz cackled again and slapped Barry on the back warmly, ever so slightly winning him round. 'C'mon buddy, let's go get you boys some tail.'

Provenz put his arms around both of us and led us out of the casino.

'So when'd you fuck a guy?' Provenz asked me as we walked the streets.

'I didn't. I got blown. It was in South Africa. I'm still not sure if it was a guy or not.'

'Awwwww,' went Barry.

'Ha!' went Provenz. 'Was it good head?'

'Can't remember. I guess so. Say what you like about the Third World, they could do with the protein.'

'Awwwww,' went Barry.

'Ha!' went Provenz. 'Have the Red Cross heard about your selfless donation? They'll give you a medal no doubt.'

We entered a nightclub at what must have been about three a.m. It was filled with people like us: night workers and general reprobates. We did a lap of the place, stopping only briefly to do a bit of perfunctory dancing on the spot. It had the neon blue lighting customary in such an establishment. Hiding everyone's physical flaws and vitamin D deficiencies.

We sidled up to the bar where an Asian American dude was standing holding court. He seemed charming and affable enough.

'Hey man, how ya doin'?' he bellowed.

'I'm doin' all right, mate. How're you?'

'I'm doin' great, man. I'm just on leave from the US Marines. You guys wanna do a shot?'

I took to him immediately. 'Let me get you one. You charming bastard. I've got a drink in mind. It's called a Flaming Burnsy.'

'Flaming Burnsy? Vegas! Whooooooooo!' He screamed my Vegas scream.

I screamed it back: 'Vegas! Whoooooooooooooooooo!'

'Looks like you've pulled already, Brendon. This one's definitely a guy though,' Barry remarked in my ear.

'Get fucked. Trust me, the other one was very convincing. I'm still not sure if it was a cock or a massive clit. You wouldn't have been able to tell if you'd been there.'

'No,' Barry shot back, 'I wouldn't be able to tell . . . anyone!'

'What's your name, dude?' the Marine asked me, ignoring Barry.

He gripped my hand. It nearly broke. If this guy said he was a Marine, I believed him. He was shorter than me but just had the build and air of a human weapon. He had broad shoulders and was a perfectly proportionate mix of brawn, gristle and body fat. Not all steroid gym muscle, rather the physique brought on by days of vigorous running through shit and having people pelt you in the stomach with medicine balls while ordering you to puke.

'My friends call me Burnsy, and this is Barry and Provenza.'

They all nodded and smiled a 'Whassup?' at one another.

The cogs started whirring in his head. 'Wait a second. Your drink's named after you?' He was amiable but displaying the intellect of a man born to take orders.

'The night I invented it at the Edinburgh Festival three shows didn't go on the next day. The performers all called in sick.'

He stood there staring for a bit, processing the information. 'You're a performer?' he eventually asked.

'Yeah, we're comics.'

Again there was a pause while he processed.

'I'm a Marine,' he said.

181

'Yeah, I know. What's your name?'

'Aaron.'

I turned to the barman. 'Well, four Flaming Burnsies for my buddies and my new friend Aaron.'

'Vegas! Whoooooooooooo!' screamed Aaron.

'I like this guy,' I yelled back into Provenz and Barry's ears.

'We can tell,' said Provenz.

'He looks like he's got a massive clit – just how you like 'em,' Barry teased.

'Ha!' went Provenz again.

I could see as they snickered at my expense that they had both moved on from their little disagreement.

I explained to the barman what was in the drink: one shot of tequila and one shot of sambuca mixed together. The barman winced. 'It gets worse,' I said. 'You set it on fire when it's in your mouth.'

The barman nodded appreciatively. 'Sweet.'

By the time the drinks arrived everyone at the bar was watching, intrigued. Spurred on largely by Aaron yelling to all within earshot, 'Check this shit out – it's a new drink!' I piqued the interest further by prompting, 'OK, now the trick is not to panic. It'll feel warm in your mouth but if you shut it too quick it'll slide down your cheeks and set you on fire.'

'Vegas! Whoooooooooooo!' Aaron screamed.

I looked at the others and laughed.

'I'll go first, just to show you,' I announced.

I ushered Barry in to light my drink. I knocked the shot back, letting it settle high enough in my mouth so Barry's lighter could reach it. Unfazed, he touched the yellow flame to the surface of the booze and a blue flame then flickered around the inside of my cheeks and atop the pool of alcohol in my mouth. Carefully I closed my lips to extinguish the flames yet not let out any of the flammable liquid. I gulped the warm gas and sticky-liquorice fluids. It burnt for a bit and then was gone. I stood up with a shiver and opened my mouth, sticking out my tongue to reveal that it had all gone.

The bar whooped and hollered. Aaron yelled, 'Whooooooooooo! Vegas!' Mildly wandering off his original theme of 'Vegas! Whoooooooooo!'

'I'm next, I'm next!' he added, dropping to his knees and opening his mouth wide.

I took his shot and the lighter from Barry. 'OK, now remember, just let it sit in your mouth and don't close your lips too suddenly.'

'I got it, I got it.'

I poured the sickly potion in his mouth and stuck my lighter in. The pool lit up and he knelt there with the flame licking away in his mouth.

'OK, now close your mouth slowly.'

He shifted his lips slowly, yet too slowly. More like the sliding-roof doors of an evil genius's volcano.

'OK, not too slowly. You have to extinguish the flame eventually otherwise you'll burn your lips—'

'Aaarrrrggh, fuck!'

The flame having burnt Aaron's lips, he instinctively bowed his head, letting out the flaming sambuca and tequila on to his chin and wrists. He padded down the flames on his jumper then slapped away at his face. The bar stood there stunned as he stood up covered in sticky hot black lava.

'Vegas! Whoooooooooooooo!' he screamed.

Everyone cheered and laughed, seeing he was OK and/or mental.

Provenz sucked his back successfully, to a much more appreciative reception now that everyone had seen how wrong it could go. Then Barry did his, with little effort, stand-ing up afterwards with the same unperturbed air with which he'd lit mine earlier.

I realized 'unperturbed' was the perfect way to describe Barry. Everything just seemed to wash over him. He'd feel passionately for a second and then return to quiet resolution. I envied him his unaffected demeanour. Even when Chris left him, he was sad, certainly, but he still managed to plod along with a brave face. He may have displayed anger at first but then he just moved on, as if to say, 'Well that's happened and now this is happening.' He'd just done the same with Provenz buying his dad a hooker right in front of him. I'd had to pull him off Provenz only twenty minutes earlier yet here he was doing shots with him like it had never happened.

I had trouble letting go. I wished everything were different. I'd still have taken my ex back. Barry had already divulged to me that there was no way he was interested in his after what she'd done. But now was not the time for this. I snapped myself out of it.

'Man, you're a cool guy,' Aaron said, slapping me on the back.

'And so are you, my friend. Most of the Marines I've met are bullies and dicks.'

'Nah man. I train hard and I party hard. I've got some girls over here. You should be my wingman.'

Provenz and Barry nodded intuitively that this would be where I parted ways with them and took off to see what else was in store.

'Sure, Aaron, not a problem. Let me get another round for the girls.'

'No way, man, my round. Lemme introduce you.'

He took me over to their table where there were three girls

and one guy. It became immediately apparent that my judgement was off and Aaron was a dick. As we sat down he started to bark and direct orders. He pointed at one girl and said, 'OK, she's with me.' He pointed at another and said, 'She's with him.' And then the third, 'She's all yours. This is Burnsy. He's a comedian from England I think.' He then went back to the bar to get the drinks.

The girl who had been appointed as 'mine' shook her head and said, 'OK, that's the final straw, that guy is freaking me out. I'm going home.' And she got up and did just that.

I stared at the girl who had been appointed to the other guy and rasped, 'OK, that was weird.'

The guy leant over and said, 'That guy has been freaking us out all night.'

'You don't know him?' I asked incredulously.

The girl next to me said, 'No.'

'Shit, I thought you were together.'

'No,' they all confirmed in unified disdain.

'He's kinda scaring me cos he just presumed that he's with my girlfriend.'

'She's *your* girlfriend?'

'Yeah. I don't give a fuck what he says. I'm going home with her tonight.' He pointed at what Aaron thought was his conquest.

'And who are you with?' I asked the other girl.

'No one.' She patted my lap.

God bless America.

'OK then. Do you want to have sex with me?'

'Yes.'

'Really? I was just trying my arm. That simple? I was only kidding. Well, no, I wasn't kidding. It's just that we're going to have to move fast with Aaron in tow.'

I leant in and kissed her. Her lips were soft. She was a slim blonde with curly hair. She lifted her hand to my cheek.

I pulled back. 'Wait a second. How old are you?'

'Twenty-three.'

I shrugged. 'I can do that.' And I leant in and kissed her again.

Aaron came back from the bar to see that the girl he'd assigned to me had gone and I was copping off with what he'd perceived to be his friend's girl. He was wrong on both counts. The guy wasn't his friend and she wasn't his girl. I almost felt bad for him being so simple.

'What the fuck?' he said to me. 'You're cock-blocking my man here.'

'She's not his girl, dude,' I said calmly as she slipped her hand on to my inside thigh and purred in my ear.

Aaron stormed off, confused.

'OK, that guy is *really* freaking me out now,' the guy said.

Before we could work out a game plan Aaron was back with a bouncer, yelling and pointing at me. 'This guy took my friend's girl!' The bouncer looked at me and the girl, then the guy and his girl. We all shrugged. He then looked back at Aaron and shrugged too. Aaron shouted 'What the fuck?' then went over to talk to Barry and Provenz.

I turned to my new companions. 'OK, that guy's a living weapon but not that bright. For whatever reason he thinks somehow that you're stealing his missus and I yours.'

'I don't want to fight that guy,' the guy said.

'We can't and we won't have to. Brains over brawn here, my friend. He's easily confused and obviously has a simple ego. He is, therefore, easily manipulated. But we have to move fast. You're going home with me, right?' I asked my girl.

'Yeah,' she said chirpily.

'And you're going home with him, right?' I asked the other girl.

She nodded.

'OK, so we just remove us from the equation. Girls, you have to turn us down in front of him.' I turned back to the guy. 'Then you and I act dejected and go to the bar. If you need to, tell him you've got work in the morning. That way as long as he knows you're not going home with anyone he won't know who to punch. Do you know where the girls are parked?'

'Yep.'

'OK.'

We all acknowledged that we understood the plan with military precision.

'OK, here he comes, mate. Go.'

As Aaron made his way over to us again we stood up and said in loud voices, 'OK, well, if you've got to go you've got to go. Nice to meet you, girls.'

'Yeah, nice to meet you too.'

We left Aaron at the table, a little befuddled by how quickly the situation had contradicted then counter-contradicted itself. We made our way over to the bar where Provenza and Barry joined us.

'What the fuck's going on?' Provenz asked. 'Everything OK? That guy seems to have it out for you.' Aaron had obviously gone and bitched to them.

'He seems to be under the impression that we somehow stole his girls so they're pretending to leave and we're going to sneak out after them.'

We all looked over to where the girls were talking to him. He was gesturing wildly and indignantly.

'You guys have got my back, right?' the guy said to all three of us as we continued to watch events unfold.

'Yeah, no problem,' Provenz assured him.

'We won't need to, and we don't want to,' I repeated. 'That fucker will take half the bar down with him. Did you see him? He's a fucken weapon. You can just tell. That's all he understands. We just want to keep him confused for now.'

In the distance the girls had obviously done a good job of placating Aaron as they kissed him on the cheek and made their way upstairs and out of the club. Aaron stood there stunned and dejected.

'OK, before he has time to think, let's go, mate. Go!'

'See ya tomorrow,' Barry said as I took off.

'Yeah, see ya,' I said over my shoulder.

I ushered the guy out while a dumbfounded Aaron continued to stare blankly at the space where the girls had been standing. He then looked to his right and made his way back to the bar to look for us as we took off to the left of his field of vision.

As we clambered up the stairs the bouncer nodded at us and smiled. 'Good night, gentlemen.'

'We're lovers not fighters,' I offered.

He nodded again, winked, and did the 'click click' pistol gesture with his fingers.

We made our way outside where the girls were waiting for us. They embraced us both and kissed us full.

'Man, that was smooth,' the guy said. 'What's your name again?'

'Burnsy,' I replied.

'I'm Todd.'

I turned to the girl I was kissing. 'Oh yeah, sorry, what's your name?'

'Katy.'

We all laughed.

'Well tough shit there, idiot Marine machine,' I said. 'Let's go and get laid, shall we?'

Todd and I high-fived as the girls led us to their car, snuggling up to us as we walked.

About five hours of rampant meth-induced pounding later, Katy rolled off me and I voiced what I thought was a compliment: 'Wow, I refuse to believe you haven't been paid for that at some point.'

'I'm sorry, what?' she replied.

'I mean . . . erm . . . is it OK if I don't speak for a bit? I'm a bit thick after I've just come.'

She giggled, shrugged her shoulders, put on her clothes and left with an affectionate toodle-oo wave of her fingers.

My kinda girl, I thought.

25

The Sunshine Boys

ABOUT FOUR HOURS later I sat bolt upright and bounded out of bed. The afternoon sun was beaming through the windows and on to my face. The drugs were obviously still coursing through my bloodstream. My throat was dry and torn to shreds now. I tried to speak and could only muster a frail whisper, as if stirring from a coma. Even the whisper seemed to induce some level of internal bleeding. Yet today was the day we were to make our sojourn to the desert to follow my vision to fruition. Spurred on by chemicals and sexual bragging rights I quickly showered, picked up a pad and pen for communication and made my way to the guys' room.

When I got there I was disappointed to see that the mood was more than a little sombre. Barry was stirring on the couch, Provenz was chilling on the bed and Keith was nowhere to be seen. I gestured at the empty bed and made a 'Where's Keith?' face.

'Can't talk, huh?' Barry asked.

I made a talking puppet gesture with my hand and a cutting gesture at my throat.

'Awesome,' Provenz snickered.

I made the 'Where's Keith?' face again, pointing at the empty bed.

'Dunno. I think he was embarrassed and took off. Came home last night and passed out on my bed. I've had about an hour's sleep in total I reckon.'

I wrote on the pad *So you ready to go to the desert then boys?* I clapped my hands vigorously then returned a palm to massage my agonizing vocal cords from the outside, hoping to stretch and limber them up like a muscle.

'I dunno, man, we're kinda beat,' Provenz replied.

I shook my head emphatically, made *pssssst* noises and stamped my feet. I felt a genuine sense of panic. I started to write on the pad: *Our lives will never—*

Barry stopped me. 'Yeah yeah, lives never the same again, blah blah, Jesus God unconscious something.'

Their reluctance soon rubbed off on me, and I had to agree this could be the worst idea ever. Bad moods mean bad trips.

'I think I know why Keith said he wasn't coming,' Provenz piped up. 'Pardon the pun, Barry.'

'Oh ha fucking ha,' Barry replied.

'Why?' I mimed with my face.

'I think he's a little embarrassed about being broke and us having to pay for everything.'

'Oh yeah, andmaybehefuckedahookeronmybedthat-youboughtforhim,' Barry noted in his best machine-gun manner.

I frowned and nodded at Provenz in agreement.

'Great, now Rain Man's playing Harpo to my Groucho,' Barry remarked. Changing the subject, he turned to me and said, 'Sohowwasyournightwiththatgirlthen?'

I did the sunshine mime again. Provenz and Barry rolled

their eyes at each other. I wrote on the pad *Holy fucken shit she was nimble.* Barry read it out.

'Sweet,' Provenz said, toking on another joint. 'How'd the meth work?'

I made a 'strong like bull' gesture with my fist.

'Oh, so you fisted her then?' Barry remarked facetiously.

I mimed a sarcastic 'ho ho ho', rubbing my belly. I then went into a descriptive series of mimes of the night's encounter. I got to my final mime and sat back.

'She came on your face?' Provenz asked when I was done.

I went to mime otherwise but Barry cut me off. 'That's one hell of a clit. You really are having your run of luck with them ladyboys!'

We all laughed. It was amazing how quickly the three of us could reinvigorate one another. Taking the piss just seemed to be done with such affection.

'You got any meth on you then?' Barry asked.

I nodded and pulled out the wrap, chopping us both a line. I looked at Provenz, eyebrows raised.

'Fuck no!' he said. 'I think somebody's going to have to play sheriff today.' He popped on his bright red hat again.

Barry snorted a line of meth. I walked over to the side of Provenza's bed and took the joint from his hands.

'Well that oughta cure your throat,' he said.

I toked on it and immediately felt like I'd swallowed burning embers from a campfire. I clutched at my throat while Provenz just grinned at me like I was an amusing experimental subject. I grabbed a bottle of Drambuie and gargled. He stared at me, still grinning. Like when watching a thirsty dog drink from a high-pressure hose then sitting back and laughing while it retches and pukes.

After swilling Drambuie I snorted back another line of

meth, which immediately woke me up but added to my apprehension about the trip. Having built it up so much in my head I was starting to feel nothing could live up to it. What if I was wrong about all of it? If there was no outrageous random occurrence, then Provenz would be proved right, Barry would be miserable and I'd be left with nothing but myself to deal with. That simply wouldn't do. I was enjoying running away far too much. If we got to my destination and there was nothing there but a bad trip, I had to admit, I'd be pretty much out of ideas.

'So where do we go?' Barry sniffed and snorted.

I wrote on my pad *I can't be fucked now*. He read it out.

'Oh no,' Provenz said, grabbing me by the scruff of the neck. 'No fuck'n way. You dragged us out here and if you think I'm gonna just sit here in a hotel room with you guys on crystal you got another fuck'n think coming.'

'Yeah, he's right, Brendon. We've come all this way.'

I nodded and shrugged enthusiastically (if such a thing is possible).

'Yeah, s'gonnabegreat!' Barry remarked, yet again with sarcasm. 'Let's go to the desert. Maybe get bitten by something. It'll be brilliant!' He dropped the 'll's in 'brilliant'.

Brilliant is Barry's favourite word. He uses it more, and frankly has more uses for it, than anyone I know. He can use it to mean almost anything according to how many times or how quickly and/or clearly he says it or what noise he prefaces it with. Here it was belted out so it sounded more like 'br-int'. That signified that something was, or was going to be, significantly shit but hilarious. Yet if he says it with the same speed and enunciation twice in a row, book-ended with a sighing 'uhhrr' – i.e. uhhrr br-int br-int uhhrr – that signifies a fond memory. If he says it slowly, breaking it up into syllables – brill-i-ant – that can be taken at face value. Yet, again, if it is prefaced with an 'oh' – oh brill-i-ant – that means everything has so gone to shit that even Barry isn't amused.

I was fearful of hearing one such 'oh brill-i-ant' when we got to the desert.

We all laughed at how shit this was shaping up to be. As my room was no longer available I checked out and moved my stuff into theirs while the guys got showered and dressed.

All sorted and ready to go, Provenz ran through a checklist while Barry confirmed and I nodded.

'Keys?'

'Check.'

'Shrooms?'

'Check.'

'Hats?'

All three of us popped on our hats.

'Check.'

We looked at one another for a bit.

'OK,' said Provenz, 'let's do this.'

26

That Movie with William Hurt and the Deaf Chick (Y'know, the One She Got the Academy Award for)

I CLAMBERED INTO the back seat of the convertible as soon as we'd taken the roof off. There was nothing I could add to any conversation beyond 'psst' when I wanted attention. I wanted time to myself in the back anyway, to bask in the sun and air.

As we pulled out of the Delta car park Provenz yelled over his shoulder, 'So which way Harpo/shaman, or whoever the fuck you reckon you are?'

'Murhurhurhurhur,' Barry tittered.

'Psst!' I spat.

They turned to see me pointing towards the sun and the mountains surrounding Vegas.

'I guess that means out there,' Barry said.

I pointed at him and put my finger on my nose, confirming he'd translated my exact sentiment verbatim.

'Out there it is.' Provenz slammed the pedal to the metal. I hate that turn of phrase but he literally did. I actually heard the *clink*.

On the way there Barry voiced his disapproval of Provenz

buying the hooker for his dad some more, while Provenz carried on justifying it as a fantastic father-and-son bonding exercise. Rather callously, Provenz then started making fun of Barry, pretended not to hear him as he carried on regardless.

'I couldn't believe it. I was just staring as you handed out the notes—'

'Sorry prozzie jizz, what was that?'

'I mean, right in front of my eyes—'

'What's that, working girl?'

'I just followed the money note by note—'

'Can't hear you, son of hooker fucker.'

It was still difficult to get a bead on Provenza's motivations, but 'son of hooker fucker' did have an amusing ring to it and I stifled a laugh. It even brought a smirk to Barry's face.

Provenz spat and dropped his cigarette at his feet. He automatically reached down to retrieve it, swerving over to the outer lane in the process.

'Look out!' Barry screamed as we headed into oncoming traffic.

'Psssssssssssssst!' was the loudest warning noise I could make.

We straightened up, and as Barry was about to chastise Provenz I held up a note I'd written earlier that read *It's a rental*. Barry read it out and Provenz laughed.

'How'd you write that so quick?' he asked.

Almost before he could finish the sentence I held up another note: *I was ready for you, dickhead*.

They both laughed.

'I love silent Brendon,' Barry managed through his giggles.

A cop car drove by and thankfully it finally made Provenz slow down to a semi-reasonable pace.

'We should take it easy,' Barry reminded him. 'We do have mushrooms and meth on us.'

'Noted,' replied Provenz.

It took about another forty minutes or so to reach the outskirts of the city. To our left I saw a massive DVD and record store.

'Psst!' I stamped and pointed.

'You wanna buy a DVD?' Provenz asked. 'We gotta get our skates on if we wanna catch that sunset.'

I wrote on the pad *I need to get some CDs for the soundtrack to our movie.*

'OK,' Barry said after he'd read it out. 'There's a café over there too. I need some breakfast.'

'Sure, I could do food.'

Provenz casually looked around for cops, then did a handbrake turn.

We pulled in to the café car park and took a seat at a table outside. The waitress was punkish and fit. I figured my not talking would make me seem more enigmatic than the others. Even though I'd just got laid I still craved the sexual attention. On some level, in every woman's fantasies lies a mute man. For obvious reasons:

1. Good listener.
2. Can't answer back.

What's more, mime and sign language leave a lot more opportunity for subliminal suggestion.

I mimed thank you with my lips while rubbing my heart and pointing at her a lot. She just blanked me. I figured her a lesbian. I'd discussed all this days earlier with both Barry and Provenz when my voice was giving in and out. They could tell what I was doing and seeing her give me no response was amusing them no end.

197

'Nothing, mate, you've got nothing.' Barry tittered, shaking his head. 'Pa*th*etic.' He accentuated the 'th' amiably and folded his arms.

Provenz changed the subject. 'Look, getting off the beaten track is going to be harder than you think. You can't just drive off the road into the desert.'

'Ask directions off the waitress,' Barry suggested. 'At least before Burnzino the mute hypnotist here completely pisses her off with his dumb thank-yous.' He performed the heart-rubbing mime spastically at me.

I wrote a note while we waited for her to return.

When she came back with menus Provenz said, 'Excuse me, miss. My friends and I want to share a moment in the desert and we need to work out how to get off road from here and over to somewhere near those mountains.'

She gave us a long and convoluted set of directions that Provenz seemed to take in expertly. He jotted down some notes on my pad, giving the customary number of 'uh-huhs' and 'yeahs' necessary to let her know she could move on to the next direction.

When they were done I handed her the note. She read it aloud: 'What are the chances you have ginger?' She looked at me blankly.

Barry stepped in to save any further confusion. 'My friend's lost his voice. He wants hot water with fresh ginger, honey and lemon in it for his throat.'

I mimed with my throat, looking for sympathy from her that never came. I figured her definitely a lesbian, or she'd had a motorcycle accident in which she lost her pussy.

She leant down to write a response on my pad. I waved at her while Provenz and Barry spoke for me, both giggling: 'You don't have to do that. He's only lost his voice.'

She stared at them blankly.

'He's not deaf.'

She nodded but was not remotely amused. She turned to me and mouthed her words carefully, as if I had to lip-read: 'OK. I – don't – think – we – have – ginger – but – I'll – try – for – you.'

I mouthed 'thank – you' then rubbed my heart and pointed at her again. She found none of this endearing or amusing. This was preposterous. How could this be? She'd gone from lesbian to motorcycle-crashing pussy-loser to born asexual in my eyes.

'You're – welcome,' she mouthed again slowly in response, nodding, then she left.

She returned before long. Again she started to write her response on my pad.

'You don't have to write it,' the boys repeated.

She pulled a look as if to say 'Don't patronize me, you're the one dragging a spastic around'. Instead she said rather huffily, 'We don't have ginger but I can do you lemon tea with honey.'

I made the 'thank – you' mime again, keeping eye contact.

The penny finally dropped that I could listen but not speak. Her tone switched to something far warmer immediately. 'You're welcome,' she chirped, and wiggled as she turned. She quickly returned with my drink and patted me as she set it down. 'There you go. Hope this helps.'

Barry shook his head.

'You should shut the fuck up more,' Provenz said from behind his menu, not even looking at me.

I drank my tea as Provenz and Barry continued to work out what they wanted to eat. When I'd finished, I held up the note that read *I need to get some CDs for the soundtrack to our movie* at them again.

'Sure,' Barry nodded.

'You wanna eat?' Provenz asked.

I wrote *Nah, mushrooms work better on an empty stomach.* Truth be told, with all the meth in my system I couldn't stomach food.

'Keep telling yourself that,' he said wryly as I made my way across the car park. 'Hey, why don't you try that mimey thank-you shit with the record counter guy? See if you get some free shit.'

I gave him the finger over my shoulder.

In the record store I wandered around looking for something to watch the sunset to. The place was easily the biggest record store I'd ever seen. I walked down the first aisle I came to and immediately had my decision made for me. Staring out at me like a beacon was a compilation of The Church. I figured it apt, given our vigil. The Church were a well-respected Australian band that stuck out amid the glut of tedious eighties drivel. Pretty much every Aussie my age spent their teens listening to them, or had it played to them ad nauseam by a guy who was really really 'into' them, like they were some sort of southern hemisphere answer to The Doors, only with a less dead front man and therefore attracting slightly less mythical devotion. I perused the back cover looking for one track in particular. Having found it I felt a newfound vigour for our journey. Whatever the perception, this would be our moment.

I flung a few more CDs into my basket, and Doug Stanhope's live DVD *Deadbeat Hero* (another sign, I figured), paid silently without incident and left.

When I got back to the café the guys were wrapping up their breakfast, Barry a variation on the full English, Provenza some LA-based muesli nonsense.

'You get what you need?' Provenz asked.

'Pssst!' I replied with a big elated thumbs-up.

Barry turned and squinted with his mouth wide open as one does when detecting a fart. It turned out he was actually listening intently to the music in the background, but it was the same face. 'There's that song again. Bum. I should've come with you. I want to get that album. I always used to listen to them when I was out here but I can't remember the name of the fucking band.'

The Jamaican in white played over my shoulder again.

27
What Happened in the Desert

PROVENZ PROVED REMARKABLY adept at following the waitress's directions. We soon veered off the road and on to a dirt track between some houses. We negotiated left after right after left after right. Attempting to get as far away from civilization as possible. Bits of corrugated rusty tin sprang up either side of the road as we navigated our way between small boulders and mounds, blocking our view either side. To the right there were rows of houses with makeshift fences made from the same corrugated tin propped up against or strapped to the wire-mesh surrounding the backyards. As we took one left I made note of a particularly large rock as our point of reference to get back to the main road.

I was sitting up on the back of the convertible with my legs dangling in the back seat.

'Where to?' Provenz asked.

'Psst.' I pointed left.

Barry was sitting in the front with his head resting on his palm. He wasn't digging this at all. I patted him on the shoulder. He smiled thinly and insincerely back at me. I made the sunshine mime at him, but it seemed only to add to the insincerity and thinness of his grin. Coupled with a noncommittal raising of the eyebrows, he could easily just have thrown his shit at me.

As we drove along we dug out the mushrooms and started chewing on them. Some of them were dry, twig-like, and got stuck in our teeth. We swilled them down with beer and stifled a puke by punching our chests and belching.

Soon the dirt track opened up, revealing the mountains and horizon beyond.

'Now where?' Provenz asked.

'Psst.' I pointed in the direction of the mountains.

He nodded and pulled off on to an even dirtier unused track, which in turn diverted to one even less travelled. We'd driven all of two hundred yards when we came to a two-foot-deep ditch and skidded to a halt.

'I can jump it,' Provenz said, slamming the car into reverse and covering us all with dust.

'Pssssst!' I spat and stamped.

'It's a rental,' he replied.

I considered exactly how many people had said that while in possession of this car and exactly how loose the engine had been knocked accordingly. I had a flash-forward premonition of us making the jump but losing the underside of the car in the process. As the wheels held the body of the car only about three-quarters of a foot off the ground it wouldn't take much for us to become stuck, lodged over a hump, with our tyres off the ground, rendering the car immobile. Even less impact could dislodge the engine.

'What do you say, Rain Man? I'm up for it.'

'Yeah, you could make it easily,' Barry concurred.

The convertible was already in a thrashed state just from us tearing round the back roads. I knew enough to know that the New York Italian and the South Londoner probably wouldn't have half a clue when it came to off-road driving. What's more, it wasn't their deposit or insurance record on the line. This called for desperate measures.

'This is the place,' I croaked, louder than expected, the honey and lemon having done some repair work on my throat.

'It speaks,' Provenz said to Barry.

They both raised their eyebrows and shrugged.

I clambered out of the car and walked off into the distance for about hundred yards to a little mound. 'This is it,' I said, pulling up a wooden box. 'This is the spot. This is where we'll have our moment. I know it.'

'Brendon,' Provenz yelled from the car, 'this isn't the fuck'n desert. We're on the outskirts of suburbia.'

A dog barked in the distance.

'You can hear the neighbour's dog barking,' Barry added.

'Nope, this is it,' I insisted. 'Right here on this mound. The Nevada skyline is behind us. Look at those mountains. This is it. I can feel it. I know it.' I didn't say 'This'll do' because in order to achieve there whatever I wanted to achieve they had at least to believe that I believed. And now that I was there I was doing a pretty good job of convincing myself.

'But we've hardly gone anywhere,' Barry protested, standing up in his seat.

'No, this is the mound.' I was already clearing a space and collecting rocks to surround a campfire.

Barry and Provenz walked over to join me. Provenz was fiddling inside the bag of shrooms. 'I think I'll need more to get off,' he explained. He already looked as if they were taking effect as he was staring intently into the bag then at his hands and fingers.

'Eat the stems rather than the caps then,' I said.

'What, aren't the caps the potent bit?' he asked.

'No, that's a myth. The psilocybin is the blue strains you see down the sides. As you can see, there's more in the stems.'

'Tastes gross,' said Barry. You could see the twigs caught in his teeth.

'Here, stuff them in these,' I said, producing some muffins I'd purchased earlier for the purpose.

I reached into my other pocket and found the notepad. On the front page it read:

What are the chances you have ginger?

'We have to leave this here for someone to find,' I said, showing it to Provenz and Barry.

'Totally,' Barry agreed.

'That's hysterical,' said Provenza with a nod.

I put the note under a rock and went back to gathering others into a circle.

'What are you doing?' Barry asked.

'I'm clearing a space for a campfire,' I replied.

'You can't do that,' Provenz announced.

'I fucken can.'

'Yeah, right, like you can light a fire out of nothing,' Barry said sarcastically.

I took this as an insult to my nationality. My accent broadened as I said, 'You fucken what? You'll be gobsmacked, mate. Look how dry this wood is, and you see all these brushes?' I gathered up some loose tumbleweed that was tumbling weedily and loosely everywhere. 'These'll go up like a shot. Better than any firelighter in a shop. You compound them at the base of a square kindling fence. Then, once they're giving off a steady open flame, you stick one of these on' – I turned over a thick dry grey log – 'and that's you set for the night. We need to dry the underside of it though by turning it over and setting it downwind of the fire.'

'What the fuck's he saying?' Provenz murmured to Barry out of the corner of his mouth.

'I know,' Barry murmured back. 'Listen to how Aussie he gets.'

'Yeah. Now he's fuck'n Crocodile Burnsy.'

'There's nothing fucken crocodile about it, you city-dwelling cunts!' I snapped. 'You're the ones that are under the impression you can jump a two-foot-deep ditch with a fucken convertible that's less than a foot off the ground!' Now that my voice had returned I was making full use of it. Deep and guttural. Like Outback Jack.

'A foot off the ground?' Provenz quizzed. 'Are you under the impression the car is levitating? Have your mushrooms kicked in yet?'

'Look at him,' Barry spat, like a Texan into a spittoon. 'He *is* a mushroom. He's probably got them growing in him.'

We all laughed.

'No, fuckheads,' I replied, 'you can't make a jump because the base of the car is so low. It'll bounce and probably knacker it completely.'

'Whatever, you can't light a fire,' said Provenz.

'I fucken can. You're insulting my heritage.'

'No, dude. Nevada state law. No open flames.'

'What?'

'Because of the bushfires.'

'What, so it's illegal to act like a fucken man?'

'Yeah.'

'Land of the free my hole.'

'Tell me about it.'

I started to giggle. It may have been the mushrooms, but for some reason I found this hysterical. 'Wait a second. So hahahahahaha ever since man stood up, our very first hahahahaha, our very first invention and that's hahahahaha illegal?'

'Yup.'

'Is it illegal to stand upright?'

'I know.'

'I'm starting a fire.'

Provenz wiggled his red sheriff's hat again. 'Not on my watch.'

Barry and I burst into fits of laughter.

'Fuck, man, give me some more of those shrooms. You guys are way ahead of me.'

Provenz dipped into the bag I produced.

'You had the same amount as me,' I tittered.

'Yeah, but I'm bigger than you.'

'Whoa, check out the big man. So old and mature.'

'No, retard. I'm literally of more mass. It'll take more.'

Provenz chomped down on some more shrooms.

'We should take a photo,' Barry piped up after staring at his hand for a bit.

'Yes, Barry, yesyesyes.'

'A'right,' Provenz murmured with a shrug.

We sauntered over to the car, popped open the boot and pulled out a six-pack. We opened a bottle each and took long swigs from them. The beers were a little warm but it seemed to add to their flavour.

Barry suddenly felt the pressure. 'I mean, I don't know if this'll be it. I just meant *a* photo. Not *the* photo. I'll put the camera on remote but I dunno if it—'

'Don't worry mate, now is the time, I can feel it,' I offered coolly.

'I can't guarantee it'll get us all in frame right—'

'It will mate, I know it, I know it.'

'I didn't mean take *the* photo—'

'Barry, this'll be it. I just know it.'

Provenz and I drained the rest of our beers, lit up a cigarette each and clambered over the boot so that we were sitting with our legs in the back seat of the car. Barry was nestling the camera between the driver's wing mirror and the windscreen, trying to get the right angle, while imagining himself in frame (this being only just before back screens became the norm).

'Don't forget to get the skyline in behind us,' I said.

He attempted to stretch his neck to peer through the little viewfinder. He stuck his tongue through the side of his closed mouth as one does in some bizarre attempt to improve perception of depth. His voice was audibly crumbling further as he fired off his machine-gun Barryspeak: 'ImeanIdunnoifthis'llbe-be-be . . . I mean I dunno if-if-if-if this'llbeitmate—'

'It will, my friend, it will,' I reassured.

Provenz just sat there silently, staring at the lens.

'I think that's it,' Barry announced at last. He pressed the button. The light started to flicker red. He climbed over to us quickly, sitting to my left on the back of the convertible, and struck a pose.

As they stared, I suddenly felt, simultaneously, very conscious and unconscious of my surroundings. I turned my face into the setting sun. The sky was now a mix of brilliant oranges, blues, purples and reds. Soft and warm, I suddenly felt as if my face were mirroring those colours.

My friend Ed Byrne once remarked of me that I would go to any lengths to create the impression that I hadn't gone to any lengths to create an impression. That's the best way I could describe my demeanour. I was so very aware that the other boys were looking directly at the camera that I turned to look a different way and in doing so became genuinely distracted by the colours of the sky. It was the most beautiful sunset I have ever seen and I smiled a big white grin. My skin was sandy, brown and dry. The dust and angle of the sun made my hair a lighter brown than normal.

None of us chose to put our arms around each other or pull any kind of matey gesture. We just sat there, each of us an entirely separate and different character.

Just sharing a moment.

Click.

Flash.

Whirr.

. . .

'That was it,' I said, breaking the silence softly and calmly.

'I dunno if we were all evenly in frame or—' Barry began to stammer again.

I stood up and patted him on the shoulder. 'Barry. That was it. That was my photo. Thank you.'

'Thank you, Barry,' Provenz said in a similar soft tone.

For the first time on our trip Barry actually looked proud of himself. But he still couldn't refrain from humbly back-tracking. 'I mean. You're welcome. I mean I dunno if it got the skyline right or it's even and we all fit in—'

'Barry. We were all in frame. I know it. That was my photo.'

I hugged him, pulled another six-pack out of the boot and walked back to sit on the mound. They soon joined me on it. As he stood over me, Provenz suddenly reached down and patted at something next to me.

I shot bolt upright. 'What? What was it? What the fuck?' I

looked around for a snake, scorpion or some other deadly animal.

'Hey man, I'm just looking for the lighter.' He held it up.

'Well fuck, man, just ask me for it. If you snatch at an Aussie in the desert like that he'll think there's something poisonous near by.'

'OK. Is there always something poisonous near by?'

'No. Not really. But we like to remind people of just how many things can kill you in Australia. It makes us feel rugged.'

'Is that why you like to pretend you're in the desert when you're not?' Barry tittered.

I ignored him and carried on. 'That's why all Oz ex-pats like to freak out anyone proposing to go there.'

I put on an extra-extra Aussie accent, mocking my native land.

'Awwwww you'll love it there, just look out for trapdoor spiders under toilet seats. One of them bites you and your kids'll explode!'

The boys were laughing so I fired off a few more.

'OK, but beware of the great white sharks. You do know they've learned how to drive now?'

Then, 'If a blue ring octopus so much as looks at you, it travels back in time and erases you from existence. Apparently you get a raging hard-on though.'

'I've heard that, is it true?' Barry enquired.

'Nah, that's the one little factoid that always seems to filter through and rear its head in any bullshit Australian death-trap tale. It speaks volumes about us that we feel that that some-how softens the blow.'

I adopted the uber-ocker voice again.

'You've been bitten by a redback spider. You've got twenty

minutes to live. You've got a raging stonk on. What're ya gonna do?'

I pointed at them like Uncle Sam in need.

They pissed themselves again. Provenza's shrooms had kicked in now.

'So how do you survive it as a kid?' he asked.

'It's the same thing the Irish say when you ask 'em about the Troubles.'

They leant in.

'Well, what you do is, don't be a fuckwit.'

'HA! HAAAAAA!' Provenz cackled. 'You oughta put that on your flag!'

'Oh, that reminds me.' I ran off to the car.

'What're you doing?' Barry asked.

'I meant to play you guys something as the sun set,' I shouted over my shoulder.

'What?' Provenz ventured.

'As part of our soundtrack,' I professed, as if it were obvious.

I rummaged under the front seat until I found the stack of CDs I'd purchased back at the store. I soon had The Church compilation out of its packaging and in the player. I made my way back to the mound where the boys were sitting serenely staring off into the distance, the opening acoustic guitar chords of 'Under the Milky Way Tonight' accompanying me all the way. Power lines skirted our view all the way to the horizon, the setting sun behind, making them the blackest of jet-blacks. As if they had been painted into the scenery with the thickest of oil paints. The full spectrum before us began to swirl and the earth beneath appeared to be breathing. I could see the transfer of gases from the shrubs on the ground as they expanded and contracted.

I sat with the two of them and not a word passed between us as we stared straight into the horizon, just below the sun. Taking in every word. The lines 'Wish I knew what you were looking for / Might've known what you would find' rang particularly true for us.

(If possible, please find the song and play it here for mood.)

As the chorus of bagpipes kicked in I was pleased to see their surprise at their rather fitting appearance. Bagpipes don't normally fit in anywhere. Not even in Scotland. That's just for tourists. Try it in a pub some time. You may as well claim you're part 'Scotch'.

The song ended, and again we sat in complete silence. Until I broke it. My voice, now bizarrely fully healed, had returned to its usual timbre. 'That was my movie, fellas. I hope you enjoyed it. I'm glad we could be here. We write our lives, gentlemen. We write our lives.' I felt happy and content that I'd made it to this point.

'Yeah. It's like ... it's like ... when ... it's like ...' Barry stammered.

Provenz cut him off: 'Note to self: when being profound, think again.'

We cracked up at this. At the time I thought he was making fun of Barry. We all rolled around in the dust in proper gut-busting hysterics. So much so we created a cloud around us like a car had just skidded.

When it settled I turned to Barry. 'Barry, I think there's just time for one more song before the sun sets. I want you to pick it.'

'No, wait, no, I couldn't. The photo was one thing but ... I can't mate. There's too much riding on it. You've invested so much in it.'

The guy wasn't just on shrooms, he was really beaten. It

was like he couldn't trust himself with anything. To him, everything seemed to turn to shit in his hands. I didn't see it that way. All we were asking of him was to pick a song but he didn't even have the faith in himself to do that.

'Dude, you totally can do it,' Provenz assured him, sensing this too.

'Fellas, I can't. It's your movie, Brendon.'

'Mate. *I know* that the picture you took is perfect. Like I just *know* that you're going to pick the perfect song to see the sun down.'

'All right,' he said. 'I'll try.'

He wandered off to the car with steely intent. Mushrooms can lend unwarranted importance to the mundane. Provenz and I nodded at each other, feeling the weight of this moment and acknowledging our faith in our friend. We hoped he could do it, yet his doubts had prompted some of our own.

We turned our gaze to the horizon once again, sipping and smoking.

Our mellow drift was abruptly broken by Barry honking the horn again and again, angrily yelling 'FUCK! FUCK! FUCK!' each time the horn beeped. He was beating his head against the steering wheel. We figured the pressure had got to him. Perhaps his broken heart had finally caught up with him and here he was, finally willing to show some real emotion. Or perhaps his fury at his dad had got the better of him, or, worse, his fury at Provenz.

Provenz and I called out to him in unison, 'What? Are you OK?'

The horn beeped and Barry screamed 'FUCK!' again. The sight of him doing so in a car parked in the middle of nowhere was quite funny.

'What?' we reiterated, concern in our voices.

213

'Some cunt's cut me up!' he yelled.

Provenz and I dissolved into hysterics. We laughed un-controllably until it hurt as Barry shook his fist at the imaginary traffic. We simmered down to a barely manageable wheeze in time to see Barry slip a CD into the player. We listened with intense anticipation . . .

'*Just a perfect day* . . .'

We screamed our appreciation and hailed Barry as a god. It was the perfect song, and we let him know it. 'You're the king, Barry! The king!' Provenz raised his beer. Again we sat and listened intently to every lyric while Barry trudged back from the car. Lou Reed's morphine-like marshmallow zithering seemed to drift in and out of the clouds and sky above.

'Perfect, Barry, perfect,' I murmured. 'Thank you again, my friend.'

It was a perfect day, however imperfect the preceding events. Again Barry seemed to have a reinvigorated sense of self. He had given us the most poignant magical gift and he knew it. It was the greatest blend of song, scenery and friend-ship I have ever known. Again, as Provenz had said, a moment shared.

Then, as Barry trudged through his own slips in the dust up the mound, he spat with the utmost conviction and vehemence, 'I'm fucking *gutted* I don't have the Mitch Benn version.'*

Provenza and I laughed loud and hard through the rest of

---

* This will make absolutely no sense if you don't know who Mitch Benn is, I know. He's a comic who used to close his set with a version of 'Perfect Day', doing an impression of all the artists who collaborated on the 1997 charity rendition of the Lou Reed hit. At the time it was the funniest thing Provenza and I had ever heard. However, it would soon shift to number two.

the song. Barry, best pleased with himself, joined in too, rolling around in the dust clutching his sides in agony. All through this, Lou Reed sang of reaping what we sow over and over.

Then, finally, he whispered, *'Just, a perfect day.'*

Eventually Barry managed to squeeze out, 'I think that might have been the funniest thing I've ever said.'

'Pwahhhhhhhh! HAAAAA-HAAAAAAAAA-HAAAAAAA-AAAAA!' We all lost it again. And again and again and again.

When eventually we managed to batter ourselves into a bearable titter, I said, 'I think that's the funniest thing I've ever heard anyone say.'

'Could be, could be,' said a nodding Provenz in a little girl's voice, sighing and wiping away a tear.

Setting us all off yet again.

We bantered until the sun went down. Totally in sync, no ego among us. No trying to top or trump one another, just our very different styles of humour complementing one another perfectly, like jazz musicians improvising, listening intently while diving in and out of segue after segue. Rolling from one subject to the next. I'd never laughed so freely and easily, nor have I since. We shared stories from our youth and on the road. Each of us affording the others space to create the scenes necessary.

Eventually the air started to cool noticeably.

'So how'd you nearly get tricked into having sex with a man?' asked Provenz.

'Oh yeah, pray tell,' said Barry. 'We let you off the hook a little easy with that.'

'All right. I was in Cape Town—'

The chill of the night air suddenly hit me and interrupted my train of thought.

'I'm going to light a fire,' I announced.

'Not on my watch,' Provenz reiterated. 'The police will come.'

I considered this for a bit, then suggested, 'That would add to the trip and the story, wouldn't it? Could you imagine my defence? "Aw c'mon!" That'd be it. "Aw c'mooooon!"' I found this particularly funny. 'Aw c'mooooon, your honour. What? Whaaaaat?' I said over and over, much to my own amusement. I've always found single words or noises way funnier than well-worded jokes. Which is probably why I've died on my arse so much. Here, I was on mushrooms and taken with a rather particular way of saying 'What?' and 'C'mon'. The kind of 'Whaaaaat?' and 'C'mooooon' an indignant drunk might produce as a precursor to:

Can't a guy get a little loaded on a Tuesday morning?

Or,

It's six p.m. in China.

Or,

Oh, like you could tell that was a guy?

Or,

How come it's OK when they say it then?

Or,

How is this offensive? It's a fancy dress party for things beginning with "c" isn't it?

Vividly imagining myself in court, I cried out 'Whaaaaat?' and 'C'mooooon' in an exasperated fashion over and over.

Provenz snapped me out of my trance. 'As much as I appreciate your pursuit of a good story, I guarantee our night won't be what it could be if we get arrested. Las Vegas jail is the last place we want to be.'

It was hard to tell if I was joking or not. Even to me.

Mocking or not, I was still sceptical. 'Why would the police come all the way out here?'

'This is the US, man. Brave New World, baby. Brave New World.'

'Bullshit. We're in the middle of nowhere.'

With phenomenally freakish timing, I swear, right then, in that instant, there was a loud chopping noise in the distance.

'What are those lights in the sky?' Barry chipped in.

All three of us gawped at the speeding row of lights, agog and agape.

'I think they're heading straight for us,' I said.

28

Close Encounters

'WHAT THE FUCK *is* that?' Provenz asked as we huddled together.

The chopping and whooping got ever louder and closer. There were three lights attached in a blur. It was still far off but it was coming for us at an alarming speed.

'Quick, climb on top of each other!' I said as I scampered on to Provenza's back.

'Why?' Barry asked as I piggybacked Provenz.

'We can pretend we're a totem pole. It works. I saw it in a cartoon.'

They both cracked up, despite the seriousness of our situation.

Barry was the first to regain his composure. 'Guys, seriously, that thing is coming for us.'

'Man, you can't tell,' Provenz offered cynically.

'Mate,' I said, gripping Provenz on the shoulder, 'as doubtful as you want to be of me about tonight, you cannot deny that that police helicopter slash UFO slash whatever-the-fuck-that-big-flying-thing-coming-towards-us-is is very definitely flying towards us. What's more, it's making a beeline for us at the exact moment you said it would.'

'I didn't say it would, I just said the cops would come for us if we lit a fire.'

'Yeah, and then he said they wouldn't,' Barry offered.

'Well some fuck'n guru he is then,' Provenz said, pointing to the massive black chopping whirring thing looming towards us.

'So you admit it's coming for us,' I yelled over the deafening sounds of the blades.

This was more than a regular chopper. It was more like a Black Hawk as it circled around our little trio then spun in mid-air to face us. We stared dumbstruck into the lights. No blinding white spotlight came forth as one would expect from a police helicopter. Just a steady, hypnotic, monotonous beat pulsed out of it. It wasn't anything like the normal deafening chopping from a (erm) chopper either. More like sonar popping that could be felt more than heard. The sound pulsed at such a slow pace with regular long intervals that we no longer even had to yell over the top of it. It was as if our voices meandered between the waves of sound.

'Mate, I don't know if it's the mushrooms or not, but that doesn't look like a regular police helicopter,' I stammered.

'No, I gotta give you that, it doesn't,' Provenz admitted.

'That looks a lot like a UFO,' said Barry, tilting his head like a confused dog.

I instantly remembered something Kevin Booth had written in his biography of his best friend Bill Hicks. The pair of them were taking mushrooms in the desert and shared the exact same simultaneous hallucination. They were taken aboard a spaceship and afforded what they described as pure truths.

'Strap in boys, I've read about this trip before,' I said as I patted them both on the shoulder either side of me.

Cut to:

Montage.

Ext. The desert – night. The boys are lifted up in the air and onboard the UFO.

Int. UFO – night: everything around them is bright white light. They stare at one another, confused.

Something appears before them. We can't see it. But they are obviously moved.

Close up – each of their faces sheds a single tear.

Int. UFO – night: Provenza is clearly being gestured to by the shadows of the alien forms. The others look on as he steps forward.

Provenza is levitated in the air and his body stiffens, as his eyes light up and his head is seemingly pumped with white light. We can only presume he is being filled with visions and information. Provenza is set back down. His eyes are white lightfor some time. They return to their normal brown. He is shivering as he stares at Barry and Brendon. All three are alert but not afraid.

The boys are facing the alien forms. They wave them farewell.

PROVENZA

What, no anal probe?

Scene.

'So anyway, I was in Cape Town—'

'You what?' Provenz spat.

'Before we started all the talk about starting a fire I was telling you about the time I might have got sucked off by a guy.'

The police helicopter/UFO was speeding off into the distance now.

'You fuck'n self-absorbed asshole. Did you not just see what happened? We were just lifted up and shown what can only be described as a complete and utter mindfuck. I can't even begin to explain what I've just seen, and you're going with fuck'n Cape Town? Does no one else think it's strange that we were just lifted on to a UFO?' Provenz was staggered now.

'Oh, did you have the UFO thing?' I said. 'I've read about it before. Plenty of people have reported that exact same trip. Experiencing contact with aliens is commonplace. The UFO trip is widely reported in particular. That's why people view them as an experiment in the unconscious mind and that they lend themselves to some sort of psychic ability, transcending space and time.'

'You fuck'n asshole. You think cartoon trees are talking to you yet you can't share in this?' Provenz was genuinely livid as opposed to expressing mock outrage – a rarity.

'The police must have taken one look at us and thought, "Fucking shit party",' Barry giggled.

I looked at the three of us standing in the middle of nowhere wearing cowboy hats and holding a solitary bottle of beer each and joined in with his giggle fit.

'Are you two fuck'n kidding me?' Provenz spluttered again.

'Look, it was just mushrooms, I've heard about it before,' I repeated.

'OK, but that was not a regular police helicopter,' said

221

Barry. 'That was definitely something else. It was heavy. It really spun me out.'

'No, you're right,' I agreed. 'It was possibly special ops. Think about it. We're out in the middle of nowhere.'

'No we're not,' Barry responded. 'I can still hear the neighbour's dog barking.'

'OK, fair enough. But we are on the outskirts of Vegas and have been for several hours with nothing but a convertible with an open boot.' Then it all clicked for me. 'Holy fuck, no wonder it was such a heavy-duty chopper! They must have figured we were burying a body!'

'Murrrrharrrrrywaharrrrhurr! And *then* they must have actually thought, "Fucking shit party"!'

'Holy fuck, how did they know we were here? It must've been via satellite or something. Jesus.' I turned to Provenz. 'I thought you were joking about it being so bad here. But that is brutal. That really is a police state.'

Provenz nodded. 'Brave New World, baby.' He was coming down a bit now. 'Look, I get it about the hallucination and all. I just think it's trippy. Don't you?'

'What did the alien say?' Barry asked.

'It wasn't so much a sound as pictures and feelings. It was fuck'n incredible. There was a stream of yellow across my eyeline yet somehow behind my eyeline. And it was a strip of data. We are all taking in billions of data per second every day. Yet we only take in what's significant to us. Thereby co-incidences are happening constantly and they are only such because we notice them. This is basic chaotic theory. We know this, but at once I was opened up to the amount of data our minds are fully capable of absorbing. It wasn't the input that had been changed but rather the system and hardwire of my mind. Normally I wouldn't be able to contain it all. If it were happening on a regular basis I'd go fuck'n mad. But for a nanosecond I was afforded enough hardware space in my conscious mind for a glimpse. It was fuck'n incredible. Man, I gotta do mushrooms more often.'

I waited a while, then offered, 'Sounds great . . . So, I was in Cape Town . . .'

I paused, and Provenz looked at me to see if I was joking or not. When he saw my wry smile we all burst into fits of laughter again.

'Yeah so anyway, I was lifted up on to a spaceship and one of the keys to my conscious mind was opened up by aliens for me – follow that!' I said at my own expense.

'HA! HAAAA! HAAAAAAA!' howled Provenz. 'Follow that!'

'Murhurhurrrrr-hur-hurhuruurrrr! So anyway, I just signed the Declaration of Independence. Follow that!' Barry pissed himself laughing.

We all took it in turns to offer variants, some highlights being:

And that's when they decided to rub all the other faces out and make Mount Rushmore just my head over and over. Follow that!

So anyway, now I'm in the Beatles everyone reckons they sound better even without the dead ones. Follow that!

So I invented AIDS just for a laugh. I've just told the crowd at the Terrence Higgins Trust gig, said your name and run off. Follow that!

So I'm half goat. Follow that!

When we'd exhausted every option and the laughter had died down to an audible calming sigh, I broke the silence, without a hint of irony, by saying, 'So I was in Cape Town . . .'

29
Weird Science

'OK,' SAID PROVENZ, 'fuck where you were. I think the key information is South African ladyboy hookers.'

'So what exactly happened?' asked Barry.

'Well, as far as I knew it was a girl. We'd been drinking at the bar with them and then the other guy declined to take one of them home. And to be honest I wasn't even that horny but, well, you know . . . When someone offers to blow you for the equivalent of five quid . . .'

'You consider the source and reasons for that?' Barry questioned.

'Yeah yeah. I know I wasn't thinking straight. Anyway, we go back to my hotel and I obviously wasn't going to go in but oddly enough a price for that was never offered.'

'What, no white board and price chart?' quipped Barry.

Provenz, for once, was too gleeful even to comment. Just taking in the tale like a wide-eyed child being told what Santa's bringing for Christmas.

'I turned the light on afterwards, which she was rather adamant about keeping off during said fellatio, I might add. I looked at the silhouette between her thighs and found myself pondering, "That's a particularly big clitoris . . ."'

'Nooooo!' yelped Barry.

'It looked like a miniature version of Gonzo's nose.'

'HA! HAAAAA!'

'I said, "I need to ask a crucial question here: are you spelling Toni with a Y or an I?"'

'No!' Barry had his hands over his eyes and mouth. 'What did she say?'

'She got upset and left.'

'You managed to offend a post-op transsexual hooker in Cape Town?' said Provenz. 'Oh that's too much. You are the fuck'n king, Burnsy.'

'By the way, Provenz,' I said, exasperated, 'what the fuck were you thinking buying Barry's dad a hooker? Not Barry, Barry's dad?'

'Brendon, please, I don't need you to do this for me.' Barry held up his palms in a calming gesture and turned to Provenz. 'By the way, what the fuck were you thinking buying my dad a hooker? Not me, my dad?'

Provenz considered his previous defence before offering the final conciliatory truth: 'Y'know what? It was the funniest thing I could think of.'

We both burst out loud laughing.

'See, it worked,' he said as we continued pissing ourselves.

'There is a line to be drawn, mate,' Barry said.

'Yeah, but that line is sneaky,' Provenz countered, tilting his hat as his menthol wiggled again.

'What a thoroughly bizarre man you are, Provenza,' I said. 'I'm never going to tell you anything bad that happens to me, ever.'

Barry and I took it in turns to offer different hypothetical scenarios:

What's that? Your mum's just died? Is your dad still alive?

What's that? You've lost your cat? Lemme buy your dad a hooker.

What did you say? Your car's broken down? I've got just the thing!

I waved my finger about on 'just the thing' and we took this as a catchphrase as Provenz joined in with the hypotheticals:

What's that? Your dad's got testicular cancer? I've got just the thing!

So you just won a car? I've got just the thing!

Huh? Your dad likes hookers? I've got just the thing!

Once we'd recovered from laughing, Barry carried on. Through tears he spluttered, 'Y'know what? When Brendon convinced me to come out here I did think to myself, "Y'know, I'm just not going to be able to get closure over Chris until Provenz buys my dad a hooker"!'

'HA! HAAAA! HAAAAAAAAA!'

You had to give it to him. This was the first time Barry had even acknowledged Chris since we arrived in LA, let alone laughed about her leaving. Here he was going after everything, and it was beautiful to see.

'Look, all right, fine,' he concluded. 'He fucked a hooker. So what? At his age someone offers him a hooker of course he's going to take it. Jesus, he's got a bung arm and he looks like a cleaning woman. Y'know, at my lowest of lows last night I was so drunk and methed up I even considered ringing the Pink Flamingo myself.'

Provenz let out a solitary 'HA!' again.

'What's the Pink Flamingo?' I asked, even though I could guess.

'It's the only legal brothel in Vegas, just on the state line,' Provenz answered.

'No way! I thought it was *all* legal here.'

'Nope. Everyone just turns a blind eye. The Flamingo is the only place where it is legal.'

'So what happened?' I asked Barry.

'Well, I was obviously feeling pretty pathetic and desperate so I checked my bank balance and worked out the very most I could overdraw by.'

'What was that then?' asked Provenz.

'Eighty bucks,' Barry replied. 'So, pathetically, I very nearly rang them asking what I could get for eighty bucks.'

'Oi, Bizarro!' I chipped in, pretending to be the Madam holding her hand over the receiver.

'Bizarro!' they hailed in unison.

'Oi, Bizarro,' I carried on, 'roll over and take your tampon out, you've got a customer!'

Naturally, after that the hypothetical Bizarro lines came thick and fast:

Oi, Bizarro! Wash your gills and clean the mould out of your flippers, you've got a customer!

Oi, Bizarro! Stop secreting stomach fluids and digesting food outside your face, you've got a customer!

Oi, Bizarro! Strap your arms back on, you've got a customer!

Oi, Bizarro! Pick the teeth out of your shit, you've got a customer!

Provenz then mimed answering the phone as Bizarro, giving her a black crack whore's voice: 'Hello, this be Bizarro.'

Barry slipped straight into the scenario as himself. 'Hello, Bizarro, what might I get for eighty bucks?'

'Ooooh Lordy, eighty dollahs you say? My my my, that gonna buy me one whole lot of flipper polish.'

Barry and I stifled laughs. I play-bumped him in the background. 'Shhh, she'll hear you. Ask her if she'll come to you.'

'Can you come to me?' Barry asked.

'I'm evah so sorry . . . what yo name again?'

'Barry.'

'I'm evah so sorry, Barry. I will not be able to come down there to you as I cannot leave my tank fo too long.'

'Well then, if I come to you, what will I get for eighty bucks?'

'You get all o' me, Barry. Every scale, nook and gill cranny.'

'Well, what do I get for fifty dollars?'

'You get to drink my tank water, you cheap eighty-dollah-havin' muthafucka.'

'OK. Sorry, Bizarro.'

'Oh please. You may call me Ms Bizarro.'

For some reason 'Ms Bizarro' was funnier to us than 'Bizarro' and we lost our shit again. Perhaps it was her failed attempt at formality. Provenz carried on with Ms Bizarro impressions for a good half-hour. I could never do it all justice but it was a comic masterpiece.

This was the greatest thing about our trip. The three of us placed one another in scenario after scenario, constantly setting each other up and passing on the baton. In hindsight we all agreed it was the greatest form we'd ever been on. Just topper after topper, not trying to outdo one another but throwing one another lob after lob, letting one another knock it out of the park. A comedian's ego would ordinarily dictate jealousy and resentment that Provenza had 'taken' Bizarro from me. But watching and listening to what he did with it provided me with so much mirth and merriment all I could do was be glad to witness it.

I certainly would never have made her black. British sensibilities don't allow for such licence, and even though I'm Aussie, London hasn't not had its effect on me. New York comedians tend to deal with race more than English ones, I guess because different cultures and races are way more represented in comedy clubs there. If everyone's there and there's a shared agreement that all is fair game, I guess all is fair game.*

* In Britain comedy is still predominantly a white middle-class art form. Rightfully, no one wants to hark back to the hateful Bernard Manning years. The working men's clubs horrible 'Paki' and 'Darkie' jokes led to a counter-culture clash where everyone stopped mentioning that races and cultures even existed. It had to happen to mend the wounds. But both manufactured environments are based on fear and presumption. Different bubbles, but a bubble nonetheless. It's a self-perpetuating situation as no one mentions other cultures for fear of being misinterpreted as hateful, and in turn said cultures stay away in droves because comedy stops being relevant to them. But in Britain all things begin in London, and like any cosmopolitan city it'll catch up with New York eventually.

Yes, I know the English are under the delusion that they invented modern stand-up, but they didn't. You're twenty years behind. Ahem. Yes you are. In terms of diversity and invention, you are. Yes you are. Stop it. Put that down. Do your research. It's a fact. Show me an ethnic minority comic in Britain who is anywhere near the calibre of Cosby in the sixties or Pryor in the seventies. Or able to go after *polite* society the way Flip Wilson did in the sixties. Never heard of him? I rest my case. (The man won two Emmys and a Golden Globe.) In fact that puts us about *fifty* years behind (and I say that as a British comic first and an Australian second). White Britain does not want to discuss race. Beyond: racism is bad, or racism doesn't exist. Anything in between will be wilfully misrepresented as an example of one of the former trite arguments.

Flip Wilson's opening line when I saw him at age nine, directed at his white band leader, was, 'Does your daddy know you work for a nigger? It'd kill him.' I have no doubt in my mind that the British press would eat him alive if he said that today. Flat out *refusing* to comprehend that the butt of the joke was received racism.

My experience of the rest of non-white Britain has been that they'd like a look-in, please. I *cannot wait* for a British ethnic comic who says, 'Fuck you, whitey. Get off your high horse.' I fucken hate whitey. And if you think I'm being racist, I mean you.

It used to *infuriate* me when New York and LA comics made this argument to me, but watching the way things have transpired it's hard to argue with. Not that it's all a bed of roses over there. If I was to totally buy into the American argument then apparently all we'd need is an influx of Mexicans to put the boot into.

Provenza even gave Bizarro a back-story. What it was like for her at school, being the only black half-fish girl at an all-Latino college. He traced her professional career, which included a short-lived stint in stand-up comedy. Apparently, being a stand-up chimera just gave 'dem damn hecklers too much to work with. Somebody yell "Show us yo titties!", that be one thing. But "Show us yo fins!"? Dere's nowhere to go. Dere's nowhere to go.' And she stared off into the middle distance. Provenz made it genuinely poignant. We could actually empathize with the poor little black mermaid starting out on her own. Fuck being in *The West Wing* and the lead in *Northern Exposure*, this was Paul Provenza's finest acting hour. Here was a six-foot-four New York Italian making two stoned comics care about some African-American fishy minotaur prostitute in the dark on the outskirts of Vegas just after being lifted up on to a spaceship . . . maybe. The mushrooms may have been a factor there.

Bizarro briefly returned her attention to Barry and the phone. 'You know, I met a man. I swear he could be yo daddy. Why don't you come down here to the Castagnola lounge and we can talk face to face?'

Suddenly Provenz celebrated his Bizarro impression by dancing like an old Wild West prospecting drunkard who had just struck gold. Holding his hat, jumping from leg to leg, jiggling them back and forth. Somewhere between Yosemite Sam and one of those mobile skeletons where one pulls the strings and the legs and arms flail upwards simultaneously. To add to this manic jumping-jack look he was working on, he started waggling his tongue about and grinning broadly, clearly enjoying all the dust he was kicking up. It was quite a sight. He was really going for it.

Unaware of Provenza's jig, Barry suddenly got defensive.

'Look, my dad might be a hooker fucker, but he did sort out the crystal meth for us.'

Provenz stopped, rejoined us briefly, let out a single 'HA!' then returned to his one-man sans-bronco, sans-bull rodeo. I gave him a double-take, then returned my attention to Barry.

'My dad might be a hooker fucker but at least he sorted the crystal meth?' I said incredulously. 'Holy fuck, Barry, that is the funniest, least self-aware sentence I've ever heard in my life. Say it back to yourself again.' I repeated it at him, my voice a pitch higher: 'My dad might be a hooker fucker but at least he sorted the crystal meth? Ha! Top sentence.'

'HA! Top sentence!' Provenz chimed in, conveying that he thought 'Top sentence' was a bit of a top sentence. Even though all three of us had used it on numerous occasions already.

Somehow, he and Barry were managing not to notice each other at all throughout this exchange; I seemed to be acting as some sort of medium. I ignored Provenz and continued. 'Holy fucken shit, Barry, the word "dad" should never even appear in the same sentence as any of those words.'

'Wait a minute, it's not like he's a meth head or a fucking dealer or something, you twat,' Barry countered. '*You* asked for it, Brendon. You're a dad and you happily asked him to too. We all wound up at that fucking meth farm. *You* asked him if he could maybe score some coke because we were going to Vegas. How many guys do you know who can ask their dad that? To be honest he wasn't that comfortable doing it but he went ahead and did it anyway because he loves us guys. His son just split up with his bird and we were going to Vegas. Vegas! Whoooooo! Remember, Brendon, you fucking idiot? And besides, *you* did the crystal meth. You can't talk.'

231

Barry had been pretty patient with me thus far, never really reacting beyond apprehensive. I was taken aback.

'Look, dude, dads aren't supposed to do crystal meth and fuck hookers,' I said.

'Again, you're a dad, Brendon, you did meth, and you just told us about getting sucked off by a guy hooker,' said Barry with his hands on his hips.

'I'm not comparing him against me, I don't count. I'm comparing him against *my* dad.'

'Interesting,' said Provenz. 'Can we bring your dad next time? I've got just the thing for him.' He waggled a finger to the moves he was busting.

'Stop it, Provenz,' I said over Barry's shoulders and folded arms. I redirected to Barry. 'Look, I'm not actually judging. I just think "My dad might be a hooker fucker but at least he sorted the crystal meth" is a reeeeallllly funny sentence.'

'Top sentence,' Provenz murmured in the background. Again seeming only to respond to my half of the conversation. As if anyone not aware of his happy feet wasn't worth acknowledging.

Barry, equally unaware, was staring off towards the car worriedly. 'Yeah, all right, fair enough,' he said, the all-encompassing comedian's 'funny' argument having sunk in. 'Maybe your boy will get to say the same about you one day, Brendon. Then perhaps this spiritual wank you're having will finally have come full circle.' He focused his attention on the sky. It was difficult to tell how long we'd been out there. 'We really oughta work out who's going to drive back. I've had about four beers and several stems,' Barry added over his shoulder.

Looking back and forth between the pair of them I wondered how Barry was managing not to see the blatant ruckus only metres behind him. Provenz had obviously kicked into a brand-new high and was away with the fairies. Bigger than me or not, he'd been consistently knocking back shrooms all evening.

'I can't,' I replied. 'I'm not insured and I can't drive on the right side of the road.'

'Provenz, you've only had a few beers.' Barry still had his back to him. 'Maybe you should drive.'

'Look at me!' Provenz exclaimed, clearly forced to respond by being addressed directly.

Barry turned to look at him for the first time and only then realized that Provenz must have been carrying on his crazy, inexplicable, unaccompanied dancing throughout the entire conversation.

'And you're making a case for me driving?' said Provenz. His tongue flapped about as he spoke and danced.

Barry couldn't help but laugh at the sight. 'I, er, I dunno. I'm pretty fucked up. Maybe I shouldn't . . .'

As suddenly as he'd started, Provenz stopped dancing and walked normally towards us. 'OK, sorry fellas, I was gone for a while there. I'm back now. Gimme the keys, I'll drive.' He said the latter in a generation-specific impression of Michael C. Hall in *Weird Science* and clapped his hands when he received the keys.

'You sure you can drive?' we both asked.

'Totally.'

He slipped on his sunglasses in the pitch black.

'Are you sure?'

'Totally.'

He clambered behind the wheel of the car, started the engine and drove off without us.

'Provenza!' we yelled after him, to no avail. Fortunately he was driving so slowly that we could catch up and jump in.

233

Barry leant over the front and I sat on the boot again, dangling my feet into the rear seat.

'Now carry on driving slowly,' I said. 'I need to get our bearings. And turn on your high beams so we can see our way back. I'm looking for landmarks.'

'Landmarks?' Barry started tittering. 'What are you saying? Turn right at the big rock or something?'

'Well, yeah, that's exactly it. We passed a big rock and turned left on the way here. So we turn right at the big rock on the way back.'

For some bizarre reason, Barry found this hysterical. 'What are you, Steve Irwin all of a sudden?'

I had no idea why he found this so amusing. This was one of the few times I was being perfectly sensible. 'What the fuck are you talking about, Barry? There aren't any street signs in the bush, so you navigate via landmarks, like a weirdly shaped tree or a particularly big rock. That's hardly the work of the bush tucker man.'

'Yeah, but we're not in the bush,' Barry persisted.

'Yeah, but there are no street signs either, dickhead. Slow down, Provenz. I need to find that rock.'

Provenz, who had picked up speed, ignored us both and carried on driving at the same pace.

'Provenz, you might wanna take your sunnies off,' Barry said, waving at him.

Provenz didn't flinch.

'Provenz, dude, seriously, we need you to slow down and flick on your high beams so we can see where we're going.'

To our right I saw the big rock I'd made note of on the way in.

'There it is! There's the big rock! Turn right!'

Provenz, still without acknowledging me, turned right sharply, sending me crashing on to the rear seat.

'See? Fuck you, Barry. OK now Provenz, we carry on this way for a few hundred yards then it's left then right then left again, then we're back on the main road.'

Provenz took all these directions without saying a word. Once we'd made it back on to the main road we took another right on to the main drag back into Vegas.

'Fuck, I'm driving!' Provenz blurted out as the rush of oncoming headlights slapped him awake.

'What?' Barry replied.

'Fuck! Sorry. I went away again. Wasn't I just dancing? What the fuck am I driving for? Those lights are way too fuck'n bright.'

'Pull over!' we both snapped.

Barry took the wheel and drove extra slowly back into Vegas. I didn't envy him. I'd stopped doing shrooms hours earlier and the lights were spinning me out. He and Provenz had been taking them consistently ever since the police helicopter/UFO incident. The blur of oncoming cars and Vegas neon had more of the appearance of words and sheet music than obstacles to be negotiated. Lord knows what it all looked like to Barry. To top things off, Barry was coming down hard off the meth we'd taken earlier.

'Awwwww man, this isn't good,' he murmured. 'I'm not having a good time of this.'

'What?' I enquired from the back. Provenz was still somewhere on space mountain in the front.

'What? What do you mean "what"? My fucking fiancée dumped me, I'm fucking broke, and the squirrels on the bonnet are fucking with my head.'

I chose to ignore the squirrels lest I ended up having to drive.

I looked at Barry and could actually see the furrows on his brow breaking free and flying about the car. They looked like gulls in the distance, then grew jagged like single shards of lightning to depict his dread as it washed over him intermittently. I wondered what I could do to bring him back to my way of thinking. It felt as if all three of us were vying for his soul. Although when it came to Provenza ... well, I had no idea what was going on there.

To confirm my impression of him, Provenz piped up irrelevantly, 'I gotta wear more yellow,' then went back to staring into space.

30

Elevator Men

MIRACULOUSLY WE MADE it back to the Delta. Equally miraculously, Provenz was suddenly compos mentis and businesslike. 'I gotta go see some people about some projects,' he said. 'Make this trip deductible. You guys wanna see a show or something while you're here?'

'Nah man, I wanna go get laid again,' I replied. 'Actually, fuck that, I wanna go get Barry laid. I won't be able to use my voice much in a club anyway. I think I'm going to have to revert to pad and pen again.'

'Thank Christ for that. Barry, you sure you don't want me to buy you a hooker?'

'No thanks, hate myself enough already thanks,' said Barry with eyebrows raised and a thin sarcastic smile on his face, which was grey. His jowls were showing. The drive and meth comedown had taken their toll. Hallucinations are a lot easier to deal with if you don't have to do anything about them. As one can imagine, 'What a pretty dragon!' and 'Oh fuck! Is that a dragon or a traffic light?' are two entirely different beasts.

I patted him on the back. 'Don't worry mate, we'll go out and get you laid.'

'Great,' said Provenz. 'You guys go get laid, I'll go see my people.'

We'd reached the lift. The doors slid open and there was a woman in front of us with her young boy. Between them they had four massive pieces of luggage. As the doors closed behind us Barry smiled at them. 'StayingtillChristmas?' he joked in his friendliest machine-gun voice.

The woman stared at him blankly, not understanding. The boy started hiccoughing nervously and pronouncedly. All they saw were three drunken cowboys getting into a lift, one of whom appeared to be blathering in French or something.

'Gotalotofbags,' Barry persisted, pointing at the luggage, nodding and smiling. 'StayingtillChristmas?'

The woman huddled her son into her and nudged her bags away from us slightly with her foot.

'Gotalotofbags,' Barry said, a little louder this time.

They continued to cower away so he figured it best to leave them in peace.

We all stood there awkwardly as the lift made its way to their floor, the only noise the sound of her son hiccoughing intermittently, his bony frame jolting pathetically with every *hic*. His mother started wishing the lift on, yet it stalled like a watched toaster. *Hic . . . hic . . . hic . . .* Again and again, with infuriating inevitability, he broke the silence in which we were anticipating another hiccough, yet as there was no rhythm to the outbursts there was zero predictability in terms of the timing. Provenz and I stifled a laugh, not wishing to add to the awkwardness.

Finally the elevator reached their floor with a *ping*. Barry had one last go: 'Do you want a hand with your bags? You've got a lot of them. It's like you're staying till Christmas.'

The woman now looked panicked. She laboriously

struggled with her four cases and ushered her little boy out of the lift, away from Barry. Once their backs were to him, Barry mockingly mimed a gut punch at them. As the lift doors shut we heard a solitary *hic* from the boy.

We burst into fits of laughter.

'Fuck, how much did that kid's hiccoughs piss you off?' I said.

'StayingtillChristmas . . . that did wonders for my self-esteem,' Barry tittered. 'Fucking hell, never mind going on the pull, I'm so charming I can't even not scare a family in a lift.'

'They did have a lot of bags though,' Provenz remarked.

'Yeah, it's as if they were staying till Christmas or something,' Barry added.

'Fucken hell, how meek was that kid?' I blurted. 'I've never seen one so young with so little hope in his eyes. You ever wanted to slap someone round the chops more? *Bam*! "That'll cure your hiccoughs. Life's gonna get so much worse. Toughen up, hiccough boy!"'

The boys voiced their approval in unison: 'Toughen up, hiccough boy!'

'Top sentence,' I congratulated myself.

'Top sentence!' they reiterated with glee.

'So your dad ain't around and your mum decides to take you to Vegas?'

'*Bam!*'

'Toughen up, hiccough boy!'

'So your dad fucked a hooker and your fiancée left you?'

'*Bam!*'

'Toughen up, hiccough boy!'

We all laughed, until Barry saw himself in the mirror and stopped dead short. When we reached our floor Barry just stood there like dawn of the dead. We led him back to the room. He didn't say a word. Keith was still missing.

Barry stared into the middle distance for a bit. Then, suddenly, he started smashing his head into the wall and punching it with his fists. 'FUCK! I'M SUCH A FUCKING LOSER! FUCK!' he said with each smash. This was not for melodrama, he was dishing out full-on head-butts to the wall. As if he were in a genuine fight with it. At one point he even feigned with a left.

Provenz and I did several double-takes trying to establish that it wasn't just hallucinogens, it was actually happening. Then we lunged at him.

'Dude, what the fuck are you doing?' I said as we yanked him back.

He tried to push past us and nearly succeeded, the combination of his stocky frame and crystal meth hulk-like fury a proper handful for the two of us.

'Get the fuck off me! Lemme at it!' Barry yelled as he clawed at the air.

I was almost tempted to let him go just to see what he would do.

'Barry, it's a wall,' Provenz said. 'What the fuck are you trying to get to?'

We both dropped our shoulders a bit and pushed him on to the bed.

'What the fuck was that?' we said as we stood up, straightening ourselves, short of breath.

'Fuck. I'm such a fucking loser. FUCK! AAAAR-RRRRGGGH!' As he screamed he started punching and slapping his face.

'OK, no more meth for Barry I'd say,' said Provenz.

'What the fuck was I thinking taking meth?' Barry shouted. 'FUCK!'

'All right, calm down Barry,' I said placatingly. 'Jesus. It was me that got it.'

'Yeah, and I bought your dad the hooker,' Provenz added, completely unnecessarily.

I winced. Now was not the time to be bringing that up again.

Barry glowered at him. 'So you admit that was a shitty thing to do?'

'No, not yet, I'm still looking to see how that plays out,' Provenz answered.

I shot daggers at him out of sight. He merely smirked and started rolling a joint.

'C'mon, toughen up, hiccough boy,' said Provenz, trying his arm.

We both glowered at him.

'What? Too soon?' he said.

We cracked up. The comedy in-joke got us both. 'Too soon?' being a play on the old adage 'Tragedy plus time equals comedy' (often attributed to Woody Allen, but it was actually Carol Burnett who first coined the phrase). Comics yelled 'Too soon!' in earnest at fellow comedian Gilbert Gottfried when he broached the subject of 9/11 at the Hugh Hefner roast. Or if a joke about Jesus doesn't go over, a comic might say sarcastically 'What? Too soon?' just to amuse his friends at the back. Comedians don't steal each other's material as a rule (and the ones that do lie about it, thereby confirming the rule), but 'Too soon?' is considered public property and a nod to the comics at the back of the room. Canadian comedian Stewart Francis uses it perfectly regarding the innocuous. After a joke about a chipmunk or something doesn't fly, he might look at the crowd wounded and ask, 'What? Too soon?'

If the tragedy/time adage rang true then we were cracking

the sound barrier. A stretched metaphor, I know, but as a time machine hasn't been invented yet there are very few ways to describe one that is travelling quickly. Provenz had done it again by being inappropriate.

Then Keith entered the room and lightened the mood.

'Hey Keith!' I greeted him. 'Where'd you go?'

'It's a surprise,' he beamed.

'Oh brilliant. Does it involve a homeless guy and a well-oiled pig?' quipped Barry.

Keith smirked. 'Look, watch it you. I will crack skulls!'

'Yeah, lay off the guy, Barry, for fuck's sake,' I said as I rolled up a note.

Barry shot a staggered look at me and slapped his hands to his head again.

'What's his problem?' asked Keith.

'Meth comedown,' Provenz replied.

'Whoa! Was that mixed in with shrooms?' asked Keith.

Barry nodded.

'Oh dear. Have you got violent yet? I looked it up. Apparently it can make you super horny or violent.'

Provenz went to open his mouth.

'Stoppit,' said Barry, like a man being tickled.

'They may as well call it crystal rape,' joked Keith. 'Good call scoring it, though, Bren,' he added sarcastically.

Fearing no sexual frustration given the previous night's exploits, I snorted a fat line. Holding in violent sneezes and tears, I held the note out to Barry.

He declined. 'No thanks, I'm good.'

I tried to offer to Keith but my voice gave out again.

'Hahahahaha!' Keith laughed. 'All meth and no voice! That has to be killing you!'

We all grinned at the genuine irony. I mimed 'fuck you' at

them with pelvic thrusts and finger pointing. I then pretended to blow my own cock and mimed jism exploding all over my face. Then I insinuated that they all fucked goats.

'Is that a goat or a sheep?' asked Barry.

'You couldn't just leave it at "fuck you", could you?' Provenz remarked.

'Extraordinary,' remarked Barry casually as I pulled money from my wallet and rutted a couch, pointing at him and his dad.

'Wow, that's actually pretty cool he's managed to convey that,' said Keith dryly. 'I'm actually impressed. Anyway, you boys don't need me in the way. I'll find my own thing to do tonight.'

'Where are you gonna go?' Barry asked.

'I told you,' his dad replied, 'it's a surprise.'

As Barry and I were on the pull, neither of us rushed to pursue the point.

We left the room and sauntered into the elevator. There was an old Texan man in an old Texan man's hat who saw us in ours and nodded, like the way I've seen black people do when they see each other on the street in Ireland or Australia.

'How're you doin', pardners?' he offered Texanly.

'I was doing OK until I looked in the mirror,' Barry replied.

The big Texan just looked him up and down, gobsmacked. Really not having expected anything beyond a customary 'Fine thanks'. No one ever does. He was especially taken aback because he'd been expecting nothing but a 'howdy' from a couple o' good ol' boys. As opposed to this couple o' limey fags with their doggone life stories and woes. There was certainly not adequate time in a lift journey to offer counsel. He was stumped, and just said nothing, barely able to shake his head in exasperation.

We completed the journey in silence. If the lift episode with hiccough boy had seemed tense, this was positively excruciating. The Texan stared at the numbers as they lit up with Texan gun-slinging intent. Wishing them on with his mind but only seeming to slow them down. You could feel him wanting to bellow at Barry 'What the fuck?' with every *ping* the elevator made at each floor.

Ping!

'What the fuck?'

Ping!

'Seriously, what the fuck?'

Ping!

'What the fuck?'

Instead he just fumed and fretted. When he got out at his floor he took one last look at us and shook his head. As the doors closed I imagined him throwing his hat on the ground, jumping on it and shaking his fist as if he'd just missed the last wagon from town.

As we walked along the mall attached to the hotel complex I scribbled on a piece of paper *Cheer up mate, it's Vegas. Everyone gets laid in Vegas.*

Barry nodded in agreement. 'You're right, mate. I don't even need to get laid really. Just think positive and enjoy myself. I mean, what are we, a bunch of desperate date rapists? Just a chat and some company would be back in the game enough.'

I nodded emphatically as a troupe of valley girls on a birthday bash went by. 'Hey cowboy,' slurred the birthday girl in the cowgirl hat as she broke away from the pack. Making her way towards Barry.

We took one look at each other and shrugged. 'Sure, why not?'

As we turned back to them, one of the girls pushed Barry and drawled 'Ewwww, not you, you're icky' as she commandeered her friend and led her away.

'Brilliant,' Barry said, deadpan, thumbs up.

The girls carried on down the mall, giggling cruelly. We stood there, feeling absolutely mint, as all passers-by had borne witness to the rejection. Barry looked like a kid holding a burst balloon that had just been shat on by a seagull.

'Thanks,' he yelled after them. 'That's, erm, great for the self-esteem. Cheers.'

I got out my notepad and started scribbling abuse furiously as I made after them.

Barry softly put his hand on the pad. 'Leave it, Brendon. S'OK. It's not worth it.'

I looked at him and scribbled something else. He took it and read it.

'Yeah,' he agreed, 'let's lose the hats.'

31
Swingers

'WHAT HAPPENED?' Provenz asked as we re-entered the room.

'We're losing the hats,' replied Barry on his way to the bathroom.

Provenz looked at me quizzically. I wrote on the pad *Some valley girls made fun of him.*

'Who gives a fuck?'

I mimed an arrow flying into my heart, then wrote *We need to get him laid.*

'I've got just the thing . . .' Provenz said, waggling his hooker-buying finger in the air again.

I shook my head furiously and stamped my feet. 'Psssst!' I hissed. *That's your answer for everything,* I wrote.

'OK, OK. What you wanna do?'

Where's a good place to meet girls who aren't hookers?

Barry came out of the toilet. 'What's up?'

On the pad I put *We're going to meet some women. I want you to wear my red jacket.*

He looked up, genuinely touched. I nodded emphatically, got the jacket and put it on him. I pulled it straight. Somehow it managed to fit both our shapes like a glove.

'No mate, I can't take your jacket,' he said, in much the same way he had on the hill when we asked him to choose the last song before sunset.

'I want you to have it,' I rasped, barely audibly. 'I've never not pulled in it. And it looks better on you. I insist.'

'Mate, I can't.'

Pssst! I stamped and pointed at my throat. Signifying that I didn't want to have to use my voice again.

Provenz and I appraised him up and down. Obviously our faces conveyed that we weren't taking the piss and his spirits lifted.

'Look, thanks,' he said, 'but isn't this your favourite jacket?'

It is, I wrote in reply. *Consider it a thank you for helping me get my photo.*

'W-wow. I don't know what to say, mate. Thank you.'

I'm guessing any women reading this won't fully under-stand the significance of handing over a 'pulling' jacket. Trust me when I say it's a big deal between bachelors. Consider handing over to your girlfriend:

1. Your partner's favourite piece of lingerie.
2. Your favourite piece of jewellery (passed on from a deceased loved one).
3. Your actual pussy.

Then you may have some indication of the weight of the moment. Until then, don't try to change us, *babay.*

'S'a nice-looking fuck'n jacket,' Provenz admitted unsarcastically.

Where's a good place for us to pull? I wrote.

'Ah, right. Lemme give you the name of a place.' He snatched my pad and pen.

As he flicked through it, it became apparent that I'd written down more than any of us had imagined. So often had I snatched at the pad desperately to get out what I wanted to say as quickly as possible that there were random scribbles everywhere and from all different angles. Provenz flipped page after page, trying to find a blank space I hadn't scrawled on in some way.

'Fuck!' he said. 'Even without his voice Brendon won't shut the fuck up!'

We easily found our way to where Provenz had suggested we go, and at the top of a casino somewhere in Vegas we started chatting to some girls. I'd made the first move by gesturing to them for an ashtray then miming thank you.

'Can't you talk?' one of the girls asked. She seemed good-natured and genuine.

This was an improvement on a girl we'd been speaking to earlier. After she'd asked me what we were doing in Vegas, I wrote a note that read *My friend and I went out to the desert to take mushrooms and watch the sunset. It was sublime.*

She'd stared back blankly and replied, 'What's sublime?'

Not 'What does sublime mean?' but 'What's sublime?', as if it were a lower-class lemon.

Never mind, I wrote.

She looked me up and down, got up and left like the end of the conversation was her decision.

'Is your friend deaf?' one of the nice genuine girls asked Barry.

'No, he's just lost his voice.'

'Awwwww,' they responded, looking at Barry with tilted heads, 'it's nice that you take care of him.'

'Yeah. He needs it.'

'Are you English? I love your accent,' purred another one of the girls in the group.

I grinned at Barry, rubbed his shoulders and slapped his back. Then I sat back and enjoyed my drink in silence. Listening to Barry work. The girls were enjoying his wit and company. He chatted to them for a good hour, made them laugh, sharing drinks and stories. When he asked one tall blonde girl what she had planned for later, they all revealed they had boyfriends.

Clang! I wrote as they got up to leave.

'Fuckin' what's the point of that?' Barry said. 'Why don't they tell us at the beginning? A whole hour I've been sitting here.'

I snickered.

'I mean, what the fuck? "I've got a boyfriend." Well how about telling me that *before* I buy a whole bunch of drinks and pretend to give a fuck about what you reckon!'

I nodded in agreement.

'I laughed at her bullshit too. Couldn't understand half of it. Fucking bitch.' His tongue was firmly in his cheek.

Bitches, man, bitches.

Barry read the note and smirked at his own clichés. I handed him another: *Let's go back to that club where I pulled last night.*

When we arrived, as it was early on a Friday morning the crowd seemed even more sleazy than the previous night. All the guys and girls danced like they were professionals. One huge muscular guy stood up next to us and said, 'Excuse me, I need space to dance,' and then went into a full-on routine involving back flips and splits. Barry and I looked on as if he were from space.

'Poof,' Barry said in my ear.

I nodded.

The guy sat down only to be mobbed by a pack of female

strippers. He was obviously some sort of exotic dancer himself.

'Still a poof,' Barry said.

I nodded again.

We went up to the bar and standing there were a couple of pretty average-looking Irish girls. We started chatting and it was quite apparent we were in when I overheard a guy in an expensive suit and sunglasses (indoors, and at night, no less) yelling at a black girl at the bar.

'Do you know who the fuck I am?' he bellowed at her.

She shook her head humbly, pensively almost.

'Listen. I'm a millionaire and my dad's a billionaire and you will never get near me or my dad's money because you're the wrong colour, nigger.'

Barry and I looked at each other utterly dumbfounded. London might have its pomposity and subtextual racism going on, but this was something else. Not even in Western Australia where I grew up, where racism is practically a national sport, had I heard anything quite so hateful and blatant.

His words hung in the air for a while as we wondered whether or not we'd let it slide, but valour, mushrooms and crystal meth got the better of us. It was my turn to get spontaneously violent. I rolled my head and neck around in preparation.

'I got your back, mate,' Barry said with a nod, seeing this.

I tapped the guy on the shoulder.

'Excuse me, mate,' I managed through my whiskey throat.

'What the fuck do you want?' he snapped back.

'You might want to take your sunglasses off, son,' I replied.

My voice was still damaged, but spurred on by testosterone and adrenalin it had an alarmingly weathered growl to it. The guy's eyes widened with fear accordingly.

'What the fuck for? Do you know who you're fucking with? Do you know who my dad is? Do you know who I am?' He flapped his arms about.

Barry cricked his neck in preparation.

'No, son, I don't know who you are. Do you know who I am? Allow me to introduce myself. I'm Brendon Burns. I'm the man that's about to hand you your long-awaited kicking.'

I know it's doubtful that I said anything that cool before getting into a fight. But I did. Barry was there.

Seeing the cold confidence in our eyes (which was actually meth and hallucinogens – equally, if not more, scary) the guy backed off immediately, yelling out at us as he did so. 'You motherfuckers! You know who the fuck I am?' It went on and on. 'I'll see you outside, motherfuckers . . .'

'Sure, let's do that!' I yelled back at him. 'It'll be a hoot! Not much fun for you though! I'll see you there!'

He babbled something back and grabbed the same bouncer who had seen me get hassle for no reason the night before. I shrugged at the bouncer and he shrugged back at the guy. As with Aaron, the guy was clearly an arsehole. Only this time he wasn't a human weapon but clearly a punchable spoiled little shit. After listening to him bellow for a few seconds the bouncer gave me a knowing nod that we had his blessing to pound the guy if we wanted to.

'Excuse me, boys, thank you for standing up for me like that,' the black girl interjected in a sweet Southern drawl.

'You're welcome, miss.' I went to tilt my hat only to remember I'd left it back at the hotel. Instead of cool cowboy swagger I now had the appearance of a man intent on tugging on his earlobes but failing.

'You really shouldn't have to put up with people talking to you like that,' Barry said.

251

'Thank you so much, it's so rare to meet such a fine pair o' genelmen,' she purred as she traced her hands down our chests.

'Well, there you go, miss,' I responded. 'Where we're from chivalry ain't dead.'

'That's awfully good to hear. Now, would you boys like to take me home and fuck me up da ass?'

We stood there for a while not entirely sure we'd heard her right. We looked at the Irish girls then back at the black girl.

'I'm sorry?' Barry asked.

'You know,' she replied casually, 'up the ass.'

'Erm, yeah, we get that,' I said. 'But you don't have to do that, miss.'

'Oh no, I don't mind. You and your friend, you can put it in my pussy, in my mouth, on my titties, up my ass. I can take both of you at the same time if you want.'

Again we stared at each other, dumbfounded.

'Sorry, miss,' I said, 'I don't want you to have to do that tonight.'

She moved in and slipped her arms around both of us. 'Now don't you boys want to come on my tits?'

I reached into my pocket and took out my wallet. 'Look, miss, I'm going to give you whatever I have just so you don't have to do that this evening.'

I pulled out a twenty. She snatched it and was gone.

One of the Irish girls piped up. 'That was freaky.'

'Yeah,' we replied.

'So, what are you guys up to now?' the other said, slipping her arm around Barry.

Just then Dickhead with the sunnies came over with a girl under each arm and started talking shit again. 'There he is, girls. You know who the fuck I am?'

'Well, I don't know about you guys,' I said, 'but right now I'm going to go pound that cunt.'

'He is a coont and needs poundang,' agreed the Irish girls. Now suddenly adopting the threatening Northern Irish accent as opposed to the soft, comical, lilting one.

'Leave it, Brendon, it's not worth it,' Barry said, much to his own chagrin this time. 'Oh God,' he added, 'now I know how you felt.'

Dickhead was now making his way to the door but still barking like a Jack Russell: 'You motherfucker! I'm going to kick your ass!' etc.

'Sure, mate, sure. I'll see you out there.' I started to remove my shoes.

'What the fuck are you taking your shoes off for?' he bellowed as he exited up the stairs.

'Because I'm going to kick your fucken head in, dickhead. And then I'm going to batter you with the soles of my shoes. In some cultures it's the ultimate insult.'

His face changed expression. It became apparent that I was very sure this was going to come to blows and that I knew more about the outcome than he.

I asked the bouncer for my jacket, which I could see hanging just behind him.

'I need your ticket,' he said flatly.

'Do you know who the fuck I am?' Dickhead bleated one last time from the stairs for the benefit of the girls he was with.

I pawed about in my pockets for the ticket, coming up short. 'Mate, just give me my fucken jacket so I can go pound that cunt.' I was suddenly furious and really felt a deep-seated bloodlust. I wanted to bite the man. That was the thought process going through my head. First move, eye gouge. Then fishhook the guy's mouth open with my forefinger, bringing him to the ground. Some ground and pound, utilizing elbows. Then bite his nose. That was my actual thought process. Get another human being on the ground and bite him on the nose.

If my son ever reads this, Boy, don't ever do crystal meth:

1. It makes you angry – fast.
2. You *will* wind up in jail – fast.

The bouncer looked at me and puffed his nostrils. 'Yeah, I hear dat,' he replied, handing me my jacket.

'Brendon, fuck it, leave it,' pleaded Barry again with the Irish girls in tow.

I steamed upstairs after the guy. It was getting light outside and he was long gone. I was kind of relieved as I was now shoeless and the hard concrete didn't give me quite the footing I would have liked.

'Ah well, where are you guys off to now?' I asked the Irish girls when they emerged with Barry. Out of the darkness of the club they ranged from sub-par to minging.

'We're going back to our aunt's place. I don't suppose you have a hotel we can go to?'

I looked at Barry. We knew that Provenz and Keith were back in the room.

'You can come back with us to our aunt's if you like,' one of the girls offered as the other hailed a cab.

'What do you reckon?' I muttered to Barry.

'Mate, I've had enough sexual frustration for one night thanks,' he whispered.

'C'mon.'

'Mate, we're not going to be able to shag them at their auntie's.'

'Mate . . .'

'No.'

'Vegas!'

'Don't start that shit.'

'Whooooooo!' I said softly so as not to scare the girls.

Meanwhile the girls climbed into their cab, waited a while for our decision, got fed up watching us argue and drove off.

I punched Barry lightly. 'Mate, we were in there!'

'Put your fucking shoes on, you twat,' he said.

I did the one-leg shoe hop for a bit and then we started to walk.

'Hold up, Barry. I gotta make a pit stop at the mall on the way.'

'What for?'

'You'll see.'

When we got back to the room, Provenz and Keith were still up. They looked us up and down incredulously as we were absolutely soaking wet from head to toe.

'What the fuck happened to you two?' Provenz asked.

'We got into a fight,' I slurred.

'What?' said Keith. 'Why didn't you call?'

We then regaled them with the entire tale, with a sense of valour and rebellion.

After we'd unfolded every detail of what had passed, Provenza said, 'I'm sorry, you're telling this story as if something actually occurred. What have you really achieved?'

We pondered the question for a bit, and eventually I replied proudly, 'Well I'll tell you one thing. We sure as hell saw to it that that crack whore didn't have to suck any dick for her fix tonight.'

'Amen,' said Barry, high-fiving me.

Provenz looked us up and down again and asked, 'There wasn't really a fight now was there?'

'Not really,' we replied, stealing glances at each other and giggling.

'So not one punch was thrown?'

'Well, not entirely true,' Barry replied, looking at me out of the corner of his eye.

'How so?' asked Keith.

'Well, Brendon did go to punch a swan.' Barry giggled.

'Where?' asked Provenz.

'In the fucken face!' I said drunkenly. 'I'll show them. Bunch of smug cunts. Fucken not better than me—'

'Not the swan,' Provenz cut in. 'Where in Vegas?'

'The mall,' Barry answered.

'Wait a second,' Provenz said angrily, 'you swung a punch at a fuck'n swan—'

'Cunts,' I said quickly under my breath.

'At the hotel where we're staying?'

'Don't worry, I tackled him into the fountain and he missed,' Barry said happily. 'Other people saw us and jumped in too. So I snuck him off before he tried to punch any of the other swans.'

'Cunts!' I yelled, and passed out.

32
Funny People

AFTER SIX HOURS of solid sleep I was stirring between reality and dream via the blend of a camera's flash, the wetness of my drool trickling down my cheek and the sound of giggling. I vaguely remembered a discussion about who was sleeping where and Keith insisting that I take the bed because I was splitting the cost of the room with Provenz. I snatched up the offer and passed out.

As I wiped away the spittle I looked down and realized I had my hand down my underpants wrapped around a raging stonk-on. Through cotton wool I was dragged further into consciousness by the sound of more snickering. I looked to my left and saw all three of my travelling companions gathered around me in a semi-circle. In the middle Barry was holding a camera. Still groggy, I looked down at my cock, pants and hand, then double-took between my package and them. They laughed again as I obviously had a morning-stirring face, my lips in a thin, downward-pointing smile producing extra dimples in my cheeks. Like a pissed-off fish. Even then I was not yet fully awake.

'You right there, mate?' Barry finally asked.

I still hadn't taken my hand out of my pants or

acknowledged them, which seemed to amuse them further. I stretched and shimmied, giving my morning horn a good push forward, like a gearstick struggling to get into fifth.

'Seriously, dude?' Provenz complained.

'So I imagine you got a shot of me asleep with my hand on my cock then?' I rasped.

'Yep,' they all replied, nodding their heads.

'Cool. Feel free to take the piss.'

'Oh don't worry, we got that covered,' Provenz assured me sardonically.

Soon we were all up and showered. Keith and Barry were really keen for us to make our way back to LA for a gig they'd organized.

'C'mon man,' said Barry.

I was reminded of the urgency I'd felt to get out on to the open roads of Nevada. Barry and Provenza's tardy apathy had bothered me then too.

A warm sense of achievement washed over me. We'd done it. We'd got my photo. I could see that Keith viewed that night's gig as equally important, but I didn't really care. My trivial needs were actually beneficial to us all, I thought. I didn't quite know how yet, but I figured the day would play out for us. But we'd had our moment together in Nevada. Admittedly I was surprised that Provenza had been the first one to get a magical life-changing gift first. OK, I may not have proved God's existence, but aliens had to come in a close second. I'd got my photo, though. For a split second I got to be exactly who I wanted to be. This morning I felt just like that guy. That was my life-changing gift.

Now there was just the small matter of healing Barry's broken heart.

'Calm down, hooker fucker,' Provenz said to Keith as he

stepped out of the bathroom, towelling the inside of his ears.

Keith bounced about like a four-year-old waiting for the fair. 'C'mon guys, it really will take ages to get back for the gig in time.'

I figured he hadn't quite considered such matters when I – I mean *we* – had to cut across LA to pick him up. Now that the shoe was on the other foot I wasn't too bothered myself.

'Dad's right,' Barry said. 'We should get on the road if we want to be there for the gig in time.'

'Yes, zere must be rules to ze fun!' I joked as I entered the bathroom, adopting a German accent.

Ordinarily Keith would have laughed this off or shot back again, but he was legitimately livid. On this occasion he just fumed.

An hour later Provenz took the wheel while Barry and Keith sat brooding in the back. I'd taken my time in the bathroom. Now it was their turn to deal with procrastination.

'We're not going to make it in time,' Keith worried.

'Shut your shit-car-havin' hooker-fuck'n ass up!' Provenz bellowed back at him.

'I'm serious,' Keith snapped back, 'I will *not* take all your guys shit all day. I *will* crack skulls. I will *not* stand for the nickname "hooker fucker".'

I grabbed my pad and pen, to save my voice, and wrote *Well don't fuck hookers then.*

I showed Provenz the note. He cackled.

'What?' Barry enquired.

Provenz passed the note back to him. He laughed too.

'What?' Keith asked.

Barry passed him the note.

Keith sat silently for a bit, then barked at Provenz, 'If I'd known you were going to give me so much shit about it . . .'

Keith's words petered out, so Barry completed the question for him: 'Yeah, Provenz, what the fuck did you buy that woman for Dad for?'

Provenz considered the question for a bit, then remembered his previous admission. 'It was the funniest thing I could think of,' he answered with a shrug.

We all blew up. I was slapping my hand against the dash.

'What better reason is there?' I rasped. 'I'll tell you what, I won't talk for the rest of the day. I need to save my voice and . . .' I scribbled on my pad: *It's the funniest thing I can think of.*

'Awesome!' Provenz said. 'Now we just have to find the funniest thing for you two to do.'

Oh, I think Keith's already done his, I wrote.

The others read it as I continued to scribble in preparation for Keith's reaction. When it got to Keith he began his catchphrase – 'I'm not going to take this' – but I cut him off with a note that read *I will crack skulls.* Then I flipped the pad to reveal *Fucken wear it.* Then over again for *Hooker fucker.*

'Yeah, keep writin', buddy,' Keith shot back. He smirked smugly and rubbed his hands together. 'You'll see. You'll all see.'

We arrived at the final casino on the border and the general consensus was to stop for lunch.

What time's the gig? I mimed.

'Ten,' Barry responded. We were all becoming very adept at communicating non-verbally. There wasn't even pause for thought between my gesturing at a fake watch on my wrist then holding a mike in my hand and Barry answering.

'I had that as "What time is all the cock getting here?"' Provenz joked.

That's your answer for everything, I wrote.

Provenz nodded.

I don't even think you're actually bisexual. It's just the funniest thing you could think of.

'Ha! You know it!'

'What?' Keith and Barry asked. They snatched at the note, read it, took it in, then sat in silence for a while.

'Erm, Brendon, it's kind of up to me when I tell people that,' Provenz said wilfully.

Oops! Sorry, I wrote.

Provenz had come out to me several months earlier, even though I'd known for about a year. My initial response was, 'So?' When I realized that telling me was a bigger deal than that to him I put my hand gently on his and said, 'Paul, you're one of my favourite people. How could you possibly think I'd give a shit about something like that?' Then, once the tenderness between us had been well received and duly noted, I asked, 'I can still make poof jokes around you, right?'

'That took you waaaaay too long to ask,' Provenz quipped out of the corner of his mouth.

Now Barry and Keith were obviously going through the same dilemma, only with more diplomatic consideration. I've never had to come out in any way before and this was proving a fascinating insight. Clearly they were replaying all the straight guy/homo jokes made mandatory by the closeness of our sleeping arrangements. One could almost hear the cogs whirring in the back seat as their minds rewound scenario after scenario. Obviously neither of them had any kind of a problem with Provenza's sexuality. Rather, they were checking their own behaviour around his sensibilities.

Hold on. Sensibilities? Provenza?

After a while common sense prevailed and they realized

whom they were dealing with. Barry spoke up first: 'We can still make poof jokes around you, right?'

'Fuck! That took you waaaaaay too long to ask.'

33

The Funniest Thing We've Ever Heard

OUR TRIP IN pursuit of the photograph was worth it, even though at that stage it remained to be seen whether or not we'd got the photo successfully. Every journey, as a wanker would say, is about what happens on the way, not the destination. Despite everything, this particular journey was totally worth it.

Because . . .

On the way back to LA, Keith said the funniest thing I have ever heard in my life.

If nothing else, our story so far has at least been one massive set-up for this, his punchline.

The funniest thing you've ever heard almost always comes with a back-story. That's why, so often, the funniest thing any of us has ever heard involves those nearest and dearest – a sibling insulting a parent, or a quip from a lover just after you've come – and is based on a very personal understanding between you and only a few others.

The timing, source and empathy required to fully appreciate Keith's remark make it one of the most joyous moments I will ever share with other human beings. I have tried my best to relay what had happened to him and, consequently, the mood he was in before saying what he said, when he said it. Yet already you must be aware that I won't be able to do it justice. The best I can hope for is for you not to *guess* that you had to be there, but rather wish you *were* there. But maybe I'm over-selling it, or maybe I'm just putting the pressure on you instead. (I've told this story to a number of people and received nothing more than a blank stare in return. Then again, they're the same people who didn't laugh at the 'orange for a head' joke.)

Enjoy. No pressure. Honest.

34

Leaving Las Vegas I

AFTER MUCH DELIBERATION we managed to convince Keith and Barry that we could easily stop for lunch at the last casino before the state line, still make the gig and see the trailer he'd hired for us. To his credit he compromised happily enough.

Barry climbed out of the back with his sunglasses slightly askew, pulled a face and pretended to be retarded. 'Are we in Vegas yet?' he asked gleefully. It was totally realistic. As stated before, Barry's character pieces are never cartoonish, always convincing. Let me just say, and it is not hyperbole to do so, Barry Castagnola's Vegas Tard has to be seen to be believed, and is believed when seen.

I think I've found the funniest thing Barry can think of. I showed the note to Provenz. He saw where I was going completely and nodded.

I scrawled again, *I dare you to play Vegas Tard the entire time we are in this casino,* and flashed it at Barry.

'Mate, I can't.'

'Psst!' I stamped my feet.

'You have to, Barry,' Provenz said. 'It's the funniest thing we can think of.'

'Barry, you don't have to do everything they tell you,' Keith said.

'Keith, shut the fuck up,' Provenz cut him off.

'I will—' Keith started, but I interrupted him with a mime of cracking skulls and mouthing the words 'yada yada yada' while making a puppet gesture with my hands.

'No, look, it's not that, boys,' Barry said as we made our way to the entrance. 'It's just I have to make some business calls while we're in there and it has to be consistent otherwise people can tell.'

Before he could finish his excuse we pointed out some phone boxes to our left just outside the entrance.

'Mate, I can't,' he appealed to me weakly.

'You can and you will,' Provenz insisted.

I did my sunshine mime next to the phones, indicating that they were a sign from the comedy gods.

'He's right, Barry, it's a sign,' said Provenz. 'Go Barry, go Barry!' He put on his Bizarro voice. 'C'mon Barry, I'll suck yo' dick . . .'

Barry froze for a bit as he second-guessed the joke.

'Oh please,' Provenz continued as Bizarro, 'you're sooooo not my type. Keith's got twice the shot you do.'

Keith flinched.

'Oh don't flatter yourself, Keithy.' Provenz drew hard on his fag and discarded it with a flick.

'OK guys,' Barry said, 'I just gotta make a call to my bank back home.'

As Keith and Provenz made their way into the casino, I patted Barry on the back.

'Mate, I know you want me to do this, but I can't,' he said. 'There's a few deals going on here. I've got to call the guy who runs the chain of English pubs and I need to make sure some cheques have cleared back home so I can pay you back for the flights.'

I frowned at him.

'Mate, I can't.'

I continued to look at him, folding my arms.

'Mate . . .'

Barry made his calls, handled his business, let out a sigh, tilted his cowboy hat, pulled a wide-eyed unaware glaze over his face and announced retardedly, 'Gonna play machines. Barry gonna win.' Then he took me by the hand, allowing himself to be led in.

'Are we in Vegas yet? Is Barry in Vegas?' he said once we were inside, much to the glee of Provenz and chagrin of Keith.

Now Vegas is a place where there are very strict, punishable-by-death even, rules. Like any microcosmic society there are sub-rules. Yet in all of these societies those rules do not apply if you have someone with you who's mentally challenged. I assure you we were not making fun of anyone with any kind of disability, we were making fun of people's reactions to disability. Not only did the rules of Vegas stop applying, the dynamic between Keith and Barry also altered dramatically. As the affectionately known 'Vegas Tard', Barry could tell his dad exactly what he thought of him, as any retribution in public would probably result in Keith getting pounded.

It began with Provenz and I leading Barry on while he pretended to be constantly distracted by everything.

'Lights!' he would yell and make his way to a machine.

'No, Barry,' Provenz would say with tenderness as we ushered him forward gently.

'Game!' he would blurt and bolt for a roulette table.

'No, Barry.' And we'd repeat the process.

'Girl!'

'No, Barry.'

Naturally no one was offended, hurt or outraged because Barry's portrayal was so convincing and human. In fact, Provenz and I were awarded many tilted heads and knowing, affectionate looks for being such good guys taking this 'Barry' of ours out for an airing.

Keith was having none of it, though. 'Barry, you've been a very bad boy. You have to stop this.' He maintained our tone but the narrative was ambiguous.

'Shut up, hooker fucker,' Barry replied, looking down at the floor and moving his right arm back and forth nervously and spastically.

This was too much for Provenz and me. We turned bright red as we struggled to contain bursts of laughter. Again Keith could do nothing. He was trapped, and now his son could say anything he wanted. The dialogue that followed was nothing short of cathartic poetry as Barry proceeded to give his dad what for in this untouchable fashion.

'Shut up. Barry didn't get a hooker. Barry one with broken heart, not Dad.'

'Now Barry—'

'Barry didn't get a hooker.'

'Barry . . .' Keith was grinning with gritted teeth.

'Fucked hooker in my bed. Not Mum. Haven't fucked Mum in years.'

Provenz and I exchanged a wide-eyed glance. I handed Provenz a note that read *Fucken Hell!* Provenz nodded as he read it. I then looked over at the roulette tables and scribbled *We are soooo going gambling with the Vegas Tard!*

'Oh you know it,' Provenz whispered back at me. 'I never knew you could get away with this much. Imagine what you can do when no one knows he's faking? This is fuck'n art, man.'

Keith, meanwhile, was maintaining his ground. 'Barry, now you've had a big day with your friends but you need to watch your mouth.' An angry bead of sweat trickled down his forehead.

'Shut up, hooker fucker. Just cos you scored meth. I didn't get to fuck hookers. Fucked a hooker on my bed. Fucked hookers on my bed. Took meth and fucked hookers on my bed. Not Mum. Mum not a hooker. Dad left, went to live in America, land of opportunity. Barry stayed home with Mum. Barry sad. Divorce your fault. Your fault.'

Astonishingly, Keith laughed in shock then turned pink as he attempted vainly to stifle it. We all corpsed a bit. My cheeks were full and red just thinking about it. Provenz and I were looking at each other with elated raised eyebrows. Well, his were raised, mine were utterly dumbfounded.

'See!' Provenz announced proudly. 'That line is sneaky.'

I had to hand it to Provenz again. Barry had gone so over the line that Keith couldn't even see it any more. And if one can't even see the line, how can they determine where it was in the first place? Keith had to realize he'd done the same himself. They were so far beyond the offence and outrage zone they were in limbo. It was a bizarrely bittersweet moment between father and son. I guess they'd always known that they were just a couple of men with weaknesses and shortcomings, but here was a big slap in the face, acknowledgement between them. It sounds sick and twisted I know, but it was, oddly, both tender and beautiful.

'OK, boys, let's go eat,' Provenz said in singsong fashion, clapping his hands.

We made our way into the buffet restaurant. As soon as a waitress sat us down at our table, Barry bellowed at her,

'Thank you. I'm Barry. Barry gonna win. I'm from London.'

'Well I hope you do, Barry, I hope you do. Welcome to Vegas.' She smiled at him sweetly and gave us all a congratulatory nod for taking this mentally challenged man out gambling. 'I hope you all have a good day.'

I mimed thank you at her. She was taken aback. Provenz was in a bright red cowboy hat and Keith looked like someone's dad. Adding Mute Boy and Vegas Tard to the mix just made our little band a tad too eclectic, even for Vegas. One too many specials on the menu for this waitress.

'Fuck, she can't tell who the carer is,' Provenz observed.

We all went up to the buffet, and Barry's commitment was admirable. He insisted on serving himself things that didn't mix.

'No, Barry,' we said as he went to put cake on his salad.

'Cake,' he blurted as the chefs smiled awkwardly.

'No, Barry, you can have cake later.'

'What about chicken? You like chicken, don't you Barry?'

'Chicken,' he agreed.

We piled on some fried chicken.

'Do you want some potato salad?' Provenz asked him gently.

'Potato,' Barry said.

'What else would you like?'

By now all the chefs were clearly nauseated.

'Sprinkles.' Before we could stop him he'd covered his lunch with sprinkles. When we started giggling everyone else watching did too. Retarded or not, funny is funny.

We sat down at our table and Barry proceeded to eat his sprinkle-covered fried chicken without a knife, fork or hands. He just stuffed his face in his plate and tore away. When he sat back up his face was covered with chicken and sprinkles. The waitress frowned at us at first for laughing but then burst into fits herself when she saw his face.

Again, mentally challenged or not, funny is funny.

'Fellas, I don't really know about this,' Keith piped up. 'This is bang out of order. We have to stop.'

I scribbled a note and held it up: *Who's to know?* Then another: *It's only offensive if we stop.*

Provenz and Keith appreciated my point while Barry spat out his potato salad.

'You know, Brendon used to work with the differently abled,' Provenz said to Keith.

I wrote in response *And do you know, the funniest thing is, you can play this game with them and they go with it.*

They nodded and laughed. I loved that they understood me. Most people require some degree of elaboration. But if you have to explain it you spoil it.

Keith was sitting where he could see the entrance, behind Barry. Suddenly something caught his eye and he gripped the table in anguish. 'Oh no no no no no no no no! Fellas, we reaaallly have to stop.' He gestured subtly with a nod.

We all turned to check out of the corners of our eyes. Approaching us was a family of three: Mum, Dad and their child, who had Down's syndrome. They walked right up to the table behind Barry and sat down.

Keith leant in towards us. 'We have to stop!' he whispered intently.

Again I held up the notes I'd written one after the other, a very calm look on my face: *Who's to know? It's only offensive if we stop.*

We all acknowledged the undeniable truth. We were committed to it.

To hammer the point home, Barry yelled, 'I want a balloon!'

The other family smiled and waved happily at us as we looked over. Keith, resigned to our unsung agreement, waved back at them.

He then whispered the funniest thing any of us has ever heard: 'I wonder if that kid's acting too.'

Oh my God!

We all spat into our plates. Barry pulled his hat firmly over his face so that no one could see him break character. He giggled into his hands, pretending to bury his head in his elbow. Having gathered himself, he then began to pluck chicken and sprinkles off his cheeks. This sight was enough to trigger our stifled giggle coasters again. It seemed like for ever as we attempted over and over again to regain composure. Sighing, wiping away tears, only to burst out laughing again. Each one of us could lay claim at some point to being the trigger that set it all off again. Giggling in fits and bursts, then a lull, then a sigh that would kick-start the whole cycle all over. The more we needed to contain ourselves the more difficult it was to do so. We went from constipated pink to birthing red as we tried.

Keith too. It was beautiful to see him drop his guard.

'That might well be the funniest thing anyone has ever said,' Provenz announced.

We all nodded.

'I'm sorry, Barry, you might have shifted to number two,' he added.

'Barry don't care, Barry love Dad,' he said, still with sprinkles on his face.

Keith beamed with pride. He was part of the gang. He took a napkin, wiped his son's face, looked him dead in the eyes, nodding slowly with warmth and intent, and said, 'Come on Barry, let's go gambling.'

'Yayyyyy!' said Barry.

As mentioned earlier, when you have a person with special needs with you, you can break a lot of the rules of convention. Here I should make an addendum: so long as you appear to be attempting to abide by them.

I handed Barry twenty dollars to gamble with. He tried to shake his head in disgust but I insisted.

We passed a roulette table.

'Hello gentlemen,' the croupier said with a smile.

'Barry,' Barry replied at them.

The croupier tilted his head quizzically.

'Barry, where do you wanna go? You wanna play cards?' Provenz asked.

Barry clapped his hands. 'Cards!'

'Or do you wanna play roulette?'

'Roulette!'

With this, Barry shoved his way in at the nearest table.

'Hey!' the patrons rightfully complained.

The security guard at the table was reaching for and about to use the taser/pepper spray or whatever disabler he had on his belt when Provenz completed the picture for everyone by saying, 'No, Barry, no. There are people sitting here. You wait your turn.'

'Barry,' Barry replied.

The staff and players took a look at his glazed eyes and excited demeanour and their faces softened immediately. Much like Provenz's forced coming out in the car, it was a fascinating insight to watch people's faces change once the penny dropped.

'Oh that's OK, take a seat over there, Barry,' the croupier said, gesturing at a place down the end.

'Barry,' Barry blurted again.

'Say thank you, Barry,' said Keith.

All three of us nodded humbly at everyone. They reciprocated, even the security guard, who only seconds earlier was about to pepper spray or electrocute us all. I can't stress it enough: you don't fuck about with the gambling at Vegas. This was unheard of.

'So what do you want, Barry?' Provenz asked. 'Red or black?'

'Red!'

Barry threw his twenty dollars on the table while the wheel was spinning. Everyone just grinned nervously and let it slide.

'No, Barry, you're not allowed to touch the table after the dealer has said no more bets,' Provenz explained, much to the relief of everyone around.

Barry waited a beat while the information sank in. Then threw his cash on the table again. 'Black!' he blurted.

The security guard and croupier flinched.

'No, Barry, that's not how it works,' Keith tried. 'You have to give the man your money. Then he gives you one of those chips.' Keith pointed at the croupier and the chips on the table respectively.

The security guard and croupier eased off again once they saw we had Barry under control.

'Twenty!'

Barry went to grab at some chips on the table. The three of us pounced on him and held him back. No one was even flinching now. Even though this would ordinarily wind up in us being taken outside by mobsters and getting our faces smashed in with baseball bats.

'No, Barry, not yet.'

'Barry,' Barry announced again, leaning over the table and staring almost through the roulette wheel.

This time the security guard even let out a thin smile.

All and sundry were now enjoying experiencing this through Barry's eyes. The wheel slowed and the ball made its eventual decision after bouncing about for a while with a few high-pitched clinks. Barry kept his eyes still and moved his head to trace its path.

'Red!' he yelled.

'Red seventeen,' the croupier agreed, nodding at Barry.

'Red!' Barry reiterated.

Everyone at the table now viewed Barry as some sort of soothsayer after his single solitary guess. Not so much a guess, more watching where it landed and saying so. But Vegas being Vegas, an omen was an omen.

He's going to win I fucken know it, I wrote. Provenz nodded. Everyone clocked me as the mute one.

'Red!' Barry said as he threw his twenty on the table once the dealer had collected the losers' and divvied out the winners' chips.

'Twenty dollars,' the dealer announced, expertly dispatching the money and sliding towards Barry four five-dollar chips.

'Red!'

Barry put all his chips on red. Every player at the table followed suit.

'Black!'

Barry changed his mind and put everything on black. The herd followed again.

'Red!'

Again, they moved with him.

'Black!'

Barry continued the charade until the croupier rang his bell, with Barry on red. 'No more bets,' he announced.

Barry watched the wheel again intently while the table watched him. The ball was soon bouncing and settling again with a few slow clinks.

Clink, clink—

'Blue!' Barry blurted on the third clink and reached across the table to move his chips.

Even the security guard froze before instinctively reaching for his mystery weapon.

'No, Barry!' the croupier spat in panic.

In Vegas you can fuck hookers, take drugs, do pretty much anything you want 24/7, but YOU DO NOT TOUCH THE ROULETTE TABLE WHEN THE BALL IS LANDING. Go to Google images right now and type in 'Mayor of Vegas'. It doesn't matter what year you're reading this, you'll still see pretty much the same guy. Have a good look at his fat drunken red nose. That guy turns a blind eye to everything. Nevada has no state income tax; how the balls is he affording to get that drunk? He doesn't care what you do while you're there. JUST DON'T TOUCH THE FUCKEN ROULETTE TABLE WHEN THE BALL IS LANDING.

Even Provenz, Keith and I were startled by the bravado of the conceit. If anyone found us out now we could well end up being shot, or at the very least walking out with broken fingers. However, as stated before, when you have a tard with you the rules don't apply.

'No, Barry!' the whole table yelled.

I kept my silence lest I cast any doubt on my muteness. In order to save us all, Keith jumped in and chastised him properly. 'Barry, no! Never do that! *Never*, Barry! Never!'

'Red,' Barry said.

'Red twenty-seven,' the croupier announced cheerily.

Everyone cheered and forgot immediately that Barry

could have blown it for all of them. 'Yay Barry!' they all cried.

The security guard took his hands off his weapon (keeping it a mystery) and sighed a sigh of relief. No matter how officious or bullying an authority figure might be, no one wants to mace the mentally challenged. It's just bad press.

'You won, Barry, you won!' Provenz hugged him.

The croupier handed him his chips happily. Barry took them and immediately reached across the table, trying to put them in the wheel.

'Yellow,' he said.

'No, Barry, no,' said Provenz, restraining him.

'You won, Barry,' said Keith. 'I think we've pushed our luck enough. Time to walk away,' he added wisely, much to the table's, and our, relief.

'Bye Barry!' Everyone waved, even the security guard.

'Let's go cash your money,' Provenz said, steering Barry to the cashiers.

'Hundred dollars,' Barry insisted, literally throwing forty dollars worth of chips at the cashier, hitting him square in the chest. 'Hundred dollars,' he repeated.

'No you don't,' the cashier snapped. 'Nice try.'

'Barry. Hundred dollars.'

'What's this guy been drinkin'?' asked the cashier.

'No, Barry, you've got forty,' said Keith.

Thus completing the picture for the cashier, whose face blatantly read, *Oh shit! Not drunk. Retarded.* His tone softened and slowed. 'Noooo, sir, you got forty dollars. You still won. Well done.' The cashier handed out his money. 'Congratulations.'

'Hundred,' Barry repeated.

'OK, bye bye now.' The cashier grinned.

I took one of the bills and signed it: *Barry, I knew the Vegas Tard would win, Brendon x.*

'Thanks mate,' he said, ever so briefly out of character.*

'That was fucken incredible!' I said as the pair of us burst out the front doors of the casino. 'Oh shit, I spoke!'

'S'OK, I'll let you off just this once,' Barry said.

Don't tell the others, I scribbled. I don't know why but it seemed important.

Barry nodded softly. 'Don't worry.' He then gestured that Keith and Provenz were coming up behind me, having broken away briefly to buy cigarettes.

'Barry Castagnola, ladies and gentlemen!' Provenza bellowed as he and Keith spilled out through the double doors.

The three of us gave Barry a standing ovation right there in the car park. He bowed humbly.

'You nearly had me with that kid acting line, Dad,' Barry said, resting his right arm on Keith's good shoulder.

'Kid acting? My God, I nearly shat when you brought up the divorce!' Keith responded, beaming.

Provenz and I gave them both an appreciative golf clap.

'The Castagnolas!' said Provenz as we made an imaginary toast.

As we made our way to the car, Barry pawed at his forehead, then at the top of his hat, and groaned, 'Ah fuck.'

'What?' asked Keith and Provenz. My face shared the sentiment.

'I forgot my fucking sunglasses. Ah fuck. I know exactly where they are too. I left them at the roulette table.' Barry

---

* When we got home he had the bill framed. Two months later some fucker broke into his house and stole it, earning him the nickname 'Barry Castagnoluck'.

went straight back into character and announced, 'Barry gotta go back in.'

He had to go it alone. We were of no use to him. We actually rolled around on the ground, holding our sides, right there in the car park.

As he stumbled innocently through the double doors we could hear him yell in dismay to no one in particular, 'Glasses!'

35
Leaving Las Vegas II

'No, Bren, I insist,' Keith insisted.

I was trying to offer him the front seat. After the casino he and I had softened towards each other no end. For the first time since we'd started out I noticed just how old and frail he was. I tried to insist back, gesturing at his shoulder.

'No, Bren, you're fine, you're fine. In you go.'

Before I could stop him he slipped into the back seat and instantly started moaning about how cramped it was. You had to give it to him. He did it to himself admirably.

Noticing that we'd all noticed exactly what he'd done, he smirked. 'Well, I need something to whinge about, don't I? What else am I going to do? Consider what the fuck I've done with my life?'

We all cracked up.

Provenz pulled out of the car park and tore off towards the state line.

'We're gonna need some gas,' he said as he veered off the freeway into a service station. After he'd filled up and made his way to the shop to pay I popped open a bottle of Drambuie and knocked back some leftover mushrooms.

'You getting ready to gig then?' Barry tittered from the back seat.

I made the sunshine mime in the car and banged my knuckles on the roof.

'Shit, I should get a photo of us on the state line with the open road,' Barry said.

We all nodded.

'Fuck!' Barry screamed. 'Fuck fucking fuck fuck fucking fuck fuck fucking cunt fuck!'

'What?' we all asked.

'I've left the camera in the room.'

He and I looked dead at each other.

'Fuck,' Barry said again.

My eyes widened and changed colour with dismay.

'Fuck.'

I mimed having a look in the car.

'Fuck. No, I can see where I left it in my head. It's back in the room on the couch. Fuck.'

'Psst.' I mimed having a good look (if one can imagine such a thing).

'I will,' he answered without skipping a beat. (Again, there was a degree of mental telepathy between us at this stage.) 'But I know I've left it there. I know exactly where I've left it.'

Barry and I clambered out of the car and started tearing our bags out of the boot, all the while saying 'fuck' over and over.

'What's the big deal?' yelled Keith from the back seat.

I stared at Barry with desperation and he looked back at me with panic. We ignored him and went back to the boot.

'Fuck fuck fuck,' Barry continued.

Provenz returned from the shop with his customary sun-flower seeds and soda.

'What's up?' he asked, seeing us flinging bags out of the boot.

Barry was now inside his suitcase, nearly dissecting it in his desperation. 'I've left the camera behind,' he replied.

'Oh,' Provenz replied. Then it clicked that my photo was in the camera. 'Oh!' he repeated, this time with more acknowledgement. Then again, dismissively, 'Oh well, now that makes things interesting.' He smirked, waggled a menthol into his lips and lit it.

'I don't see what the big deal is,' Keith insisted as he climbed out of the car. 'I've got friends in Vegas. They can just go pick it up for us.'

'Psssssssssssst!' I stamped my feet hard. My eyes were wide open. I tried to convey as much as possible through facial expression alone just how much I couldn't let that happen. My cheeks wobbled as I did so. A lot like the bloke from the movie *Scanners* just before his head explodes.

'We can't,' Barry said, sighing resolutely. 'We have to go back. Look at his face.'

I scribbled quickly on my notepad on top of the car, *I need that photo!*

'What's the big deal?' Keith asked again. 'I really can send some friends to pick it up. It won't be a problem, I swear.'

I underlined the word 'need' on my notepad again and again.

'I can sort this out for you, honest,' Keith persisted. 'We won't make it to the gig on time.'

I lay down on the ground and started slapping it. '*Psssssssssssst!*'

'We can't,' Barry told Keith.

'Why? What photo anyway?' Keith asked.

Provenz said nothing. Just looked on.

'The photo is the reason Brendon lent me the money to come out here,' Barry explained. 'We took it of all three of us out in the desert. He wanted to be the guy in the photograph for spiritual reasons. To prove to him and me that we can choose the paths we take from here. That anything is possible, we are masters over who we choose to be, and that we write our lives.' Barry was rattling this off dispassionately. I was impressed. I couldn't have put it better myself.

'Well, my friends will get the camera for you, I promise,' Keith said.

I stood up, stamped my foot once and pulled the *Scanners* face again. I pointed at the ground, signifying that I was not moving. Then pointed back down the freeway towards the hotel.

'What's he saying?' Keith asked.

'He says we're going back and that he's staying put until we do,' Provenz finally muttered, casually.

'But you'll miss the gig,' Keith pointed out. 'This means a lot to Barry. It could be a big thing for him. If it's regular he could be out here all the time. We'll get to see each other more.'

Fuck the gig! I mimed.

He managed to understand that. 'You fucking hypocritical prick!' Keith snapped at me. 'So we all have to bend over backwards when it's important to you?'

I didn't have enough of a comeback, beyond *Pssst!* and stamping my feet again.

'That's enough out of you,' Keith warned. 'Fucking with me is one thing, but you don't fuck with my family. I will crack skulls!'

I went to do the cracking skulls mime to mock him, but before I could Keith clocked me one in the jaw. It was a surprisingly powerful blow from the old man. My head rang and my jaw winced. I raised my fist in retaliation, but for a second reconsidered hitting an old injured man, which was just enough time for Keith to follow through with a stinging right. He was surprisingly spry and strong, like Barry. Even with a bad shoulder it was a good shot. He put the shoulder in, twisted the wrist, the lot. It landed square on my nose. Old man or not, a punch in the nose is a punch in the fucken nose. My eyes filled with water and the back of my head pulsed, letting my entire skull know that my bell had been well and truly rung. A good shot in the nose is a bit like violently awakening one's third eye. For seconds you can't see but you bear witness to a visual spectacular nonetheless. As if viewing the world from where your brain meets your spinal column. You can see your forehead and eye sockets from within.

When my vision returned to the front of my face I saw Keith gearing up for another one. I instinctively ducked and popped a couple of short shots into his ribs. He shrugged them off and kneed me in the balls. I went down and he rained blows on me. Then Barry and Provenz pulled him off. I was relieved they'd stepped in as, much to my surprise, Keith was kicking my arse good and proper. If they'd let him, I'm actually quite certain he would have cracked my skull.

I stood up like a shot and stamped my foot.

'*Pssssssst!*'

'Knock it off,' Provenz snapped. 'We're driving back.'

I patted my stomach and jaw, letting Keith know that he'd got me good and that I didn't care so long as we were going back. This seemed to sate him. There is an understanding among men that anything one is willing to come to blows over is to be respected.

I climbed in the back, with Barry letting Keith have the front seat. He may have come to life but the exertion had obviously done his shoulder a lot more damage.

However, the tension between us almost seemed to dissolve immediately after the adrenalin comedown.

Instead, it was Provenza ranting and raving from the driving seat, punching the steering wheel. 'You dumb camera-leavin', Vegas Tard-actin' motherfucker!' he yelled at Barry. 'And you,' he bellowed at Keith, 'you Tina Turner hair-havin' fuck'n mute-puncher!' Then he turned to me and was just about to hurl some insults in my direction when he saw that I was swigging Drambuie and munching on shrooms. 'And what the fuck am I driving for when he's in the back getting high? Fuck that!' He immediately screeched the car into the dirt at the side of the road. 'Fuck this shit. You're driving, Barry.' He climbed over the top of Keith, making him yelp in pain, and pulled Barry out of his seat. 'Hand me those mush-rooms, Burnsy. I'll be fucked if I'm not going to enjoy this.'

I held up the booze and shrooms with a big grin. Barry settled into the driver's seat while Provenz and I threw shit at him and Keith.

'Drive, bitches, drive!' Provenz bellowed.

36

Adaptation

IT TOOK US ABOUT an hour to get back to Vegas. Barry was really beating himself up the entire way. Constantly smashing his head against the steering wheel and yelling, 'Fuck fuck fuck! I'm such a fucking loser!' We got to the hotel and Barry stormed in while the rest of us sat with the car and smoked. By now the mushrooms had kicked in well for both Provenz and me.

After quite a while, Barry emerged with the camera bag.

I gestured at an imaginary watch and shrugged my shoulders quizzically.

'It had already gone to lost property and I had to prove we were in the room,' he replied.

'OK, well, at least let's get to the gig on time,' Keith said, looking me up and down.

'It's all going to plan,' Provenz said to Barry.

Barry ignored him and slumped into the driver's seat. Keith sat in the front passenger side. Provenz and I got in the back, our spirits returned to us now we had the camera. Keith and Barry sat brooding in the front, Barry continuing to beat himself up. 'Fuck, I'm such a fucking loser,' he said over and over.

'You guys seem to be enjoying yourselves back there,' Keith said, changing the subject.

'Different world, baby, different world,' Provenz responded.

He was right. As far as we were concerned we were having a blast. Having a giggly road trip with some buddies.

Provenz started his Bizarro impression again: 'Now why you boys so sad up there in the Castagnola lounge?'

I tittered. Keith didn't know what he was doing and Barry was still way too busy hating himself.

'Fuck your mum,' Barry spat.

'Now why would you say that?' Bizarro replied. 'My momma's not even here. That doesn't make any sense. You've wasted everyone's time.'

I giggled noiselessly. *I am sooo in the mood to do a gig,* I scribbled on my pad.

Provenz nodded.

I saw one of the pages with a note from the previous night. I scribbled on a blank space *Last night I showed this to a girl.* Then I turned over to the page that read *My friend and I went out to the desert to take mushrooms and watch the sunset. It was sublime.* I wrote *She asked me what sublime meant.*

Provenz read it and cackled.

Then she stormed off like the conversation being over was her idea.

Provenz cackled again.

'Fuck! Fuck, I'm such a fucking cunt! Fuck!' Barry blurted at himself in the mirror, then started banging his head on the steering wheel.

I felt awful for him. It was truly painful to watch. I wrote on a new page *Dearest friend, I wish you could see that you are actually having the time of your life but only you are that powerful.* I showed it to Provenz and he nodded. I handed it to

Barry who took it, read it, flippantly flipped the page to see if there was any more, then raised his eyebrows as if to say 'Is that it?' He harrumphed and fobbed it off to Keith. Keith read it, did the exact same thing, then tossed the notepad in the back.

Provenz and I were startled by the flagrant symbolism.

Now that's what sublime means, bitch! I wrote.

Provenz cackled again.

That was Keith and Barry in a nutshell. Here we were, offering them a way out of their blue funk and all they could muster was 'Is that it?' *Flip.*

'How long do you think mushrooms last?' Keith asked Barry as they shared thin smiles and giggles between them.

They were fucking with us. I didn't know the extent of the Socratic irony until much later.

Totally out of the blue, Provenz started an Elvis impression, singing 'Viva Las Vegas'. He warbled the first few lines then substituted some of his own to the same tune:

> *You buy your Dad a hooker*
> *He fucks her in your bed,*
> *You pretend you're a retard and you bet on red,*
> *Viva Las Vegas! Viva Las Vegas!*

Barry joined in with his own rendition:

> *You get dumped by your missus*
> *And ring the Flamingo,*
> *You take some shrooms with a man dingo,*
> *You only have two bucks*
> *So you get Bizarro,*
> *Viva Las Vegas!*

Then Keith threw in the biggest curve ball of all:

You take your hooker money and you bet on black,
It goes the way you wanted
And you get more money back,
So shut the fuck up you cheeky twats,
And cut me some slack!

With that he produced a thousand bucks in cash and started throwing it about the car. He peeled off $500 and threw it at Provenza. 'Take that, you dago-wop-hooker-buying-cock-sucking-pussy-licking-channel-changing-chaotic-spanner-throwing-leather-trousered homo!' Then he peeled off another $300 and threw it at me with a giant grin. 'And as for you, you delusional-God-bothering-hypocritical-meth-taking-photo-seeking-no-driving-no-hat-for-me-buying-grubby convict prick, here's the fucking money for flying out my engaged-to-a-girl-with-a-boy's-name-camera-forgetting-Vegas-Tard-pretending son of mine. Pow! In your face, fuckers! Ha ha!'

Keith leant back and howled. It was so infectious. Our faces turned pink with both glee and shock. We sat there staggered for a while.

'Keith, what the fuck?' said Provenz as he and I sat there with piles of cash in our laps. I'm quite certain that the exact same words were written all over my face too.

'That leaves me with two hundred to spare,' Keith continued. 'So the drinks are on me tonight, boys!'

'Wha? Bu ... bu ... meh ... wh ...' we all spluttered. Myself included. Noises being all we could muster.

'Hey, like I said, when I have, I give, boys, I really do.'

Keith was fucken beaming. I know it seems like a limited

vocabulary, but trust me, Keith was fucken *beaming*. So were we. Flabbergasted wasn't the word.

'But Dad, why the hell didn't you tell us earlier? Why'd you . . . sorry . . . what the fuck?' stammered Barry.

Keith paused for a while. 'I guess it was the funniest thing I could think of.'

Everyone cracked up and started a 'Keithy! Keithy! Keithy!' chant. I pumped my fist to join in.

'Teach you all not to take the piss out of me, though, won't it? Look at you now, you smug little bastards. I'm the old man and I *will* crack skulls! Ha-ha-ha-hahaha! Wankers!'

Keith reprised the chorus of the song and we all joined in at the top of our lungs:

> *Ah Viva!*
> *Ah Viva!*
> *Las Vegaaaaaaaaaaaaaaas!*

I clapped enthusiastically. The vehicle itself seemed to be pumping along on sheer goodwill. I've never been so happy to be proved wrong. My cheeks fill with blood even now.

When the sighs had subsided, Keith turned to me and spoke softly and with genuine intent. 'I'm really sorry about earlier, Bren. I don't know what came over me. I just got suddenly uncontrollably furious.'

I thought of Barry punching the wall and my wishing to bite the guy in the club and scribbled quickly, *Keith, might I enquire when was the last time you took some crystal meth?*

Keith took the note, read it and replied, 'Hmmm, now that you mention it, I had a dab this morning in order to keep up with you boys today.'

I mimed back at him, through pointing, punching and pulling faces, that Barry and I had done exactly the same. And that all was water under the bridge. Quite literally, even from the back seat, 'bridge' and 'water' were quite easy to get across, so adept at guessing my mimes everyone had become. I reached across to the front seat and we shook hands genuinely.

'Sorry, Bren,' Keith repeated. 'I don't know what came over me.'

I produced what was left of the rock.

'Oh yeah, that's what came over me.'

I gestured that I was throwing it out.

'Good idea,' said Keith emphatically.

I hurled it out the window.

Seeing all this unfold in the corner of his eye, Barry realized out loud, 'Oh yeeeeah, the meth. No wonder I'm so fucking angry. Good idea ditching it. All I did was forget a camera. Don't know what I was so upset about. That stuff is shit.' Looking from the notepad to his father and back again, Barry asked, 'What did Brendon write?'

Keith read out the note in a proper manner: 'Keith, might I enquire when was the last time you took some crystal meth?'

Provenz let out a single elated 'HA!'

'Top sentence,' said Barry.

'Sublime even,' said Keith.

Provenz and I nodded at each other in the back.

'Can I have that notepad?' Provenz asked. It was handed to him and he let out another booming solitary 'HA!' as he eyed it.

I scribbled in the pad as he held it, *I want you to keep this pad when we're done.*

He read it aloud to the others and said, 'Oh, I will.'*

There was a short silence, then Barry said, quietly inspired but assured, 'We should write about this.'

We sat for a while thinking.

'Seriously,' he said, 'we should write about this. It'll be hilarious.'

Everyone thought more about this. Mental cogs audibly whirring, clearly replaying all the comedic possibilities.

'Seriously, we should totally do it,' Barry insisted.

'I'm in,' Provenz said flatly after considering it for thirty seconds.

'What'll we call it?' Barry asked.

I wrote something and Provenz read it out: 'Fear of Hat Loss in Las Vegas.'

Barry pissed himself. 'Brilliant!'

I continued to scribble excitedly: *For ever! Change our lives for ever! I promised didn't I? There's your proof!* (I actually honestly didn't think the story particularly had legs, but the notion supported my agenda.)

I showed the note to Provenz.

'What'd he write?' Barry asked.

'Y'know Brendon. He still won't shut the fuck up.'

I think we should leave this bit out though, I added on the pad.

'What'd he write?' Barry asked.

'He thinks we should leave this bit out,' Provenz said. 'We may as well have an "I dreamt the whole thing" ending.'

'Yeah, that is a bit hack,' Barry observed.

'Although it'd be cool to include something like that,'

---

* He still has it in his flat to this day. The Keith enquiry is his favourite page.

Provenz continued. 'A device leaving us pondering what's real and what's not. A device that defines a balance between Burnsy's faith and fate bullshit and my own sense of chaos.' He considered this for a bit, then added, 'We should definitely leave out this bit, it'd just be for the benefit of *total* fuckwits.'

Why would you say that?

'What'd he write?' Barry asked.

'He says his mum's not even here,' Provenz replied.

That's in though! I scrawled in response.

'I got it!' exclaimed Provenz. 'Gimme that.' He snatched my pad and wrote GINGER in big bold letters.

I looked at it and nodded knowingly.

'Can I be in it?' Keith asked.

Provenz laughed. 'Of course, Keithy. Without you we don't have any comedy.'

Barry and Provenz discussed details and logistics excitedly for a good while until finally Keith said, 'Ah fuck. I'm going to get fucking slaughtered, aren't I?'

37

Long Way Home

'I can't fucken speak,' I screeched girlishly, barely above a whisper, as we got closer to LA.

'Holy fuck, is that your voice?' Barry queried from the front.

I nodded.

'How the fuck are you going to do a gig?' he asked.

I shrugged.

'But you're my fucking headliner.'

I shrugged again.

'I thought you weren't going to talk for the rest of the day,' Provenz said.

'Sun's gone down,' I whispered.

'That can't be your voice,' said Barry. 'Are you fucking serious?'

I nodded.

'We'd better get him some stuff.'

Provenz looked at Barry, worried.

Keith sneezed.

'Bless you,' I croaked, then clutched at my throat in agony. It was one too many at this stage.

'Thanks, Bren, I really appreciate that when you've got no

voice,' Keith said genuinely. 'That's really really thoughtful of you. I appreciate it. Really.'

An hour or so later I was beginning to understand his apprehension about turning around to fetch the camera. It really was a long road back. We'd been driving for six hours solid and we still weren't there.

The rest of the journey was pretty uneventful, and we arrived just in the nick of time. As we pulled into the car park, Barry's sister and her friend were there to greet us.

'Don't fuck 'em,' Barry said.

'Don't tell 'em about the meth either,' Keith added.

'I'm not making any promises on either count,' Provenz joked.

'No, mate, don't, don't,' pleaded Barry meekly.

I looked at him disappointedly. I couldn't believe he was beyond seeing humour at this late stage.

'Don't look at me like that,' he said to me.

I continued to frown.

'Mate, mate!' he called after me.

Inside the pub venue Provenza's red-headed friend Ali and Doug's wife Renee were also there.

Where's Doug? I wrote.

'Doug's a drunk,' Renee slurred. 'Then again, so am I. You want a drink?'

I pointed at a bottle of Drambuie behind the bar and stuck up two fingers. She ordered for us both and we took our drinks outside.

'Have you lost your voice?' she asked.

I nodded.

'How're you going to gig?'

I made my sunshine/grin mime.

'Oh my God, I think I just came,' she whispered under

her breath. She patted away at her chest.

Barry came over and squatted down next to us. 'Mate, I really don't want you to do anything about my dad in front of my sister. He's really worried and so am I.'

I looked at him, totally offended. How could he possibly think I would do anything to intentionally hurt him after the time we'd just had together? After going back for the photo and everything? That's why I was upset. That's what I should have said. But unfortunately, what came out was, 'Don't tell me what I can and can't say onstage.'

His head reeled back on his neck from the blow. 'Aw mate. How can you say that?'

'I'm not going to. Why would you think I would?' I carried on, but the damage was already done.

Barry wandered off, muttering, 'How could you say that to me?'

Provenz and Ali came to join us.

'How you wanna do this?' Provenz asked.

'Ask Barry,' I croaked.

'How're you going to gig with your throat so fucked?' asked Ali.

I did the sunshine mime again.

'Jesus Christ, he's fucking gorgeous, isn't he?' Provenz muttered to Ali, who nodded. Like I said, the sunshine mime thing appealed to people with social disorders. Anyone sane would simply decry, 'Good God, what a prick!'

Barry returned to the fold. 'OK, Provenz, are you OK to compère? I'm feeling fucked. I'll go on first, then Brendon.'

'Sure.'

He tore off, continuing to fret.

'I don't think he's up to this,' I said to Provenz.

'I think you underestimate our friend,' Provenz replied.

38

What Happened at the Gig

'SO HOW WAS Vegas?' Ali asked.

Provenz and I looked at each other. I gargled then swigged a shot of Drambuie. As I slammed my glass down we said in unison, 'Sublime.'

Barry returned. 'OK, the line-up's sorted. Everyone OK for drinks? Dad's put up a tab and the publican says we can help ourselves for the rest of the night.'

We all nodded thanks at him.

He tilted his head, tuning into the music playing in the background. 'There's that band again! I can't believe it! I haven't heard it in years and now that's three times in a row. I can't quite place it . . .' He walked back into the bar scratching his head, trying to remember.

'Let's do it,' said Provenz, slapping his hands together. 'Y'know, this is the first time I've done stand-up in America in three years.'

I shrugged. Remarkably, I couldn't understand what the big deal was. Here I was with no voice and only a few hours' sleep in as many days under my belt. Yet I couldn't possibly conceive how it could go wrong. That was always working in my favour in those days. I honestly didn't give a fuck. That's the upside of delusions of grandeur: one still gets to be grand on occasion.

'What's going on in there?' I overheard some guy ask another on my way in.

'They got some Brit comedy or something,' the other replied.

'There used to be a pool table in here,' he said tellingly.

I was reminded of a joke comedian Bob Dillinger used to make about the exact same thing happening somewhere in rural England – word for word. I viewed it as another sign. I told Barry, 'Two blokes just did the Bob Dillinger joke near me.'

'Wha?'

'Oh, he was before your time maybe. A bloke called Bob Dillinger used to tell a story about a shit gig in, I dunno, Glebe, or somewhere equally shite. Anyway, he remarked that some bloke moaned in the middle of the gig, "There used to be a pool table in here."' And some bloke just said, "There used to be a pool table in here."'

'Greatgigshouldbegoodthen,' Barry rattled off, raising his eyebrows.

'Yeah.'

Provenz starting the show cut us short. Despite our reservations and everyone being ushered in shambolically, they still paid him full respect and attention, whooping and cheering as he sauntered onstage. I say stage. It was just a cleared space in the corner of the room. There was no sound system either, just a PA with a short mike lead and a tiny mike. Provided by a friend of Keith's who ran a karaoke shop. This struck a chord with me. I was yet to figure out why.

'Good evening, ladies and gentlemen,' Provenz said, raising his arms in a welcoming embrace to the whole room.

The crowd continued to cheer him. Say what you like about Americans, they presume they're going to have a good time over a shit one first and foremost.

'Good evening, ladies and gentlemen. Welcome to Brit Laughs. I am in fact American.'

The crowd whooped and hollered. (Although, to be honest, it's hard to know the difference. In nineteen years of stand-up, never have I heard a compère say, 'Hey, tanks for all the whooping, but what happened to the holler? *Whoop sans holler? Qu'est-ce que c'est ça?'*)

Provenz continued to tower over the pub crowd as if he were playing to the back of the room at the Old Vic, such was his stage presence. 'So, ladies and gentlemen, I will be your MC this evening, bringing you some of the finest comics working in the UK. The reason I'm here is I've been working in the UK for a year or so now and I have to say the Brits really appreciate the art and craft of stand-up comedy. It's truly a freedom-of-expression art form out there. We all believe in freedom of expression and freedom of speech here in the US, don't we?'

The crowd whooped and several people hollered, definitively this time, correcting my earlier presumption.

'Yeah, we should be able to say anything we want, yeah? This is America, dammit!'

The crowd hollered even more at the notion. All liquored up on US of A juice.

'So I'd really like to thank the Jews for killing Christ on a cross, giving us something to burn on nigger lawns.'

If this were a film script, here there would be a large 'BEAT' written in big bold letters.

Then perhaps another.

I should have warned you earlier. Provenza often confuses freedom of speech with a complete lack of manners.

One could argue that that just isn't the world he's living in yet. He would simply throw back the views of Lenny Bruce, who once remarked that being offended by the word 'nigger' gave it its power and if we all went round calling one another kikes, niggers, micks and polacks then that would somehow create some sort of multicultural Utopia. Although, everyone seems to forget, Lenny Bruce, in the end, was a fat unfunny junkie who died on a toilet. This really pisses off American acts when I say it but, fuck him, say what you wanna say onstage by all means, but kick your addictions and raise your fucken kids first. Then you'll impress me.

But Provenza is Provenza. If you had plans to talk sense into him he'd probably just buy your dad a hooker. If you bought the guy a bag of spanners he'd throw a spanner in it.

If you've found it difficult to get a read on the guy, that's purely intentional. He's for the most part unflappable yet immovable. He fails to see the difference between desensitizing the power of any given word like 'nigger' through overuse and scaring a black family in a diner. Yet if he was served food in a basket in that selfsame diner he would lose his fucken mind. I mean go seriously apeshit. So bizarre are his boundaries. One could fuck his exes in his bed and he'd be thrilled, but the mere mention of food in a basket sends him properly berserk. I've never seen someone serve him food thus, but if he even sees a picture of food in a basket he goes into a hysterical fit, screaming, 'What the fuck is that! I'm not a fuckin' animal! Gimme a goddamn plate!', starts sweating profusely and pounds his fists on the nearest flat surface. It's like me and swans. We all have our 'food in a basket', a trivial beef with some banal idiosyncratic minutia that confirms for us why the world is fucked. And everyone's trivial beef seems just that to everyone else, yet damning, irrefutable, insurmountable evidence to the individual. I think it's one of the most interesting things about humans, that very single specific piece of bullshit that drives us crazy.

The room was dumbstruck. Barry and the landlord were shitting it. Then, suddenly, a row of black people howled with laughter. That's a freaky unwritten rule in stand-up comedy: if black people are laughing, apparently it can't be racist. Mexicans and Oriental people don't even get a look-in here. Afforded licence, the rest of the crowd followed suit. Barry and the landlord's stomachs visibly fattened with sighs of relief.

'C'mon folks, you have to take the rough with the smooth,' Provenz went on. 'So hey, is it just me or was I the only one who found those torture photos from Abu Ghraib hot?'

There was a pop, an intake of breath, a collective 'WHOA!' then a laugh.

Bear in mind this was November 2004. The dust had barely settled and America was split on the matter. Liberals were outraged and Conservatives were outraged at said Liberal outrage. Ironically, I'd probably defend this joke way before I would the first, the butt of the joke actually being the coalition of the willing and our collective complicity. The first gag was more like an excuse to say something really mean.

Provenza belted out a few more gags, did a bit of crowd work, then went to bring Barry on. I didn't want to watch so I stepped outside. I felt angry with him that he didn't feel more confident, in himself and us.

I smoked outside, and then went past the stage to the bar. Our eyes met ever so briefly as he caught me not staying put for his set out of the corner of his eye. Nothing gets by a comic onstage. Our senses become so acute we can smell a mosquito fart two blocks away. There was a panic in his voice inaudible to anyone else as he begged to be liked. Admittedly that's what we're supposed to do, but it's never supposed to look like we are. That's what's so damn hard about it. With the Barry Castagnola I knew there was a negligible difference between his on- and offstage personas. It was something I'd always admired in him. Not unlikeable, quite the opposite. At his gig in Kingston he'd get up in front of the same audience week in and week out with brand-new stuff every week. Somehow coming up with gold based purely on his day. Way better than I ever could. We'd just had the funniest trip of our lives. How could he not translate that to stage? Here he was doing his regular set on auto-pilot. I don't know why but I was angrier about it than I had any right to be. I ordered my drinks and stepped back outside to smoke.

Barry wrapped up his set to rapturous applause. He'd obviously got them on board, as he'd done at the Laugh Factory. Provenz brought up the interval and everyone made their way to the bar and toilets, whichever felt more vital.

Ali and Renee joined me outside for a smoke.

'How the hell are you going to do this with no voice?' asked Renee. 'I can't understand a word you say at the best of times.'

'You should have someone ring a bell every time they can't understand you, then have someone translate,' Ali suggested.

'Yesyesyes! That's genius!'

Barry came out and joined us.

'Barry, can the publican get us a bell of some sort?'

'Dunno. I can ask. Maybe you should say hello to him and thank him for the gig.'

'Why? It's just a gig innit?'

Barry stared at me for a bit. Then wandered off, shaking his head.

He returned with a bell. 'Will this do?'

'Great. Thanks. I'm ready when you are,' I said to Provenz.

Barry grabbed my arm gently as I went in. 'Please don't say "cunt". This is America. They don't like it.'

I shot him a look with my arms wide open that read 'Now, would I let you down?'

He glowered back.

I pointed at Provenz indignantly. 'He said "nigger" for fuck's sake.'

'You're gonna have to shower that in white light and let it the fuck go,' Provenz said. This time it was hard to tell to whom.

Barry shook his head at both of us, exasperated yet again.

I went for my customary pre-gig piss. At the urinal I over-heard the same pool table guys talking.

'I thought it was Brit comedy.'

'I couldn't understand him.'

'The sad thing is, the American's the only funny one.'

I found this remarkable. At least I knew what my opener was.

Provenz was back onstage already, again handling every-one masterfully, getting them settled. After a few gags and some crowd work he brought me on.

'Ladies and gentlemen, we now have one of the top comics working in the UK. He's from Australia originally. We've spent the past few days in Vegas and now he's lost his voice. I have no fuck'n idea how this is going to work, but please welcome, Brendon Burns!'

I bounced into the corner of the room.

'Ha-ha-haaa! OK folks, this doesn't bode well as I heard you two earlier saying while the other acts were on, "There used to be a pool table in here."'

The crowd laughed as I pointed out the two guys from the urinal.

'I've actually heard another comic say that before, but it actually just happened,' I admitted. I wasn't about to put it into my act as my own. 'And I just overheard you two in the urinal. You said you couldn't understand the others and that the American was the only one that was funny. If that's the case, how can you tell, you cunts?'

There was a gasp then a pop of shocked laughter.

'What, you don't say "cunt" here? You should. Your country's run by one.'

This got a round of applause (this, remember, was California during the Bush era, not the current Obamathon). Hardly high satire, I know, or even remotely provocative anywhere else in the world. But I urge you to remember what happened to the Dixie Chicks. The fact that the second half of that sentence is both a statement and a question should speak volumes.

A Latino woman in the front row was staring at me blankly. 'I can't understand you,' she said.

'Well, the feeling's mutual,' I responded. 'You sound like cats to me.' I went on to do a Mexican impression, arching my back, moving my hands around in spastic fashion and bobbing my head up and down: 'Meow! Meow, meow! Hey, Ese. Holmes. Meow, meow, meow!'

The Latino and her daughter cracked up laughing.

'Fucking Mexicans,' I chanced.

The room erupted. Barry, Keith and Provenz were slapping their sides in the corner.

'What the fuck is up with you people? Why is that an all-purpose punchline in this town? Every comic I've seen just says "Mexicans steal" and you all lose your shit laughing.'

The room was staring at me blankly. Eventually someone piped up, 'What are you saying?' Then the whole place fell about.

'Did you understand anything other than "cunt"?'

'Not a lot,' someone replied.

'OK. I'm prepared for this.' I walked to the back of the room and took Renee by the hand. 'Renee, will you help me please?' I led her to the front of the room and gave her the bell, which I'd placed on the side. Remembering how well the translator thing had worked at the Laugh Factory, I ushered Provenz back onstage. 'Ladies and gentlemen, please welcome back Paul Provenza!'

They all clapped.

'Now, ladies and gentlemen,' I croaked, 'every time my accent is too strong or I use a word that Renee doesn't know, she'll ring the bell and Paul here will translate.'

With perfect timing, Renee rang the bell. Provenz picked up another mike and said, 'Every time his accent is too strong or he uses words we don't understand, Renee is going to ring the bell and I'll translate.'

The crowd laughed and clapped.

'That's what I fucken said,' I replied with mock indignance. Renee rang the bell.

'That's what I fuck'n said,' Provenz fired back.

More clapping.

'This is the weirdest gig I've ever seen,' someone said.

'This isn't the weirdest gig I've ever heard of,' I responded. 'I once heard about two guys in the Australian outback . . . I've never told this story onstage before. Do you want to hear it?'

Provenza echoed all of it and the crowd cheered and nodded amiably. I went on to tell them the story in every detail. With Provenza mirroring me. We weren't getting many laughs but there was no malice in the room either. Just baffled ambivalence.

I got to the bit where the sound effects comic wound up

onstage with just a small PA. 'And he gets onstage, but there was no stage. Just a cleared corner of the room.' I looked at the ground around me. 'Just like this!' I exclaimed.

Provenz repeated it word for word. People continued to stare blankly.

'And all they had was a tiny little pen microphone, with a lead only a metre long leading to a shitty little PA.' I looked at my mike, lead and PA. 'Like this!' Then I connected even more tenuous dots. 'Oh my God, from the Mexican call back, to the translator bit, to this! I'm in the fucken story I told. I'm in my favourite death story!' I exclaimed to Provenza ecstatically, 'You gotta admit there's something in this. This is a bit fucken weird. I told you everything we're doing is interconnected.'

'The UFO was weird,' he said. 'This is you making it weird.'

By now Renee was ringing the bell off its handle. The people who hadn't already filtered out of the room concurred.

'Don't even bother,' Provenz responded, 'I couldn't even begin.'

Everyone took his word for it.

'Carry on with the story,' Provenz said.

I continued the story I had practised so well. Again, no one was really laughing but they were awkwardly transfixed, listening to my ramblings then Provenza's translation intently. I may have been bombing but not to my knowledge. I didn't care one jot. I cared way more about the art and the parallels. I wasn't thinking about Barry's ongoing bookings, getting to see Keith more often or anything. I just felt this was more important.

I got to the end. 'So this bloke stands up and says nervously, "Erm, not sure what you're doing. I'm sure it's very good. But we've all come a long way to be entertained . . . and it's just not working out. It's probably best if you just left."'

I spoke slowly and concisely. Everyone had understood the words I'd used. I waited for the bell that never came. They just sat there staring in silence.

Eventually the Latino woman offered, 'I don't get it.'

Someone else agreed: 'That doesn't make sense.'

Then someone else: 'We're not sure what *you're* doing.'

And, 'This isn't working.'

Finally, most perfectly, came this: 'Why would you say that?'

I howled with laughter. Then and there, uncontrollably, right onstage. No one other than Provenz, Barry and Keith having a clue at what or why.

'You're fucken kidding me,' I said. 'Are you joking? That's perfect!'

The crowd stared back blankly. They weren't joking. Provenz and I were wide-eyed and gleeful, like when the cartoon tree did a 'what's up with that?' joke.

'OK, that was weird,' Provenz consented. He knew when to wrap up. 'Brendon Burns, ladies and gentlemen!' The room clapped, but it had gone awry. In the process we'd torn apart what was meant to be the stage. There were tables and chairs everywhere and it had descended into a bemused bedlam, if such a thing exists. The landlord had taken off and Barry was furrowing his brow at us again. But then the music started up and something in him clicked. His face changed immediately and he suddenly didn't give a fuck that we'd blown what could have been an ongoing contract for him.

Provenz and I went straight outside where Ali was smoking and waiting.

'Did it work?' she asked.

'Thank you for that, my dear, it was perfect.'

I clasped my hands either side of her cheeks and kissed her

full on the mouth. She slipped her tongue in and we went for it then and there.

'Tongues! I wanna see tongues!' Provenz exclaimed.

Renee came out and saw us making out. 'Ah fuck!' she swore aloud.

'Do you wanna get outta here?' I asked Ali.

'Sure,' she replied.

39

Barfly

Ext. British pub beer garden – night. Barry and Keith come bounding out of the pub towards Brendon, the girls and Provenz.

Background SFX: Sublime's 'What I got'

> BARRY
> (enthusiastically)

Brendon, Brendon! I remember the name of the band now!

> BRENDON

Wha?

> BARRY

The band! I remember the band! Playing in the background?

> BRENDON

Yeah?

BARRY

They're called Sublime.

Barry stands there with his arms wide, flapping his palms up and down for extra gravity.

BARRY

Brendon, you were right. You got me my gift. I get it. I get it!

BRENDON
(dismissively)

Yeah, great.

Brendon puts his arm around Ali, turns his back on Barry, Keith and Provenz and saunters off into the night, leaving them staring at one another, utterly befuddled.

BARRY
(tittering in disbelief)

'Yeah, great,' he says. Unbelievable. Un-fucking-believable.

They all make their way back into the bar.
Provenz puts his arm around Barry.

PROVENZA

This calls for brown spirits, and lots of it. Want me to buy your dad a hooker?

Barry gives him a steely look.

Int. British pub – night.

Montage: Provenz, Barry, Keith, Renee, Barry's sister and her friend are at the bar.

SFX: Sublime plays over the top of the whole scene.

Renee drinks up and makes her farewells.

Barry's sister and Keith start fighting. Barry looks on, dismayed.

Keith, Barry's sister and her friend storm off.

Keith returns. He and Barry go at it.

Keith storms off, leaving just Barry and Provenz.

The barman puts a consolatory drink in front of them both.

They both drink.

And drink.

They get drunk.

SFX: End

EXT. Car park – night.

BARRY
(hammered)

You'd better drive. I'm wasted.

PROVENZ
(equally hammered)

I thought you were driving. That's why I got hammered.

BARRY

You cunt. I thought you were driving. That's why I got hammered.

Provenz clambers into the car and vomits the moment he sits down.

BARRY

Well I guess that answers our question of who's more hammered.

Provenz continues to vomit profusely. His hacking is incessant. Barry climbs into the driver's seat.

BARRY

This is so fucking stupid. Maybe we should get a cab?

PROVENZ

We're in Pasadena. A cab from here is going to cost about two hundred dollars.

Provenz reaches for a bottle of water. It's actually his ashtray bottle filled with butts. Before Barry can stop him he necks it.

PROVENZ

Ah fuck!

He leans out the car again and vomits even more profusely. It becomes apparent he'd actually swallowed a mouthful of butts as they project violently out of him. Barry howls with laughter and retches in revulsion himself.

BARRY
(still laughing and retching)

Oh (retch) my God (retch) that's (retch) disgusting.

Provenz vomits for an inordinate length of time. He is laughing too, much to his own peril.

PROVENZ

Fuck! I can't believe (retch) I did that (puke). Am I in a fuck'n sitcom or (barf) something? Is there a fuck'n camera on me right now? (gag) That was too perfect!

He continues to vomit while Barry cackles yet sympathizes.

BARRY
(eventually)

I guess alcohol *and* nicotine poisoning outweighs just drunk.

Provenz slumps into the passenger seat.

PROVENZ

Drive.

Scene.

40
Ali

'IT'S OK, SAMMY, it's just that friend of mine again,' Ali sang as we left her place in Malibu the next morning. She really had such a kind voice that it would soothe any beast.

She'd proved this the previous night when we pulled up at her flat and the selfsame Sammy, the neighbour's dog, had started barking.

'It's OK, Sammy, it's me and just a friend of mine,' she sang to it gently in her soft hybrid LA/Southern country girl accent.

The dog gave a bark of recognition and stopped.

'That was a rather complex notion for him to comprehend,' I observed.

'I can talk to animals.'

'Bullshit.'

'No, I can.'

We made our way up the stairs and into her flat. It was hippy yet sexy. With white chiffon curtaining practically everything and only faint mood lighting in every room but the kitchen. Her cats ran to greet her. It didn't smell like a cat owner's house though.

'Your house doesn't smell like cats,' I said as she expertly prepared her bedroom for us. Switching on the appropriate lights for sex seemingly with a wave of her hand.

'No. I ask them to eat, poo and pee outside.'

'Oh yeah? And that works does it?' This chick was crazy but I liked her. Go figure. 'Doesn't it set the dog off?'

'No, I introduced them.'

'You do know you can't actually talk to animals, don't you?'

'No . . . no I don't,' she replied.

The cats meowed at her.

'Steve, Tom, this is Brendon.'

Freakishly, the cats looked right at me and meowed.

'OK,' I conceded, 'I can see how that might make you think that—'

'Whoa,' she said, undoing my belt and taking my dick out. 'Fortunately I only have extra large condoms.'

This was bullshit. I've seen a lot of porn, and that ain't me. It's not that I minded being patronized, it's that I didn't need to be.

'Erm, that's going to be a problem,' I replied.

'Why?'

'I fear I'm only average at best.'

'Oh no, believe me, that's bigger than average,' she said, almost too assuredly. 'It's a nice cock. Nice size.'

Nice.

Yeah, that's what a guy wants to hear.

Evil.

Staggering.

Behemoth.

These are words men want to hear regarding their cock.

Nice?

As the saying goes, biscuits are nice.

Still, girls, at least in the bedroom 'nice' guys finish last.

Behemoths will just pump into you, come, slump over and yell, 'Ha! Beat ya!'

Ali grabbed me and pulled me on to her bed. Kissing me full. She stopped and said softly, 'Hi.'

'G'day,' I returned in a more ocker tone.

'Meow,' the cats said in unison.

I turned, and they were looking at me weirdly. I could almost see jealousy in their eyes.

'Erm, can we lose the cats?' I asked.

'Why?'

'Because I don't like animals watching me fuck. I feel like it's their revenge for Attenborough and the like perving at them for years and putting it on telly without their consent.'

Ali sighed. 'OK, sure. Tom, Steve, can you leave the room please?'

The cats meowed back at her.

'Because he doesn't want to be watched.'

They looked at me, meowed and left. 'Meow!' they yelled again from down the corridor, indignantly.

'I know, I know,' she replied as she shut the door on them.

She took off her top, revealing pendulous breasts. I snapped out of the all-encompassing titty interlude and stared at her, quite shocked and impressed.

'How the fuck did you do that?'

'Oh, you like them?' She fondled her boobs at me.

'No, not that. Although well done, they are lovely. No, they did what you said.'

'I told you, I can talk to animals,' she insisted, clambering over me, pressing her pale porcelain skin against mine and adeptly dimming the lights.

'Woof!' Sammy replied in response, ceasing his barking immediately thereafter.

*

Ali smiled sweetly. 'You want a lift back to Venice?' she asked,
reiterating the offer she'd made earlier that morning.

We climbed into the car. It was a beautiful sunny LA day. I
wound down my window and turned on the radio. 'She Will
Be Loved' by Maroon 5 was on again. I turned it up.

'They're playing our song,' she said. It had been on four or
five times in the ten-hour period we'd been together.

I listened in and sang along.

'So who was she?' she asked.

'What?'

'The girl this song reminds you of.'

'My ex.'

'Wife?'

'Nah. We were engaged.'

'What happened?'

'We were in a long-distance relationship and she started
seeing someone else.'

'And this song reminds you of her?'

'No. It reminds me of him.'

She considered the strangeness of this for a while.

'I like the idea that someone gets to look after her at least.'
I stared out the window and continued singing alone.

The song receded softly into the background. It was the
longer version with the word 'goodbye' tailing off into a
distant echo. We sat in silence as the DJ back-announced the
track.

'You loved her, right?' Ali said eventually.

'Yeah,' I admitted softly from beneath a furrowed brow.

'I could tell.'

'Well, well done Sherlock,' I replied sarcastically.

'No. I mean days ago I could tell.'

'Well, I guess that puts me, cats and dogs in the same category.' I grinned my sunshine grin again.

'So that's what this little trip is really about, isn't it?'

'Sorry, what?'

'You're not doing this for Barry at all.'

I didn't like where this was going. I changed the subject. 'Pull over. I wanna get a beer.'

'It's a little early for that, isn't it?'

'It's after twelve and I'm on holiday.'

'OK, fair enough,' came the reply.

Pretty soon we pulled up at Provenza's.

'Thank you, Mr Burns,' Ali said. 'You've been a positive light and it's been a pleasure to meet you.'

'It's been a pleasure to meet you, Ali-who-can-talk-to-cats.'

I saw her back to her car. As she drove off, I waved and did my sunshine mime.

She did it right back at me.

Six months later she killed herself. I didn't know it at the time but she'd been diagnosed with full-blown bi-polar disorder and couldn't hack the pain of the 'downs' any more.

Provenz and I didn't get to talk about this until January 2006. The night before I checked into rehab. When I woke up the next day I'd rubbed my shit all over myself and my bed and I had zero recollection of doing so. I figured I didn't want to go out the same way. Provenz was one of the four people outside my immediate family I told that I was going in. He said he was relieved, that he loved me and was super proud that I was doing something. The fact that anyone still cared about me made me weep uncontrollably for about three days.

41

Provenza's Revisited

'SO WHAT HAPPENED with you two?' I asked them both as I walked into Provenza's flat.

'We drove home,' Barry replied flatly.

'No way,' I said. 'You were already hammered when I left.'

'Yeah, we both figured the other was driving and continued getting hammered.'

'Barry?' I turned to Provenza. 'Provenz?' It was my turn to chastise in a singsong tone.

'I know, I know,' Barry admitted, 'it was fucking stupid. If we'd got stopped we were *so* going to jail.'

I continued to stare at Provenz with my hands on my hips, like a nagging wife. 'What were you saying to me about jail ruining our trip?'

'We know, we know,' Provenz said, adopting a rare kow-towing tone.

'It was terrifying,' Barry chipped in.

'So what happened?' I asked.

'I caved in and offered to drive when Provenz threw up,' Barry tittered. 'Then he went to clear his mouth with the ash-tray bottle in his car.'

'What? Aw fuck! Aw, gross!' I exclaimed.

'It was hysterical. He necked half of it before he even realized.'

Provenz giggled sheepishly at his own pain. Like when you cop a dead leg so hard you're almost amused by the surprising intensity. 'Oh man, I cacked so fuck'n hard I could feel it in my balls.'

They re-enacted the whole inglorious scene for my benefit.

'That's hilarious, it has to go in,' I said. 'Oh God, I can picture it so vividly.'

'Anyway, fuck knuckles,' Provenz said, 'we need to get our shit together for Outlaw Radio.'

'What's that?' I asked.

'They may as well call it the ADHD hour. It's completely loose. They get millions of listeners online around the world. It's just this guy that holds a radio show in his yard by his pool. He gets together a really eclectic group of people and you just shoot the shit for hours. I told him you guys were in town and he's really keen to have you on.'

'Cool.'

'How was your night?' Barry asked.

'We fooled around for a bit and ended up just talking. I didn't seal the deal. She just switched off at one point and I didn't want to be just another notch on her bedpost.'

'Well there's a turn-up for the books,' Provenz stated, staring wide-eyed at the hypocrisy.

'What?' I replied flatly.

'That little worm turned, it would seem.'

'What do you mean?' I asked.

'Just that the shoe was on the other foot for once.'

I stared back at Provenz. 'Sorry, still nothing.'

'You've been fuck'n around trying to be "that guy" in everyone's sexual history. Then you met your match in terms of statistics and you didn't like it one bit.' He hammered the point home.

'Now why would you say that?' I responded curtly. 'My mum's not even here.'

Provenz slapped his hands on the counter. 'Asshole.'

'I'm going to shower,' Barry interjected, and took off upstairs.

'I gotta ring the radio guys and double-check they're expecting us.'

Provenz resumed his battle with his touchtone phone. Stopping and starting as it failed to register what he was pressing, then doubling up on the beeps when it did, making him have to start over. 'Fuck! Cunt! CUNT!' he yelled over and over. As always, by the time he got through he was furious. 'When the fuck do you want us there?' he bellowed angrily at the man on the other end of the phone. Who was totally none the wiser.

I had an idea and popped out. I waved at Provenza as I did so.

'Fuck!' I heard him shout. 'Yo Burnsy, hurry up wherever you're going, we gotta be there in an hour!'

'Sure. I can get this done while you're showering.'

I slammed the door behind me and raced to the electrical store down the road.

By the time I got back, Barry was out of the shower and Provenza was in.

'What you got?' he asked.

I pulled out a brand-new touchtone portable phone system. 'Just to thank him for having us. You wanna go halves?'

'Of course,' Barry replied.

We plugged it in and set it up. Then threw out the old phone that had caused so much grief.

Provenz got out of the shower and came down wrapped in a towel with some plastic rubbish in his hands. As he pulled open the kitchen disposal bin he saw his old phone sitting atop the pile. He was about to yell at us then looked at where his old phone used to be and blushed ever so slightly.

'See? Now you don't have to do all your dealings in such a shitty mood,' I said.

Again, the tenderness between the three of us hung in the air.

'You couple of fags.' Bisexual or not, Provenz was not above the straight man's way of saying 'I love you'.

The phone rang.

'Ooh, my first call,' he said with mock campness. 'Provenz,' he answered. 'No fuck'n way!' he said while we looked on excitedly. 'No fuck'n way!' he repeated. 'That's great fuck'n news. Thanks, man.' He put the phone down.

'What?' we asked in unison.

'*The Aristocrats* just got selected for Sundance.'

I looked at him and the phone smugly. He tilted his head sarcastically.

'For ever!' I said. 'Change our lives for ever! Wasn't that my promise?'

'Oh yeah, it's all about you,' he responded.

'No, it's all about *us*,' I countered. 'That's the point.'

'Don't be a dick. I've been working four years on this fuck'n thing. If anything, this supports my argument. You're just noticing it because you do.'

'It's still one hell of a first call, you gotta admit.'

'Yes, it is,' agreed Provenz. It was impossible to tell if there was any irony in his voice.

42

Outlaw Radio

'FUCK, FUCK, FUCK! This fuck'n town! Doesn't make any motherfuck'n sense! Fuck!'

We'd driven around in circles for fifteen minutes now. Trying to get on to the overpass above. We'd reversed and turned round at least ten times. All the while looking at the concrete above us, wondering if we could just attach springs to the car like Inspector Gadget.

'There!'

Barry pointed to our left but Provenz was already turning right. Provenz locked the steering wheel in the other direction, sending the car into a fishtail. This was Barry's first experience of Provenza's 'rental' driving.

'What the fuck are you doing?' he screamed.

'It's a rental!' we yelled back through yet another layer of thick acrid rubber smoke.

'What does that even mean?' Barry shouted as he was firmly pushed into the passenger door by centrifugal force.

Provenz locked the wheel again, turning into the slip road on to the overpass of the 110. Narrowly skirting the concrete barriers. Flitting through traffic, we exited only two exits away. Down a slip road, one right, a staggering left and a generous tug on the handbrake put us on the drive of a fairly regular-looking house.

'Four o'clock on the dot,' Provenz announced happily.

'You're a madman,' Barry spluttered. Having nearly torn a chunk out of the upholstery.

'You get used to it,' I slurred and croaked, my voice strained and raspy again.

'C'mon.' Provenz hopped out of the car and we followed him through the head-high side wooden gate of the house.

In the back yard everything was just as he'd described it. There was a bunch of guys sitting around a table in a hut next to a pool.

'Oh, and who's come to join us? None other than the great Paul Provenza and his friends,' came the live on-air welcome of the host of the show, the aptly named Mr Cigar, or 'Magic' Matt Allen. His voice was that of a typical LA DJ – warm as hot nuts. (The street-vending kind. No, wait. That's still innuendous. Yes, I know it isn't a word, but it really should be.) He was sitting behind his own bar in the hut talking into an overhead fully adjustable mike. Littered around the table were regular mikes on stands, picking up everyone else's conversation.

Today we were in luck as two of the guests were none other than a representative from The McCallum whiskey and another from Habano cigars. Each of whom had brought more than enough samples to go round. As we sat down they poured us whiskey and handed us cigars.

I would later find out that the show's slogan is 'We smoke, we drink, we interrupt'.

In the corner were two smoking-hot bisexual girls in bikinis, occasionally making out. When I asked later, it turned out no one knew them. They'd just showed up and started making out. As they were hot, no one had bothered to ask them who they were or why they were there.

This was a show you wanted to be on. This was a fucken show for *guys*, dammit!

'So folks, here they come. Joining us here in the cigar lounge we have the great Paul Provenza and . . . ?'

'Barry,' Barry said as he took his seat.

'And with Barry we appear to have a pirate of some sort.' He gestured at my bandana.

'Get fucked. I'll board ye!' I exclaimed in my raspy voice and best pirate accent.

'Whoa!'

'Whoa!'

'Whoa!' went everyone at the table.

'Easy on the "F" bomb,' Mr Cigar warned.

'Oh shit, sorry, I thought this was pirate radio,' I said.

'Well it is now with you here,' came the reply from my right, from a massive New York Italian, Frank D'Amico. He offered his equally quaffing paw. I'm quite certain it drank some of me as we touched.

It turned out Frank was a former mobster and collection officer turned actor and stand-up comedian. It's hard to talk about him without saying his full name – Frank D'Amico. It just seems to sum him up so perfectly. Frank D'Amico was at the head of the table so that he could fit and sit comfortably in his wheelchair. It was Barry and mine's immediate assumption that he had been shot and got out of the game accordingly.

'I'm sorry about that fellas,' I apologized to the table. 'I was told we could say what we want here.'

'No, that's later when we're online,' Mr Cigar explained without chastising, 'but now we're on long wave and we have to keep the "F" bombs to a minimum.'

'Is shit OK?' I asked.

'Yeah, shit's OK.'

'Shit yeah.'

'I think shit's the line,' came the murmurs from the table.

'Keep it at shit and bastadd,' said Frank D'Amico as if he were straight out of *Goodfellas*.

It turns out he was. Pretty much every gangster film going he was either in it or at the very least telling the actors how to speak. I don't generally approve of people benefiting from criminal behaviour but it was really hard not to like the guy. Even when discussing baseball-batting someone in the boot of a car it was still difficult not to look at him with glee. As if you were fighting back saying, 'Gee, mister, you're just like the movies, aren't you?'

'So, Paul, we still don't have the pirate's name.'

'Ladies and gentlemen, these are two of my friends from the UK, two of the top comics working anywhere in the world: Mr Brendon Burns and Mr Barry Castagnola.'

The table clapped and cheered.

'So where you guys been?' Frank asked.

'Vegas,' I croaked.

'Oh Vegas.'

'Vegas.'

'Vegas, hahahahahaha!' came more knowingly from the rest of the table.

'Blah blah blah Vegas . . .' One guy carried on a bit too long in a crocodile-hunter accent, mocking my raspy voice. 'Hey guys, listen to Crocodile Dundee over there.'

'Marty, shut the fuck up,' said Frank D'Amico.

The rest of the table joined in, really hammering the guy.

Marty, it turned out, was Mr Cigar's little brother and the show's fall guy. I thought it a little over the top.

'Whoa, settle down, he was only making fun,' I said.

'Don't stick up for me, Crocodile Dundee,' he snapped back.

'See? He bites the hand that feeds,' Mr Cigar exclaimed.

Clearly we'd come in just in the middle of something. Judging by the vehemence, about twenty years in.

'Oh why pick on me?' Marty replied.

'Kill yourself,' Frank D'Amico snapped at him.

'OK, we gotta go to commercial,' Mr Cigar announced, and we were off air.

Barry and I looked at each other, assuming that the Marty battering was all part of the show. We were wrong. The animosity towards Marty was very real.

'Hey boys, welcome to the show.' Frank shook our hands again and introduced us quickly to everyone around the table. When he got to Marty he continued his diatribe: 'And that sack o' shit at the end there is Matt's little brother Marty.'

'Hey, thanks, Frank, I always hold you in such high regard,' Marty responded. Almost like a shot from the ground.

'Shut up. You have no talent. This show sucks when you're on it. Go drown yourself in the toilet, you fuck.'

It was hard for us not to laugh along with the mobster's ball busting. No matter how stemmed in reality it appeared.

'And we're back,' Mr Cigar interrupted, banging the bar.

'Can I ask a question?' said Marty.

'You just did, now shut up,' everyone chorused.

'I wanna get back to The McCallum and these great, great, great cigars brought to us here by Mick . . .'

'Can I ask a question?' Marty interrupted again.

'Ah Christ! What?' Matt barked at his little brother.

'Oh, now why are you even letting him talk?' Frank said.

'Yeah,' someone concurred, 'you're an idiot.'

'Let him talk,' I interjected.

'Don't patronize me,' Marty said.

'See! He bites the hand that feeds again!' Mr Cigar exclaimed yet again.

I continued to stand up for him. 'Look, just let him ask the question.'

'Thank you,' Marty said this time. 'I like you now.'

'Ask your question,' Mr Cigar said.

'Ah Christ, this is gonna suck!' Frank spat.

We sat there for a while, waiting for his question.

'Your question, dummy,' Frank barked at him.

'Where'd you get your tattoos?' he asked Mick the cigar guy.

The table exploded.

'You asshole!'

'This is radio!'

'You stopped us for that?'

'Kill yourself!'

'Again!'

'You suck!'

'You're an idiot!'

'Goddammit!'

'Who let him on?'

'I told ya, this show sucks when he's here.'

Frank sat there genuinely glowering at him and muttering behind his teeth. Then he smashed his fist on the table and yelled, pointing directly at Marty as if his finger were a gun barrel, 'You're lucky I'm out of the game cos I would love to turn you into paste with a bat. Go stick your dick in a fish tank then toss in a toaster, you frikken mook.' He turned to me and Barry. 'This guy,' he said, gesturing at Marty with an open palm.

'Oh now wait,' Mr Cigar interrupted. 'Everybody calm down, this show's getting sloppy.'

329

'What?' I said. 'You host a show about whiskey tasting and you're surprised when it gets out of hand? Are you retarded?'

Everyone laughed.

'Strike one for the pirate, I'll wear that,' Mr Cigar announced, laughing good-naturedly. 'Anyway, we have our friend on the line. A guest of the show. A friend of the show. Ladies and gentlemen, please welcome, Greg Brady himself, Barry Williams!'

Everyone applauded.

'Hey, thanks, guys. Man I wish I was with you,' Barry Williams, aka Greg Brady from *The Brady Bunch*, said down the phone. (You know the one. He was Greg, the oldest one.)

'Is that Greg Brady?' I said, ecstatic.

Barry and I exchanged wide-eyed looks.

'Yes sir, it is. Who am I talking with?'

'Barry, these guys are two of the top comedians from the UK and friends of the great Paul Provenza: Barry Castagnola and Brendon Burns,' Mr Cigar said in his LA DJ patter.

'Oh great, maybe you guys can help me with my UK accent,' Barry Williams said. 'That's actually what I'm filming now, as we speak.'

'OK, in a sec,' I replied. 'Barry, I just have to ask: as a child star, exactly which drug was it that ruined your life?'

The table fell about, and to his credit so did Barry Williams on the other end.

'Yes! Yes! Yes!' I cheered as I punched the ground. 'My life is now complete! I just got to ask Greg Brady that!'

'Congratulations, Mr Burns,' said Mr Cigar. 'Let's face it, folks, he's a bit hit and miss, but when he hits it's out of the park.'

'Answer the question, Barry Williams aka Greg Brady from *The Brady Bunch*,' I said.

'Well, I do believe The McCallum had a say in it,' Greg replied.

'A fantastic endorsement! And we'll take it!' said Angus the McCallum representative.

We all clapped.

'Look, I'm serious, can you guys give me any tips on my English accent?' said Barry Williams aka Greg Brady from *The Brady Bunch*.

'I can't help you there,' I replied, 'I'm actually Australian. Barry should sort you out though.'

Like a hot potato, the attention was passed to Barry. Again I felt nervous for him. This wasn't selecting a song in the desert, this was being asked to be funny on cue in front of millions of listeners. Ordinarily I wouldn't have sweated it but he'd really been way too hard on himself over the past twenty-four hours. If he failed and wound up in the 'Marty zone' I feared his brittle self-esteem wouldn't be able to handle it. Not right then anyway. I prayed for him to be funny. No one else had even heard him speak yet. The floor was his. We all listened intently, hopefully.

'Well, as I'm from South London originally, my accent might not be what you're going for. But if you're looking for the traditional cockney accent as portrayed by Americans in films I'd go for something like' – and here he adopted the preposterous Dick Van Dyke cockney voice – 'Orright me ol' china rub a dub get yerself down them lubbly apples and pears if you know wha' I mean half a pound to the pound me ol' china roll out the barrel why dontcha it's a lubberly ol' game though innit nyaaaaaaa!'

The table fell about, as he never even stopped to breathe. He received a spontaneous standing ovation simultaneously with humility and pride.

'Well, he doesn't say much, but what he does is gold,' Mr Cigar offered as part of his bizarre running commentary on proceedings. 'You should take notes, Mr Burns. You keep using words we don't even understand.'

'You can't insult me with your ignorance,' I said. 'That's like fisting yourself and bragging you're giving me the finger from within.'

Again Mr Cigar laughed along happily.

'Thanks for the advice me ol' china,' Barry Williams aka Greg Brady from *The Brady Bunch* (you know, the oldest brother) said. 'Thanks guys. I'll see you soon.'

'Thanks Greg,' chimed Mr Cigar. 'Catch up soon, buddy.'

'Can I ask a question?' Marty said.

'You just did!' everyone chorused again.

'Shut up Marty, you dick.'

'Asshole.'

'Kill yourself.'

'Who let him in?'

'Why you always pickin' on me?' Marty whined.

Something clicked in me. 'I've got it!' I said, slapping the table for attention. 'I know why they pick on you, Marty.'

'Oh great,' Marty shot back. 'Crocodile Dundee's gonna solve my problem.'

'No, wait! Marty, I feel for you. I want to help.' I meant it.

'Screw you,' he responded.

'Again he bites the hand that feeds!' said Mr Cigar, utterly exasperated.

'Marty, Marty, Marty,' Provenz interrupted from behind the bar next to Mr Cigar's position, a bisexual girl under each arm, 'Marty, Marty.' He had the floor and lowered his tone as he leant into the mike. 'Now, I'm going to talk about Brendon like he ain't here for a second. As you know, gentlemen, I've been around the block.'

'Sure.'

'Yup.'

'Uh-huh.'

'I've been in this business some thirty-odd years now and in that time I have lived and worked with Seinfeld and countless others. I've interviewed Hicks, Kinison, Pryor, Carlin, and I gotta tell ya, Brendon Burns is one of the greatest comics I have ever seen. Marty, you have no idea what you are up against.' Provenza folded his arms for extra gravity.

There was a silence as everyone turned from him to me. Such glowing praise clearly did not come lightly around this table.

Provenz spoke up again before I did: 'Now why don't you girls make out for a bit?'

The bisexual girls made out while we all catcalled and whistled.

'Now make out with me,' he asked.

They blushed and were about to oblige when Mr Cigar objected: 'Stop that crap! This ain't Howard Stern.' He refocused the attention to me. 'Back to Brendon and Marty. Brendon Burns. The great Brendon Burns, as commended and endorsed by the great Paul Provenza, has a solution for my brother Marty's problems.'

I had the floor again.

'Right,' I said, looking directly at Marty. 'Now, I'm presuming that this has been going on for years.'

'Yeah,' said Marty.

'Right. I've managed to figure out this dynamic as an impartial witness in a matter of minutes. It's that apparent. Marty, this show is about taking the piss.'

Everyone stared blankly.

'Busting balls,' Provenz translated for me to a sea of nods and noncommittal 'for sure's.

'I took the piss out of Mr Cigar. He took the piss out of me. Frank takes the piss out of everyone. No one really takes the piss out of Frank cos they might get shot.' Everybody laughed. 'See! I'm busting Frank's balls and no one's batting an eyelid. That's what happens on this show. Guys sit around, smoke cigars, drink whiskey and give each other shit. The reason everyone dumps on you so much, Marty, is because when it happens to you you act like you're the only one. You lack empathy. And it's gone on for so long now that everyone's forgotten why they started.'

'Oh my God, that's it!' yelled Mr Cigar. 'This guy's been here only minutes and he's nailed you dead to rights!'

'It's true.'

'The man's a genius.'

'For *years* I tells ya.'

'Brendon Burns, ladies and gentlemen. What'd I tell ya?' Provenza started the applause and the table gave me a golf clap.

'Asshole,' said Marty.

'What?' I said, flabbergasted. 'No, I just said that with love. You could change all this today just by agreeing and laughing your arse off.'

'I was just starting to like you,' said Marty, ever the victim.

'See, you can't help him!' exclaimed Mr Cigar.

'You idiot!'

'He just helped you!'

'Kill yourself!'

'You're a moron!'

'This show sucks when you're here!'

334

'Go suck a tail pipe!'

'Drown!'

'Die!'

'Puke!'

'Asshole!'

'Unbelievable,' declared Mr Cigar. 'Now, during this beautiful interplay the great Paul Provenza has brought something to my attention. Apparently these three men united together for a purpose.'

The hubbub died down. I waited for Mr Cigar to reveal the nature of our spiritual vigil and the pursuit of my photograph.

'Apparently, Mr Castagnola here has just gone through a rough break-up.'

'Whoa.'

'We hear dat.'

'Broads, man.'

'Yeah, broads.'

'What are you gonna do?'

'Chin up, buddy.'

My hackles were up as the attention was taken from me.

'He was engaged and she left him only weeks before the wedding,' Mr Cigar continued.

I very nearly uncontrollably blurted out *Hey, what about me! The exact same thing happened to me! Why's nobody noticing that?*

The table continued to empathize with and console Barry:

'Ouch.'

'Dat's tough.'

'Broads, man.'

'Yeah, broads.'

Frank D'Amico spoke up, resting a consolatory paw on

Barry's shoulders. 'Barry, my friend. You seem like a stand-up guy—'

'Barry, can I ask a question?' Marty interrupted.

This was too much for Frank D'Amico. While the table was halfway through bellowing their customary 'You just did!' exclamations, to Barry and mine's utter shock Frank bounded up from his wheelchair, hurtling it backwards, wheels spinning in the air, and pounded his mighty fists on the table. 'You fuck'n mook! This guy's got a broken fuck'n heart and you're spouting your fuggen bullshit—'

Mr Cigar attempted to intervene. 'Frank, ixnay on the uckfay, we're not online yet.'

'I don't give a fuck,' Frank D'Amico snapped back. 'This fuggen prick. I oughta shoot you, you fuggen prick. You have no talent. I oughta drown you in that fuggen pool. Go watch *Barney* you fuck'n infant, or better yet climb inside that purple dinosaur fuck and never be seen or heard from again. You fuggen twat!'

Frank then calmed down with alarming speed. Coolly, he picked up his chair and nestled into it, again addressing Barry, who was as startled as I was. 'Now, Barry. Here's what you do.' He put his hand back on Barry's shoulder 'You sit back, you drink a few McCallums with me and the boys, you smoke a few cigars, and then later you give me twenty dollars and I send you home with Alice.'

Barry burst into fits of laughter, and we all joined him, relieved that Frank had returned to a more jovial mood. The guy was good fun but he was also terrifying.

'Go fuck yourself,' Alice said in the background, speaking for the first time, her boobs sagging unsupported in her pink boob tube stained with spilt whiskey and fag ash, her hands on her hips like a cartoon hooker past her prime. 'Him I do for free.'

Frank led the table in wails of cackles again.

'Am I the only one that's a little startled that Frank can friggen walk?' I interjected to more fits of appreciative release.

'I hate queues,' Frank put in. 'Fuck that shit.' He'd completely given up on trying not to swear. 'It's a great leveller too. You find out a lot about people if they think you're in a chair. And congratulations, you two passed.' He put his arms around me and Barry. 'Forget the broad, Barry, you'll bounce back.' Frank raised his whiskey glass. 'To Barry!'

'To Barry!' Everyone toasted and drank.

Barry was quietly beaming and nodding. 'Thanks, fellas, thank you.'

I was glad to see it, but a burgeoning, shameful jealousy still lay beneath. Provenza caught my stifled rage and smirked.

43

The Seventh Day

'I JUST NEED an hour's sleep and I'll be up for partying,' I slurred as we entered Provenza's flat.

'You sure?' asked Barry.

'Yeah man, it's our last night. We gotta party. I'll call up that Mexican girl from the Laugh Factory. We can get her to bring some friends. Just an hour. That's all I need.'

I remember saying that much, then lying face down on the couch.

Int. Provenz's flat – night. Provenz and Barry are watching Brendon pass out on the couch. He snores almost immediately his head hits the cushion. They look at each other and start snickering.

PROVENZA
(sarcastically)

And on the seventh day he rested.

Scene.

I came to with the sun beaming in through Provenza's windows and a cushion in my mouth again. Clearly I'd been trying to drink both during slumber as some sort of sun-based cushiony cocktail. Such was my thirst.

I staggered to the kitchen sink and placed my mouth over the tap. Noisy quasi-onomatopoeic slurp after slurp rang through the house.

'Fuck, you even drink loud, Burnsy!' Provenza hollered from his study.

I mumbled something back that came out as a gargle. Almost through a survival instinct I was unable to interrupt the quenching of my thirst by pulling my mouth away from the tap.

'What?' Provenz asked as he entered the kitchen, scratching his dick and balls through his 'company' tracksuit pants. Upon seeing me still latched on to his kitchen tap he barked his Provenza laugh again. 'HA! Take your face off the sink to speak, you fuck'n retard.'

'Ahhhhhhhhhhh,' I gasped and belched.

Provenz went to the toilet. 'Goddammit my pussy aches,' he yelled as he pissed.

'Why would you even say that?' I asked. 'You don't have a pussy. I don't think you've quite understood what you've said. You're wasting everyone's time.'

'Ow, the burning!' he yelped as he continued to tinkle loudly.

'Where's Barry?' I asked as I pulled on a shirt.

'He went to say goodbye to Keith and his sister.'

'Righto.'

'I gotta talk to you about that.'

'What about?'

'The whole Barry thing.'

'OK.'

'Go pack first. We gotta return the rental before I drive you guys to the airport.'

'Sure.'

It took me only ten minutes to pack. By the time I'd finished, Barry had returned.

'You all right then?'

'Yeah, good, thanks.' Though I was still a little sore in the head.

Provenz grabbed his keys. 'We should go. Barry, you take the rental, I'll take my car. Burnsy, you come with me.'

'All right,' I replied.

When we got to his car, Provenz took the top off. I looked at the dimensions of the interior.

'Remind me why we didn't take your car again?' I asked.

'That's why.' Provenz pointed at the rental as Barry drove off. The underside was covered in mud and the panels were all scratched to shit. We still didn't know if it had been shot or not.

'Oh shit. We're not getting our deposit back, are we?'

We climbed in and set off.

'What did you want to talk about?'

'I think you owe our friend an apology,' Provenz said.

'What for?'

'We were talking last night and he feels that you really patronize him. Over his dad, his break-up, his comedy, as a man – everything.'

'Yeah. I guess a lot of that stems from my own issues as a dad.'

'Ya think? You do know what you did the night of the gig, right?'

'Nope.' I honestly didn't remember.

For the rest of the drive Provenz filled me in on what happened when Barry was trying to talk to me as I left the club, him trying to tell me about Sublime playing in the background. A deep, deep feeling of shame wrapped itself round the back of my neck and face.

'Fuck,' I said. 'What a cunt.'

'Look, it's not just that, man. He really feels patronized by you. And he has every right to. He's going through what he's going through at his own pace. He knows what's up. He's a grown-up.'

As we pulled up at the rental place, Barry could see that we were talking about him and he was obviously a little abashed. I got out of the car and went to nip it all in the bud immediately.

'Mate, Provenz told me about the Sublime thing. I can't believe I did that. After all we've gone through. After everything I've tried to impart. And just when you come round to my way of thinking I blank you. I'm really sorry.'

At first he looked at me angrily, but seeing the genuine regret in me he smiled at my complete lack of self-awareness and flagrant hypocrisy. Utilizing his character-acting skills, he replayed the scene for me perfectly. From the elation in his eyes right down to my parting, dismissive 'yeah great'.

'Oh no. I didn't, did I?'

Alas, his retelling was so pinpointed I couldn't deny it. He squeegeed my beer goggles and it all came flooding back. Yet he did it with such good humour, although still embarrassed, I had to laugh along with him.

Meanwhile the rental guy was looking around the battered car. We prepared for the worst. We still weren't sure whether or not Exit Wound had given the car an entry wound. Fortunately it was covered in enough mud and shit.

'Mate, we're sorry,' Barry said. 'We took it out to Nevada.'

The guy just shrugged. 'It's a rental,' he said.

'Mate, do you mind if we take a photo of you looking distressed sitting in the car?' Barry asked. 'Just for posterity.'

This being LA, the guy obliged immediately, with perfect acting skills. He sat in the battered car and pretended to tear his hair out.

Click.

Whirrrrrrrrrrrrrr . . .

'I'm out of film,' Barry said. (This, remember, being just before the days when everything went digital.)

'It's OK. We have everything we need in there, don't we?'

'Yup.'

Barry stuffed the camera in his shoulder bag. Not willing to let it leave his sight now.

'That was perfect, mate, thanks,' I said to the rental guy.

'You want me to cry on the bonnet?' he offered.

We declined, pointing at the whirring empty camera.

'I fuck'n love this rental company,' Provenz exclaimed as he swaggered up to meet us. 'You faggots made up yet?' he asked, slapping us both on the back.

'Yeah,' Barry replied.

'Let's get you two to the airport then,' he said.

'Fuck, I can't believe I did that,' I said, back-referencing the LA gig night.

'Yeah, one sniff of fanny and our spiritual journey goes out the fucking window,' Barry tittered, again good-naturedly.

'Fuck, I'm such a prick.'

'Don't,' Provenz interrupted.

'What?'

'Just don't.'

'What?'

'Make it about you. You've apologized, now move on.'

'OK. I'm sorry, Barry.'

'No worries, mate,' he replied.

We hugged and moved on into Provenza's convertible, talking as we picked our seats.

'Still, at least you've got the regular US gigs huh?' I said.

'What?' said Barry.

'The gigs. What did the landlord say?'

'Erm, no, I don't think he wants us back.'

'Why not? It was awesome.'

'Brendon, you got drunk and cleared the room,' Barry reminded me.

'What?'

'Burnsy, you died on your hole,' Provenz backed up.

'What, the whole bell/death story thing? That was hysterical,' I insisted.

'Erm, no. You moved a bunch of furniture around and no one could understand you but us,' said Barry. 'The publican left in the middle of your set.'

'But I thought I did well and *you* struggled,' I said to Barry in all brutal honesty.'

'Erm, no, Brendon,' he replied. 'We got laughs, you died on your hole.'

I checked both their faces. They were nodding in earnest.

'Fuck off. That's not how I remember it at all.'

'We don't doubt that for a second,' said Provenz.

'But I told the death story.' I was genuinely perplexed. 'That shit is hysterical. Fuck 'em. I was being hilarious . . .' I trailed off and reconsidered. 'And then when they responded in exactly the same way as the people in the outback? What the fuck is wrong with those people? I thought that was hilarious!'

They both laughed. 'Well that was apparent,' observed

343

Barry, 'but I think you couldn't hear the audience over your own laughter.'

'You might want to look into that,' said Provenz.

'So what happened with your dad and sister this morning?' I asked as we cruised with the top off one last time.

'We had a bit of a fight about you and the gig,' Barry replied. 'I'll tell you what. That is me done with bringing my dad along with my mates ever again. It just complicates things.'

Provenz stared at me through the rearview mirror. His gaze hit me like a bolt between the eyes.

'What? No, don't. That's bullshit, Barry,' I pleaded.

'You what?' he asked.

'Fuck that. I'm the cunt here. You know what? Yesterday I could've fucken killed you when they were giving you all the sympathy on the radio.' I'd opened the floodgates now and almost felt as if I were speaking outside myself. 'I didn't come out here for you, Barry, I came here for me. I figured if I could heal your broken heart then maybe I could finally get over me and Mary Lou breaking up.'

'Finally he says her fuck'n name!' Provenz cheered.

'And you know what, mate? It hasn't worked for either one of us. I've been trying to control you in an attempt to get some sort of grip on my own shit, and how fucken dare I? You feel whatever the fuck you wanna feel, mate. How could I possibly think I was going to fix you with a few trite soundbites? "We write our lives" – what the fuck is that? And as for your dad, that's just my own bullshit and perception of what I think a father and son's relationship should be. That's my bullshit, not yours and not his. Fuck that.'

'The penny drops,' Provenz declared.

'But if he wants to forget he's a dad and go wild with his son and his mates on, quite frankly, one of the wildest weeks of my life, then that's awesome. And good on him. I'm begging you, Barry, here and now. Don't let me stop that. Don't let me do that, Barry. Do not afford me that power. I'm begging you, please.'

'OK mate, will do,' Barry replied calmly, more than a little surprised yet still taking it all amiably in indomitable Barry fashion. 'He did fucking crack me up in the car though when you two were on mushrooms.'

'I've still got the notepad!' I exclaimed, producing it. 'That was hysterical when you two flipped over the pages as if to say "Yeah, is that it?"'

'Yeah, we knew,' said Barry.

'It spoke volumes about you two.'

'Yeah, we knew.'

'What? You did it on purpose?'

'Yes, Brendon. Do you think we don't know what Socratic irony is?'

And that's Barry in a nutshell. He can put anything behind him in a heartbeat yet there's always so much more going on inside than he'll ever let on. His thin smile, his eyes ever darting, so much muttered under his breath. All the while so self-aware that he'll purposefully give you the impression he isn't. If he doesn't wear his intelligence on his sleeve he can find out how truly stupid someone else is being.

Almost reading my consideration of said self-awareness and catching me in a rare moment, he asked, 'What did you want out of this, Brendon?'

His question sat in the air for a while. The truth was I hadn't done anything for anyone but me. They'd bent over backwards to help me in my aim but when it came to anything they'd wanted I couldn't have cared less. I was nothing short

345

of detrimental to their own personal causes. Barry got me my photo but I'd blown his gig for him and any chances he may have had of making it an ongoing thing. Then flat out ignored him the very moment he received his own 'sign' that this was all interconnected. Keith desperately just wanted to hang out with his son and perhaps set something up where they got to see each other more. And I bulldozed over all of them just to get my photo back. And why?

Why?

Click.

Flash.

Whirr.

. . .

'I wanted to win,' I replied.

They both sat there with raised eyebrows.

'What, win her back?' asked Barry.

'No. Fuck that.' I considered this long and hard. The answers only occurring to me as I said them. 'I just wanted her to want me back. Maybe if I sent her a picture of me having more fun and looking cooler than I am then she'd miss me and want me back. Then I'd have won.' If I'd said it in front of anyone else I would've felt deeply, *deeply* ashamed. But here, with these two, I felt safe, open and fearless.

'You came out here to take a cool photo of yourself just to make a girl jealous and regret leaving you?' Barry asked. His tone was inquisitive not judgemental.

'Isn't that why you came?' I asked him.

'Nah. I came for a laugh, Brendon.'

'And I guess I figured if I could somehow make you OK about your break-up then I'd be OK too.'

'You did, Brendon. Whatever you reckon about all this, we still fucking did it. I'll be all right. Honest. Thanks. It was briiil-li-ant.' He even gave me a brand-new 'brilliant'.

'See?' I said. 'It worked. I told you I'd have a magical gift for you.'

'All right, don't try and sell the spiritual vigil shit again,' Barry said. 'You took a bunch of drugs, did some fucking and got shot at. Just let it be that. It's extraordinary enough.'

'I think you've found my problem,' I said.

'What's that?' Barry asked.

'Well, basically, I'm a top bloke but I'm a bit of a cunt about it.'

'That's really funny.' They both nodded without laughing – again, the greatest comedian's compliment.

'That's got to be the four levels of morality,' I continued. 'Down the bottom, bit of a cunt and a cunt about it. Then, bit of a cunt and a top bloke about it, which has to be inter-changeable with top bloke and a bit of a cunt about it. And at the very top, top bloke and a top bloke about it.'

'So why'd you drag me along?' asked Provenz.

I pondered his question long and hard too.

'You're clearly a top bloke about being a bit of a cunt,' I answered, 'and Barry's a top bloke about being a top bloke.'

They laughed.

'The aliens were right,' blurted Provenza as he blew his nose.

'What, you should wear more yellow?' asked Barry.

'Funny,' he acknowledged legitimately but without actually laughing. 'No man. We're all just data. Burnsy's right too. We do write our lives, only what you gotta take into account is there are a few billion people experiencing the exact same shit all over the world at the same time. Perception can be reality so long as you're willing to accept everyone else's too. We can look at all of this any way we choose to. We could take this from all three of our perspectives and there'd still be the data to back up each of our stories if we wanted. Nobody's wrong.'

'There were no aliens, it was mushrooms,' I responded.

'Yeah, but I bet you can see why I think there was, right?' Provenz fired back.

Barry and I nodded. 'Yeah.'

'And when you retell this story you'd be fucked if you left that out, right?'

We nodded again. 'Yeah.'

'And Brendon, would you have had one tenth of the time here without Keith?'

'No, no I wouldn't,' I concurred.

'And Barry, maybe Burnsy is a little nutty . . .'

'Yeah,' said Barry.

'But you wouldn't have come along if he hadn't felt that way so passionately, right?' Provenz strayed from his point somewhat.

'And Burnsy, you can accept that belief is such that you'll dramatize all that supports it and dispel anything that refutes it, right? You can understand that, right?'

'Yeah, totally. I'm not stupid.'

'So you can accept my way of seeing this?'

'Yeah. But you have to accept my way of thinking does—'

'Hey man, I don't have to come round to your way of thinking,' he cut me off. 'I haven't been mad at anyone. I'm just along for the ride.'

And that's Provenza – doesn't believe a fucken word he says half the time just so long as he sounds enigmatic. If you still feel in the dark about him then I've done my job. I told you. The longer you know him, the less you know about him.

We sat there sharing another comfortable silence. Allowing the moment of honesty and vulnerability between us to sit.

For me it was undeniable that faith and belief had given me something very rich and powerful. I'd gone out to the desert with two associates and come back with two friends for life. For all of us, faith in a stranger had paid off.

'That was fucken beautiful, wasn't it?' I eventually said.

Provenz dragged on his fag. 'Yeah, it was.'

Barry smiled thinly. 'Fucking beautiful. I think we're going to be OK, Burnsy.'

Then it hit me. That's really why I'd been so jealous of Barry the day before at Outlaw Radio – they'd shown him empathy. And that's all I'd really wanted all along. Here I'd dropped my guard and been truly honest just for a second and got it. It was that simple. The trip wasn't about spirituality, God, chaos or any single incident or set of beliefs. It was about the three of us sharing the trip. This was my magical present. We had done it. We'd got our photo, and in that single snapshot we'd captured what it was like to be on our own and together at once. No one will ever know what it was like to be one of the guys in that photo but the three of us, and that's something I will treasure always.

Certainly I'd got it wrong as much as I'd got it right, and that was OK. They'd forgiven me in a heartbeat. The beautiful truth I'd been searching for was that no matter what any of us is feeling or thinking at any given time, we are not alone.

Then I threw up.

As the top of the car was off, it shot directly up in the air. I vomited so matter-of-factly that it almost appeared like a bloody brown speech bubble out of the corner of my mouth. Both Barry and Provenz burst into hysterics as I carried on the conversation unaffected.

'Well, I guess it was my turn,' I said.

'Here, do you want a drink?'

Barry offered a bottle. I looked closely to check it wasn't Provenza's ashtray bottle. As I focused in I saw Barry's forefinger and thumb wrapped round the rim in a ring shape.

'Ha! Last goal wins!' said Barry triumphantly.

'Oh, you got him!' cheered Provenz.

'Yeah, he got me,' I said.

I also got the chance to meet up with and apologize to Keith for being such a judgemental, hypocritical, petulant prick before he passed away a few months ago. Like Barry, he didn't sweat it for a second. 'Not a problem, Bren, I had a blast. You weren't that bad.' He even got the round in.

He had a pretty bad run after Vegas. He had an operation on his shoulder but they left on the saline drip warmer next to him while he was out. It gave him third-degree burns under his arm and slowly seared all his nerve endings. After a long court battle, which pretty much only paid for itself in the end, he was diagnosed with pancreatic cancer. Barry travelled back and forth to be by his side the whole time and it was a long, painful process for them both.

Keith kept his dry wit though. Shortly after being diagnosed, with only a little time left, he and Barry went to buy a blender back in London. He was so frail and weak at this stage that when the woman behind the till offered him a twelve-month warranty he looked at Barry, rolled his eyes and said, 'You don't do three months, do you?'

My biggest regret about the trip was I wish Keith *had* fucked the hooker. I'm sorry. There's no way we could have known, but given the circumstances he wound up in, I do. I'm glad we got to be one of his more debauched memories before a shitty end. If it could have been just that little bit more debauched then good for him. Pancreatic cancer has a survival rate of nil, and although I totally *love* being clean and sober now, if in later life I'm single, lonely and get diagnosed with it? My son had better damn well take me to Vegas. Barry and Provenza know the way. Hell, my dad had better come too, if he's still around. I'm sure Provenz will have quite the surprise for us both.

Keith is remembered by all who knew him as a hilarious comic character whose son could talk to him about anything. They literally spoke every other day. He truly was a dad and a best friend.

I'm also absolutely *gutted* that he's not in the front cover photo. Our photo. So I've decided to put him in where he belongs. I might have altered the picture to suit my needs but it's a better picture for it. And for Barry and Provenz, it's the closest I can come to giving them my photographic evidence – my proof as promised. But if I have to explain it I'll spoil it.

I've been around Barry and Provenz plenty of times since the trip. We always have a blast, but I guess each time I see either of them a little part of me wishes all four of us were there.

'You must admit that thing with seeing Owen Cavanagh after ten years was weird,' I demanded as we made our way into the terminal.

'Stop,' said Provenz.

'Yeah, that was weird,' Barry concurred. 'Ya gotta give him that.'

'It was just a coincidence,' Provenz insisted.

'There are no coincidences in life,' I said.

'Yes there are. Life itself is one massive coincidence. Do you have any idea of the odds of any of us existing? When you consider how many sperm are in just one load?'

'Miraculous odds, one might say,' I offered.

'No, mathematical odds,' he fired back.

Provenz considered his response for a bit, then nodded in concession. 'Look, the Owen Cavanagh thing was something all right, and without it I probably wouldn't have got you your convertible. I admit. But again, there's so many stories being lived out in the world by so many that if you make enough predictions they'll happen to someone eventually.'

'That sounds like faith to me,' I insisted.

'No, it sounds just like chaos,' Provenz responded.

'Sounds brilliant,' tittered Barry.

We walked in silence up to the gate. Although this wasn't any kind of long goodbye, we were still very aware it was some sort of ending. What could possibly be our parting words here? We each put on our hats and searched for the last magical 'top sentence' to sum up all that had transpired.

We looked at one another, dumbfounded.

'There aren't words,' Provenz eventually declared ecstatically.

He was right.

Epilogue

Ext. Nevada desert – day. A tumbleweed blows across our eyeline.
We trace its path. Eventually it passes over some feet wearing sandals. They belong to man (26). We stay on the feet.

There is another gust of wind. A note gets caught in it and is plastered against the man's ankle. His hand reaches down into shot and clutches at the note, scrunching it slightly as he does so.

We pan up, staying tightly on his hand and the note. From his P.O.V. we see him unfold it and read it.

Close up – the note:

> *'What are the chances you have ginger?'*

Cut to wide.

We see just the man's face as he stares around his surroundings, utterly baffled. We pan around him as he looks for the source of the note. But all he can see through the full 360 degrees is desert. He looks up to the sky, still flabbergasted.

Cut to full body wide.

We see the man from behind as he looks left and right. Over his shoulders there are straps reaching round to the front that hold up the large ice-cream vendor tray he is carrying. He turns to fact us, revealing that the tray has 'ginger' written across its front in big bold letters. He looks to the heavens and scratches his head.

Fade to black.

Scene.

Acknowledgements

Firstly, and most of all, I'd like to thank Sarah Emsley and all at Transworld for taking a punt on what has been a wish-list pet project for nearly six years. Sarah's tireless understanding and commitment have left me nothing short of staggered – without her there would be no book. Period. She's probably even constructed that sentence properly after I've put a full stop in the wrong place. And this bit too. Seriously though, back in 2007 Sarah came up to me at the Edinburgh Festival and announced, 'You're a writer, you should write a book. It'll be a lot of work but you can do it,' and she has had to tear her hair out arguing subtle nuances with me ever since. I thank her for giving in and holding her ground in equal measure. Together I think we've wound up with the right decisions.

My thanks go to Daniel Balado-Lopez, Doug Young and Kate Tolley for helping with the editorial process, and to Polly Andrews for convincing the press that a foul-mouthed lout like me is reasonably competent at putting pen to paper. I'd also like to thank Danny Julian, Addison Cresswell and all at Off The Kerb who've patiently been biding their time to get a book out of me for nearly a decade.

Colossal thanks go to Barry Castagnola, who unwittingly

became a script editor and damn near co-author when all was required of him was to simply read the damn thing. Without his good humour and literary know-how this would have been little more than the ramblings of a mad man. Thank you, Barry, for putting so much of yourself into this, even at the toughest of times. To Paul Provenza, for not giving a fuck what was written about him to the point of almost being disappointing. And for busting his arse to get my career started in America. A separate issue I know, but sometimes you don't get to thank people like this until you write a book, so fuck you. (It shows a special level of anal-retention for you to be reading this in the first place, so I feel a 'fuck you' should rear its head just to reward your dedication.) To Keith Castagnola, for his dry wit, tagging along for the hoot, and forgiving me in an instant.

To 'Mary Lou', no hard feelings, kiddo. Things worked out pretty damn good. I *genuinely* hope you've found happiness, wherever you are.

To every comic mentioned herein, thanks for the road stories and being odd enough to mention.

And lastly, I'd like to give extra-special thanks to my beautiful wife to be, Laura, for putting up with my impenetrable temperament and focus while trying to write a book about my previous debauchery and madness. Oh, and for being smoking hot, hysterically funny and saying 'yes' – which is nice. Maybe I should've just said that about everyone . . . *Thank you all for being smoking hot, hysterically funny and saying 'yes'.*

Brendon Burns was born in Perth, western Australia, in 1971. Apparently he was a funny baby, so venturing into stand-up comedy in the UK in 1990 seemed inevitable. He began his TV career on *The 11 O'Clock Show* and has since been seen on *Comedy Cuts*, *Stand Up for the Week* and *The Green Rooms with Paul Provenza*. In 2007 he won the Academy Award of live comedy in Edinburgh, the if.com (formerly the Perrier). Critically acclaimed, world-renowned and highly respected Burns is an outspoken writer, actor, comedian, playwright and now author. He has recorded two live DVDs, *Sober Not Clean* and *So I Suppose This Is Offensive Now*, but this is his first book. Excited? We are.